24 AND PHILOSOPHY

The Blackwell Philosophy and PopCulture Series
Series editor William Irwin

A spoonful of sugar helps the medicine go down, and a healthy helping of popular culture clears the cobwebs from Kant. Philosophy has had a public relations problem for a few centuries now. This series aims to change that, showing that philosophy is relevant to your life – and not just for answering the big questions like "To be or not to be?" but for answering the little questions: "To watch or not to watch *South Park*?" Thinking deeply about TV, movies, and music doesn't make you a "complete idiot." In fact it might make you a philosopher, someone who believes the unexamined life is not worth living and the unexamined cartoon is not worth watching.

SOUTH PARK AND PHILOSOPHY: YOU KNOW, I LEARNED SOMETHING TODAY
Edited by Robert Arp

METALLICA AND PHILOSOPHY: A CRASH COURSE IN BRAIN SURGERY
Edited by William Irwin

FAMILY GUY AND PHILOSOPHY: A CURE FOR THE PETARDED
Edited by J. Jeremy Wisnewski

THE DAILY SHOW AND PHILOSOPHY: MOMENTS OF ZEN IN THE ART OF FAKE NEWS
Edited by Jason Holt

LOST AND PHILOSOPHY: THE ISLAND HAS ITS REASONS
Edited by Sharon M. Kaye

Forthcoming

24 AND PHILOSOPHY: THE WORLD ACCORDING TO JACK
Edited by Jennifer Hart Weed, Richard Davis, and Ronald Weed

BATTLESTAR GALACTICA AND PHILOSOPHY
Edited by Jason T. Eberl

the office and philosophy
Edited by J. Jeremy Wisnewski

24
AND
PHILOSOPHY

THE WORLD ACCORDING TO JACK

EDITED BY JENNIFER HART WEED,
RICHARD DAVIS, AND RONALD WEED

g nss

© 2008 by Blackwell Publishing Ltd

BLACKWELL PUBLISHING
350 Main Street, Malden, MA 02148-5020, USA
9600 Garsington Road, Oxford OX4 2DQ, UK
550 Swanston Street, Carlton, Victoria 3053, Australia

The right of Jennifer Hart Weed, Richard Davis, and Ronald Weed to be identified as the authors of the editorial material in this work has been asserted in accordance with the UK Copyright, Designs, and Patents Act 1988.

All rights reserved. No part of this publication may be reproduced, stored in a retrieval system, or transmitted, in any form or by any means, electronic, mechanical, photocopying, recording or otherwise, except as permitted by the UK Copyright, Designs, and Patents Act 1988, without the prior permission of the publisher.

Designations used by companies to distinguish their products are often claimed as trademarks. All brand names and product names used in this book are trade names, service marks, trademarks, or registered trademarks of their respective owners. The publisher is not associated with any product or vendor mentioned in this book.

This publication is designed to provide accurate and authoritative information in regard to the subject matter covered. It is sold on the understanding that the publisher is not engaged in rendering professional services. If professional advice or other expert assistance is required, the services of a competent professional should be sought.

First published 2008 by Blackwell Publishing Ltd

2   2008

Library of Congress Cataloging-in-Publication Data

24 and philosophy : the world according to Jack / edited by Jennifer Hart Weed, Richard Davis, and Ronald Weed.
    p. cm. — (The Blackwell philosophy and popculture series)
    Includes bibliographical references and index.
    ISBN 978-1-4051-7104-5 (pbk. : alk. paper)   1. 24 (Television program)   I. Weed, Jennifer Hart.   II. Davis, Richard Brian, 1963–   III. Weed, Ronald L.   IV. Title: Twenty-four and philosophy.

    PN1992.77.A215A15 2008
    791.45′72—dc22

                                                                                    2007033950

A catalogue record for this title is available from the British Library.

Set in 10.5/13pt Sabon
by Graphicraft Limited, Hong Kong
Printed and bound in the United States of America
by Sheridan Books, Inc., Chelsea, MI, USA

The publisher's policy is to use permanent paper from mills that operate a sustainable forestry policy, and which has been manufactured from pulp processed using acid-free and elementary chlorine-free practices. Furthermore, the publisher ensures that the text paper and cover board used have met acceptable environmental accreditation standards.

For further information on
Blackwell Publishing, visit our website at
www.blackwellpublishing.com

12:00 AM-1:00 AM

Classified: 24 T.O.C.

12:00 AM–1:00 AM
Classified: 24 T.O.C.   v

1:00 AM–2:00 AM
Dedication: To Edgar   ix

2:00 AM–3:00 AM
Philosophy? If You Don't Know 24, *You Don't Know Jack!*   xi
Tom Morris

3:00 AM–4:00 AM
CTU Orientation   xiv
Ronald Weed

4:00 AM–5:00 AM
Acknowledgments: Chloe, We Need You!   xviii

5:00 AM–9:00 AM
SPECIAL AGENT JACK BAUER   1

5:00 AM–6:00 AM
*What Would Jack Bauer Do? Moral Dilemmas and Moral
Theory in* 24   3
Randall M. Jensen

6:00 AM–7:00 AM
*Between Hero and Villain: Jack Bauer and the Problem of
"Dirty Hands"*   17
Stephen de Wijze

Classified: 24 T.O.C.

7:00 AM–8:00 AM
Beyond the Call of Duty   31
Richard Davis

8:00 AM–9:00 AM
*Truth and Illusion in 24: Jack Bauer, Dionysus in the
World of Apollo*   43
Stephen Snyder

9:00 AM–12:00 PM
THE OVAL OFFICE AND THE HALLS OF POWER   55

9:00 AM–10:00 AM
*President Palmer and the Invasion of China: The Beginning
of a Just War?*   57
Jennifer Hart Weed

10:00 AM–11:00 AM
*Jack Bauer as Anti-Eichmann and Scourge of Political
Liberalism*   67
Brandon Claycomb and Greig Mulberry

11:00 AM–12:00 PM
Palmer's Pickle: Why Couldn't He Stomach It?   76
Georgia Testa

12:00 PM–3:00 PM
CTU HEADQUARTERS   89

12:00 PM–1:00 PM
The Ethics of Torture in 24: Shockingly Banal   91
Dónal P. O'Mathúna

1:00 PM–2:00 PM
Loyalty and the "War of All Against All" in 24   105
Eric M. Rovie

2:00 PM–3:00 PM
Who Dares Sins: Jack Bauer and Moral Luck   118
Rob Lawlor

3:00 PM–6:00 PM
MOLES, DOUBLE-AGENTS, AND TERRORISTS   **127**

3:00 PM–4:00 PM
*Living in a World of Suspicion: The Epistemology of
Mistrust*   129
Scott Calef

4:00 PM–5:00 PM
*The Cruel Cunning of Reason: The Modern/Postmodern
Conflict in* 24   142
Terrence Kelly

5:00 PM–6:00 PM
The Knowledge Game Can Be Torture   155
R. Douglas Geivett

6:00 PM–9:00 PM
TECHNOLOGY, OBJECTIFICATION, AND THE CLOCK   **167**

6:00 PM–7:00 PM
How the Cell Phone Changed the World and Made 24   169
Read Mercer Schuchardt

7:00 PM–8:00 PM
24 *and the Ethics of Objectification*   181
Robert Arp and John Carpenter

8:00 PM–9:00 PM
Jack in Double Time: 24 *in Light of Aesthetic Theory*   195
Paul A. Cantor

9:00 PM–10:00 PM
Classified: CTU Personnel   208

10:00 PM–11:00 PM
Classified: Assets and Sources   214

11:00 PM–12:00 AM
Classified: The Codes   216

Dedication: To Edgar

To Edgar,

I miss you. You wouldn't believe the new recruits Division has me working with; they can't redirect a satellite, let alone encrypt a database with a 5-bit encryption key. I know you said I was the best that CTU had, but you couldn't have predicted that they were going to replace you with FBI rejects. I'm really sorry about what happened. I promise to remember you every time I run an extra backup on the server because someone else forgot to do it.

Love,
Chloe

Philosophy? If You Don't Know 24, You Don't Know Jack

A neighbor of mine served for many years as a Secret Service agent personally guarding four US presidents. His name—of course—is Jack. He tells me that he and his wife, a former CIA bio-terrorism expert (no, I'm not making this up), watch the television show *24* religiously, but surely, no more fervently than I do. One of my former students is a member of the FBI's current counter-terrorism SWAT team. I can't tell you his name, but I can tell you that he's sent me some of their official shirts. I feel like I should put one on every time I watch Jack Bauer in action. My wife comes into the room and laughs when she sees me standing 5 feet in front of the TV, poised on the balls of my feet, ready to spring into action and help Jack if he ever needs it. But, of course, he never does.

After the first three or four seasons of the show, I was talking on the phone one day to one of the country's top experts on Homeland Security, and I happened to ask whether he was a regular viewer of the show. He told me, to my great surprise, that he had never seen it. The old philosophy professor in me came out and I gave him an assignment: to go get at least the first couple of seasons on DVD and then watch them as soon as he possibly could. He laughed and wondered why I was so insistent. I told him that nearly every ethical issue imaginable comes up at some point or other in this truly remarkable series. It's vivid, it's gripping, and it's immensely thought provoking. You could orient an incredible philosophy seminar around watching episodes of this show and then discussing what happens in it. And that is exactly what this book does. These essays will help you to understand in new ways not just the timely topics of terrorism, global conflict, and national security, but more personal issues as well that impinge on our lives every day.

What is a hero? What is the nature of moral obligation? And what are the limits of duty? How bad is human nature, anyway? Is the political realm inevitably corrupt? How can we balance the various commitments and loyalties that we have, and what should we do when they come into conflict? What are the conditions for rational action when the outcome could be catastrophic? Have cell phones and the Internet changed the world forever, and how do they affect the way we think and act? Is it ever morally acceptable to torture a murderous individual in order to obtain crucial information that might save the lives of many? Surely, it's permissible to be seriously unpleasant to such a person. But then, what are the limits of that unpleasantness? Finally, if you whisper a question to someone whose actions may threaten your whole way of life, and you don't get an answer, is the next logical step to shout the same question into that person's face, as loudly as possible, and as close in as you can get?

Okay, some of these aren't everyday issues, and I'm clearly joking a little bit now, and of course this is most likely the one thing that Jack would never do. I don't think I've ever seen him crack a smile—at least, not at a joke, or even at some aspect of a situation that's so absurd you and I would just have to laugh at it. Admittedly, there's not much giggling or guffawing around CTU generally. Saving the world can be a bit stressful. But still, it's worth pointing out that among all the human virtues identified long ago by Aristotle, wittiness is the one—and, perhaps, the only one—that Jack does not seem to have. Is this his only flaw? Or does he have others? Granted, we don't see him except when he's rather busy. So we really have no idea whether he has hobbies outside of work, likes Italian food, or enjoys walks on the beach. We don't have a fully rounded sense of his personality. But what we do see is fairly impressive.

I think it's safe to surmise that agent Jack Bauer has become preeminent among present day fictional heroes as a paradigm of virile valor and virtue in the eyes of a great many fans of the show. But what image of the heroic does he model? Is he a modern day Stoic? Or could he be the quintessentially twenty-first century American version of a classic Samurai warrior? Is he a Homeric hero bound by honor and loyalty, and torn only by the unexpectedly strong bonds of love that he never fully understands? Or is he creating a new model of heroism?

Let's face it. Jack is not necessarily someone it would be great fun to sit around and have a beer with, but I can't think of anyone I'd rather have with me on the wrong side of town, or in case I discovered that someone had just slipped a small nuclear device into my carryon luggage. Not even an open phone line to Chloe O'Brian would give me a fraction of the assurance that Jack could provide. In this character, the actor Kiefer Sutherland has clearly found the role of a lifetime. He's engaging, immensely entertaining, and endlessly provocative in his actions both as a counter-terrorism agent and as a man. He embodies so many philosophical questions and issues so vividly that he is guaranteed to stimulate your thinking in new directions. In these pages, you'll find an explication of what we can learn from him and his associates about good and evil and life that not even the best analysts at CTU could match. I suggest that you read it now. The clock is ticking.

Tom Morris
Author of *If Aristotle Ran General Motors*, *The Stoic Art of Living*, and *If Harry Potter Ran General Electric*, among other books of very serious philosophy.

3:00 AM - 4:00 AM

CTU Orientation

Ronald Weed

Another day begins at the Los Angeles Counter Terrorist Unit (CTU). Meanwhile, we pan across the world to the skyline of Seoul, South Korea late at night. Our eyes quickly descend upon the dimly lit corner of a warehouse from which we hear bellowing shrieks of suffering. We see just the corner of a torture device, as its technician carefully adjusts the dial. While the prisoner writhes and contorts under the grip of a metallic contraption, with a vacant expression the technician calculates how much suffering will extract a truthful disclosure. With barely the strength of a breath, the prisoner whispers his secret into the ear of his captor, who quickly dashes across the dark and shadowy corridors of the warehouse to deliver his results. A small cohort of anonymous operatives assembled in a barely lit workroom nervously await an answer to what is apparently their only question: "When?" The messenger tells them what they need to know: "Today." We don't yet know what is happening today that could be so dreadful that it would have set into motion the complex machinery of the offices of the president, vice president, the cabinet, a myriad of shadowy friendly and hostile associations within and beyond government and of course CTU and its most valuable, albeit, difficult asset—Jack Bauer.

This is the realtime world of *24*, a fragile world full of danger and intrigue. While it is a fictional world, it certainly resembles the real world. And the realtime dimension can bring a brief moment in a Los Angeles afternoon under microscopic, dramatic scrutiny, causing us to feel more keenly what is heroic, dreadful, and unexpected. Moreover, we have realtime access to events, associations, and conversations across the world, forming plotlines that are complex, overlapping, and nearly always bound to converge in captivating ways.

While its viewers always look forward to the beginning of a new season, it is never a show with a beginning. *24* always plunges its viewers into crises that have already begun, into the middle of things (*in medias res*). Characters and organizations can never make a truly fresh start. There is always some previous action or situation that complicates the next challenge or opportunity on the horizon.

It's no surprise that *24* has been hugely popular not just in North America, but also in Europe, Latin America, Asia, and Australia. The success of the show has been overwhelming and strikingly international in scope, despite the sensitive and controversial nature of its material: terrorism, covert action, intelligence gathering, torture, racial conflict, and profiling. In North America, the fan base extends across the political spectrum with celebrity fans ranging from Rush Limbaugh, Antonin Scalia, and John McCain to Bill Clinton, Rosie O'Donnell, and Barbra Streisand.

There have been plausible criticisms of *24*. For example, in an article in the *Guardian*, Slavoj Žižek makes the case that the show uses its realtime feature to heighten the viewer's perceptions of urgency and thereby manipulates sympathy for torture as the only way to avert dangerous situations. Other criticisms have included worries about the use of convenient stereotypes in the depictions of heroes, villains, and a cast of suspicious characters in between. But it may be that the interest in the show goes beyond political lines because it so artfully depicts interesting characters immersed in complex situations that generate wildly intriguing and unpredictable plot twists and outcomes. While the show doesn't resist depicting terrible crises fraught with urgency and unattractive alternatives, it certainly doesn't offer easy answers to those problems, nor a one-dimensional presentation of their causes. Nearly every crisis that Jack Bauer helps avert through questionable means brings damage of some sort upon Jack himself and those around him.

It may be that *24* appeals to familiar stereotypes, if only to test both their limitations and usefulness. I won't risk spoiling too many stunning surprises of *24* for new viewers. But it's fair to say that those who prove to be the actual villains and heroes of a season cut across lines of race, gender, age, and background, though the show doesn't go out of its way to manufacture appearances that conform to politically correct intuitions. Nevertheless, after six seasons, *24* has had two African-American Democratic presidents, who were brothers. The elder brother, David Palmer, was a revered and beloved character whose assassination sent shockwaves throughout his *24* constituency. In alternate seasons, the show had Caucasian Republican presidents who were far less attractive characters, one of whom was complicit in a plot against the US, and had to be rescued by David Palmer in a moment of crisis. Of course, Republican Defense Secretary James Heller (who bore a striking resemblance to Donald Rumsfeld) and hawkish political strategist Tom Lennox have been presented as very able and somewhat respectable figures, though not unflawed. Democratic Vice Presidents Jim Prescott and Noah Daniels are treated as dangerously ambitious and sometimes myopic. The bottom line is that both major political parties are presented with mixed qualities.

In many respects, the dramatic intensity and realtime elements of *24* help illuminate philosophical problems and dilemmas that philosophers have thought about for centuries, but which continue to be relevant across new and challenging contexts. The question of how we should live is as old as philosophy itself. Socrates asks us, "What is the good life?"—a contentious question that has sparked inquiry, debate, and a vast array of responses from philosophers over the centuries. But how we take up this question may already imply answers to other critical questions such as what we can know, the nature of reality, the scope and character of our ethical and political commitments, and perhaps even whether there is meaning in life.

This book gives a guided tour of CTU and the wider world of *24* with the help of the great philosophers—no stun gun required. The realtime dilemmas that characters like Jack Bauer, David Palmer, and Michelle Dessler must face are problems that help us think about the big questions of philosophy. This book's contributing authors have probably never met Jack Bauer or Nina Myers, but they nevertheless know how to tell us about them and what Aristotle, Kant, or Nietzsche might have to say about their problems.

How should we think about controversial actions such as torture, lying, and killing? Are they ethically acceptable, so long as they lead to very good consequences or avert very bad ones? If not, are there some actions that are always wrong, no matter what the circumstances or expected consequences? Is Jack Bauer off the hook ethically when his torture sessions help him save the day? Is it ethically permissible for Jack *not* to use force or deception in grave, catastrophic situations?

Is there such a thing as just war? If so, what conditions would have to be met for a justified use of force? And what are the appropriate limitations that should be placed on the execution of that force? Is there any justification for a covert incursion into the Chinese embassy and subsequent kidnapping of one of its citizens? Is it reasonable for the Chinese to treat Jack Bauer as a prisoner of war for leading the incursion? Would David Palmer have had any justification for a preemptive military strike against a state, had it tacitly supported a nuclear attack, albeit a failed one, in the US?

How do you know when to trust someone? How much evidence do you need in order to believe someone? What is the difference between belief and knowledge? *24* asks all of these philosophical questions because the currency of CTU is Intelligence. CTU needs to know when to trust someone and when to be suspicious; when to believe an Intelligence report, such as the Cyprus tape, and when to dismiss it. Some of these decisions are made in minutes if not seconds, but all of these decisions assume a particular epistemological framework that asserts various things about evidence, trust, belief, and knowledge.

"You're out of time!" Why is time so important to the show? Why is time so critical to how we assess particular situations? The fact is, human beings are subject to the constraints of time, and time is always of the essence for CTU. But that condition heightens the dramatic tension of the show, and challenges an armchair philosophy that puzzles over moral dilemmas in leisure. Jack has no such armchair. He is rarely seated—he's always moving, unless he's in restraints. Jack knows that events can happen simultaneously, that one must think and move quickly, and that mere seconds can sometimes be the difference between averting a nuclear disaster (like in Season Four) or experiencing one (as in Season Six).

The problems depicted in *24* are our problems. While they are sometimes overstated and other times understated, they bear enough resemblance to our world for us to take them seriously. So let's wrestle with these problems with the help of the great philosophers. We'll have to navigate the minefields of CTU and the world of *24*. But, don't worry! You don't have to be a field agent.

4:00 AM–5:00 AM

Acknowledgments:
Chloe, We Need You!

This book came about as a direct result of the collegiality at CTU. Perhaps no other counter-terrorism unit in the world has ever decided to edit a volume in philosophy, and completed that project before the personnel were eliminated or transferred.

Unlike most CTU operatives, we have enjoyed working with Division, especially Bill Irwin, Series Editor for Blackwell, and Jeff Dean, Senior Acquisitions Editor for Blackwell, who supported this operation from the very beginning. Gratitude is also due to our Oval Office and its inhabitants, especially Special Aide Will Kinchlea, whose security clearance had to be upgraded to scan Interpol "high probability chatter" for signs of trouble. Many security breaches were thereby avoided. We also thank our colleagues Brad Faught (MI5) and Scott Veenvliet (CSIS) for sharing intelligence and preemptive strategies.

Needless to say, CTU is nothing without Field Ops. A team of highly skilled agents provided us with critical encouragement, insider advice, and indispensable backup. Thanks are due to Glen and Angela Meyer (for parting for nearly a year with all those 24 box sets!), to Siegmar and Patricia Bodach (for sharing the obsession), and especially to Caroline Davis. Caroline viewed hundreds of hours of security footage, provided expert intel, and happily agreed to countless lengthy but delightful dialogues on the philosophical riches of 24. Each of these agents deserves a day off at the beach—or at least a free Coral Snake tattoo!

Most importantly, however, we would like to thank our students at Tyndale University College for their enthusiasm for philosophy. They keep us from being mere desk agents.

5:00 AM–9:00 AM

SPECIAL AGENT
JACK BAUER___

What Would Jack Bauer Do? Moral Dilemmas and Moral Theory in *24*

Randall M. Jensen

The later episodes of *24*'s first season open with Kiefer Sutherland's weary and heartfelt voiceover introduction: "I'm federal agent Jack Bauer. And this is the longest day of my life." In fact, every one of *24*'s day-long seasons competes for the title of the longest day in Jack's life. Bauer's days are long for a perfectly obvious reason: they're jam-packed full of surveillance, investigation, pursuit, political wrangling, interrogation, and combat. By the end of each season we feel we must have lived through more than just one day with Jack. But his days are long for another reason as well: Jack is constantly forced to make agonizing and gut-wrenching decisions. Time after time he has to decide who lives and who dies, often at his own hand and all too often with the life of someone he cares about hanging in the balance. Such moral dilemmas are one of the true hallmarks of *24*. Not only do they help keep us glued to the screen, they show us what Jack and the rest of the characters on *24* are really made of. Sometimes we see something to admire and emulate; other times we react with pity or disgust.

Fortunately, we don't often find ourselves in situations where the stakes are so high and the options so frightening. At times, however, most of us face moral dilemmas that have the same *structure* as the ones Jack confronts, but on a much smaller scale, of course. And if we spend some time thinking about some of *24*'s many moral dilemmas, we'll have the chance to explore some really interesting territory in *ethics*, the area of philosophy that has to do with what's right and wrong and

3

what's good and bad in human affairs. In particular, we'll be able to think about the idea of a *moral theory*, which is a general and systematic account of how all of us, including Jack Bauer, ought to live our lives. A moral theory potentially offers us a way to navigate through difficult moral terrain. But a moral dilemma may test our limits—and the limits of moral theory as well. Sometimes, like Jack Bauer, we may find ourselves in a kind of "moral hell" with no clear way of escape.

Jack's Dilemmas

Not every difficult decision is a moral dilemma. Many decisions are daunting for reasons that have little or nothing to do with morality. For example, some of Jack's decisions are tough calls because it isn't obvious what the outcomes of his various options are going to be, and so it's unclear which course of action is tactically preferable. Here the problem isn't really a *moral* one; instead, it's *epistemic*, which means that it concerns what we do and don't *know*. If an enemy agent—Nina Myers, for example—has some valuable intel, then Jack will be forced to comply with her demands, perhaps even to the point of letting her try to kill him. But if she doesn't actually have any important information, he might do something quite different, like put three rounds into her to make sure she's good and dead. Jack's strategy in dealing with Nina thus depends crucially on his figuring out what she does and doesn't know, and that's no small task. Although Jack's training, experience, and well-honed intuition equip him to handle such disturbing uncertainty, we ordinary folks are often paralyzed by our lack of knowledge even in less dire circumstances. But while our ignorance is a real problem for us, and while the resultant paralysis may render us incapable of making a decision, we're not yet in the grip of a moral dilemma. You see, if the problem is our ignorance of certain facts, the solution is obvious: more information. A true moral dilemma, however, is not resolved simply by more data-mining.

We have a genuine moral dilemma when there is a compelling moral reason to perform action A as well as a compelling moral reason to perform action B—and here's the kicker: we cannot do both A and B. So, a moral dilemma is the result of a conflict between competing moral reasons. What's a *moral reason*? Well, to begin with, it's a *practical* reason, which means it's a reason to *do* something (or not to do something) rather than a reason to *believe* something. And a moral reason is a reason to do something *because it's the right thing to do* and not for some other reason, such as *because it will impress someone* or *because it will please me* or whatever else. While moral philosophers argue about *exactly* what counts as a legitimate moral reason, it's pretty safe to say that moral reasons usually concern how we treat other people. Let's have a look at how competing moral reasons create a moral dilemma.

When Jack is on a mission, he often has some really important *end* in view: he's trying to stop an assassination or to prevent someone from deploying a nuclear, chemical, or biological weapon. This end supplies Jack with an overarching moral reason—*because it will save people from a threat*—that explains why he's doing many of the things he does. However, as we know, sometimes Jack's only *means* of pursuing this end involves doing something that strikes us as morally questionable, or sometimes even morally horrific. And don't we usually think we have moral reasons not to do things like that? Let's call this a *means-end* moral dilemma, since the conflict arises because we approve of Jack's end but disapprove of his means.

In Season Five, for example, Jack is tracking down a large supply of nerve gas that terrorists are planning to use on American soil. Thousands and thousands of lives are at stake. He's just captured Christopher Henderson, his former CTU mentor who is somehow involved in all this. Henderson won't talk, and Jack knows that standard interrogation techniques won't work on him because of his training. Thus, in desperation, Jack shoots Henderson's wife in the leg to try to force him to reveal the location of the nerve gas canisters. Clearly, we endorse Jack's end, which is to stop the release of the nerve gas and save numerous lives. But we also strongly disapprove of his means of achieving it: shooting someone who is an innocent bystander in all this. Doesn't morality tell us not to threaten or attack innocent people? Jack seems to have a moral reason to shoot Henderson's wife (*because it will save thousands of lives*) and a moral reason not to shoot her (*because it would harm an innocent bystander*).

So how should we evaluate what Jack has done? The answer is not obvious to everyone, which is why this strikes us as a dilemma.

24 supplies us with any number of additional means-end dilemmas. In his efforts to stop terrorists and save lives, is there anything Jack Bauer won't—or shouldn't—do? We've seen him shoot and kill an unarmed man (who is admittedly not a nice guy, but he's in custody and is no threat to anyone) and then cut off his head! We've seen him interrogate people in many cruel and unusual ways. In Season Three we even watched him execute Ryan Chappelle, a loyal and blameless Division operative, because a terrorist demanded it. And Jack doesn't just do such things to other people. We saw Jack get himself hooked on heroin to keep his cover, and it goes without saying that he's willing to sacrifice his own life in pursuit of a good end. Now all of these things are done for a good cause. But aren't there moral limits to what can be done even for a good cause?

The second kind of dilemma we often see on *24* is a *personal* moral dilemma. Here the conflict is between what strikes us as the morally right thing to do and what we feel compelled to do for personal reasons. By a personal reason we mean a reason that's based on our particular projects, commitments, and relationships; the reasons of love, family, and friendship are at the center of the realm of personal reasons. Notice that these personal reasons needn't be *selfish* ones, for many of them arise from our relationships with others. *24* began with an ongoing personal dilemma way back in Season One when Jack's family was held by terrorists who were forcing him to do whatever they wanted. Recall, for example, that Jack was forced to smuggle a weapon into a secure location and give it to a man who would assassinate Senator David Palmer. Surely Jack had some kind of moral reason not to cooperate with these nasty characters and not to endanger the life of a presidential candidate. But he also had very strong personal reasons to do whatever it took to save his wife and daughter! And it isn't just Jack who is caught in such a predicament, either. In Season Three, Tony Almeida must decide what to do when Stephen Saunders is holding Michelle Dessler and asks for his help in escaping, and then later in Season Four, Michelle faces the same awful choice when it's Tony who has been captured. In the end, Tony caves to the terrorist's demands to save Michelle, saying along the way, "I don't have a choice. I wish I did, but I don't." But Michelle refuses to go along with Tony's captors when his life is on the line, because, as Bill Buchanan puts it, "You can't put Tony's life ahead of the lives of millions." Who's right here? What should any of us do when forced to choose between love and morality's rules or the greater good?

Whatever the exact nature of the dilemma, Jack and his friends (and even his enemies) are all too often caught between a rock and a hard place. How do they deal with it? Can we learn anything from them? Or can we instead offer them some helpful moral advice, perhaps by way of a moral theory that will help them and us know how to handle a moral dilemma? After all, we face means-end and personal moral dilemmas too. We find ourselves trying to decide whether to tell a lie if it will prevent someone we know from suffering, for example, or whether to help a friend if it involves doing something morally dubious.

The Utilitarian Solution: Don't Be Squeamish!

Our first reaction to a moral dilemma is probably to find a way out of it. Sometimes we're lucky enough to think of a creative exit strategy that helps us to avoid making a seemingly impossible moral decision. Other times no such strategy is available and we're forced to choose between what look like two evils. But we want desperately to make the right choice! Perhaps a good moral theory will equip us to do just this. In fact, a moral theory may even *eliminate* many of our moral dilemmas by showing us that there's a morally correct choice after all—even if it's a hard choice to make.

The moral theory known as *utilitarianism* maintains that morality can be summed up by a single principle: you should always do what maximizes utility, where utility is to be understood as happiness or well being. Morally speaking, then, what really matters for the utilitarian is *the greatest happiness of the greatest number of people.* And given that its ultimate concern is to maximize happiness (and to minimize unhappiness), there is only one very general utilitarian moral reason for doing anything whatsoever: *that this action will produce the greatest balance of happiness over unhappiness.*[1] As a result, if the

---

1 The founding fathers of utilitarianism (consequentialism) are British philosophers Jeremy Bentham (1748–1832) and John Stuart Mill (1806–1873). Peter Singer is a well-known contemporary utilitarian.

end in an apparent means-end dilemma produces more happiness than whatever unhappiness is produced by the means, there's really no moral dilemma at all. For the utilitarian, the moral objection to shooting Henderson's wife, for example, is that it will cause her a good deal of pain and suffering, and it no doubt has other bad consequences. But in this case a utilitarian might judge that *not* shooting her would lead to even more suffering! So there's no dilemma. If we're not willing to do what will maximize happiness just because it seems wrong, the utilitarian diagnosis is that we're just being squeamish or that we're too moved by what is nothing more than a moral taboo or superstition. After all, morality sometimes demands that we do something we really don't want to, and that we get our hands dirty while doing it.[2]

If someone were to be unwilling to do what would maximize happiness for personal reasons, a utilitarian would regard this as a straightforward case of selfishness or partiality. A utilitarian might very well understand why it would be very difficult for Jack to sacrifice someone he loves simply because the sacrifice will maximize happiness. And a utilitarian might even partially *excuse* his failure to do so, as Tony Almeida apparently does in Season One when he says that while he doesn't agree with Jack's methods, Ryan Chappelle can't convince him to condemn anything Jack did while his family was being held hostage. But a utilitarian won't see Jack's personal reasons as having anywhere near enough moral force to create a moral dilemma when so much is at stake.

Utilitarianism doesn't assume that moral decisions are easy to make. Often, we face an epistemic problem: it may be nearly impossible to *know* which course of action will lead to the greatest happiness. Thus, while Jack thought that shooting Henderson's wife would force him to talk, it didn't. All utilitarianism requires is that we do what is *expected* to bring about the best results, and we don't always know what that is. Other times it may seem that our options lead to roughly the same amount of happiness, in which case we are facing a real moral dilemma, and the only kind a utilitarian would recognize. Suppose that canisters of nerve gas have been placed in two buildings,

---

2   For a detailed treatment of the "dirty hands" phenomenon in morality, see the chapter by Stephen de Wijze.

each of which contains roughly the same number of people, for example, and Jack only has time to get to one of these canisters. But except for situations like this, utilitarianism leaves no room for moral dilemmas. In this way, utilitarianism offers us a way of solving some very tricky moral problems: just figure out what course of action maximizes happiness. And while that might be hard to do, it's not spooky or mysterious in the way some moral systems might be.

Utilitarian reasoning should sound very familiar to *24* fans. Anyone who talks about what must be done for the greater good is probably talking the utilitarian's language. Think of the Season Six opener where Morris O'Brian says that if anyone understands what has to be done for the greater good, it's Jack, who's about to be handed over to a terrorist after being released by the Chinese government. And he's right, since Jack's own actions often seem motivated by a concern for the greater good. Of course, *24* fans know that villains who talk about the greater good are sometimes just using such language as a cover for their own agenda. In contrast with such thoroughly political creatures, real utilitarians actually mean it when they say something is for the greater good!

The Deontological Solution: You Just Can't Do That!

The unfamiliar word *deontology* is derived from *deon*, a Greek word that means duty or obligation. So it's no surprise to hear that the aim of a deontological moral theory is to say what we're obligated to do and what we're forbidden to do. Such a theory is often expressed in a series of rules or principles that together make up the moral law. Different deontologists endorse different rules, of course, but nearly all deontological theories include prohibitions of deceit, assault, murder, and the like. For a deontologist, a moral person is someone who does the right thing for the right reason, and this may or may not lead to the best consequences.[3] Such a moral theory may also help us to eliminate moral dilemmas: Jack should follow the moral rules, never mind the consequences.

---

3   Immanuel Kant (1724–1804) is the key figure in the history of deontological ethics.

Randall M. Jensen

In Season Five, CTU decides to allow the release of one canister of nerve gas in a mall filled with shoppers because it seems to be the only way to track the terrorists back to the other 19 canisters. The reasoning for this decision is clearly utilitarian: sacrifice a large number of lives to save an even larger number. But Audrey Raines strenuously objects to this decision in fine deontological fashion, saying that they have no right to sanction the deaths of innocent people, presumably because it's wrong to treat these people as pawns in a strategy to beat the terrorists, rather than seeing them as persons who must be treated with respect. Think also of Kate Warner's very deontological moral revulsion (or is it just squeamishness?) in Season Two when she thinks that Jack has killed the son of a terrorist he's interrogating—even though she knows very well that thousands of lives are at stake. Now Jack didn't really kill the boy; he faked it, which was good enough to get the boy's father to tell Jack what he wanted. But most deontological theories would prohibit Jack from using deception as well as torture and murder, even if his cause is a good one. For the deontologist, then, it's *always* morally right to act on principle, regardless of the consequences for the greater good or for those we love. If the moral law prohibits torture or shooting someone who's innocent, then it's wrong to do so no matter what Jack or anyone else might be trying to achieve. No means-end or personal dilemmas here.

Finding a Compromise?

We now have two potential ways of handling moral dilemmas. But it may seem that all we've accomplished is to shift the dilemma to the theoretical level, for we may now feel torn between these two theories, unable to accept either one of them wholeheartedly. Is there some way to forge a theoretical compromise?

The version of utilitarianism we've been considering is called *act-utilitarianism*, since it evaluates *acts* in terms of how much happiness they produce. *Rule-utilitarianism*, on the other hand, determines what set of *rules* produces the most happiness and then requires that we live according to those rules. So a rule-utilitarian might consider the various rules regarding torture and decide that a rule that's too permissive of torture—allowing it in any case where it will do even *slightly* more good than harm—will have bad results over the long haul if we were to accept and follow it. A more restrictive policy might thus be more beneficial for all of us. CTU might well operate along rule-utilitarian lines, as might any number of bureaucracies.

Alternatively, we might consider a version of deontology whose principles aren't absolute. Suppose torture is prohibited for the deontological reason that it treats another person as a mere means to an end, and thus we shouldn't torture someone just because it leads to a somewhat greater good. It's possible to think that this moral reason against torture can at some point—call it a threshold—be overridden by a highly compelling utilitarian reason, such as that thousands and thousands of lives can be saved.[4] This form of deontological theory is founded on moral principle, but it doesn't simply ignore the consequences of acting on principle. And so the deontologist moves some distance toward the utilitarian.

Each of these compromise strategies involves making moral theory a much more complicated business. And in the all too complicated moral landscape of 24, this is probably a good thing. However, such strategies make two assumptions that we might not want to assume: first, that we should indeed make a choice between utilitarianism and deontology, and second, that it's a good thing if a moral theory works to eliminate moral dilemmas. But—as 24 shows us on any number of occasions—we should be very careful about what we assume!

Now It's Personal!

Think back to Season Three when Jack stages a prison break to spring Ramon Salazar. They're in a chopper headed for Los Angeles. Salazar is a very dangerous man, so of course the US government doesn't want him on the loose. President David Palmer is asked whether or not they should shoot down the helicopter. His response? "I can't give the order to kill Jack Bauer." Why does the president say this? No doubt it's because of all Jack has done for him and for the country and because of his own friendship with Jack as well. Thus he has strong personal reasons for refusing to let CTU shoot down Jack and Salazar. But Wayne Palmer replies: "You have to think about

4 For more on the utilitarian argument for torture and its perils, see Dónal P. O'Mathúna's chapter.

national security, David . . . You have got to make this decision as if it wasn't Jack Bauer on that helicopter." Wayne is urging President Palmer to consider the greater good, to think about this decision from a utilitarian perspective rather than a personal one, which is no doubt something a president often has to do. Now it may very well be that Wayne is right to urge President Palmer to have the helicopter shot down. A utilitarian would think so. After all, the damage Salazar could do if he got away far outweighs the cost in happiness of shooting them down. And it may be that a deontologist would see this action as Palmer's duty as president. We might agree. But is it obvious that Wayne is right to tell his brother to make the decision *as if Jack wasn't involved*? A utilitarian or deontological morality seems to ask us to treat someone who's a friend—someone we're connected to—as we would treat anyone else, because friendship has no real moral weight.

One of the complaints sometimes lodged against both utilitarianism and deontology is that they're *impersonal*. It isn't that love and friendship don't matter at all on a utilitarian or deontological scheme. Rather, it's that they don't matter enough, and they matter in the wrong way. Consider utilitarianism first. Suppose Kim Bauer is being held hostage somewhere and Jack's trying to rescue her. And suppose further that Jack finds that a small group of five people is also being held at the other end of the fairly large building from Kim. Who does Jack go after? Utilitarianism doesn't tell Jack to ignore Kim entirely. He can factor into his calculations the fact that he'd be very saddened by her death. But that's not going to move the scales of utility very much when we weigh that against the deaths of a few more people and the sadness of those who'll mourn for them. The fact that Jack is Kim's father just doesn't count for much here, morally speaking. In effect, he does have to make this decision as if it weren't his daughter at the other end of the building. Psychologically speaking, no doubt Jack feels nearly compelled to save Kim. But that's not a moral compulsion, at least not according to utilitarianism.

But wait a minute. Is it possible that Jack has overlooked some more remote bad consequences of his deciding not to save Kim? After all, what if his failure to save Kim meant that he'd wind up a broken man, unable to continue saving the world? Much unhappiness might come of that. What if his failure to save Kim in some strange way led to other fathers caring less for their daughters? Even more unhappiness! Maybe an ingenious utilitarian can make it turn out so that Jack is allowed to save Kim after all. Whew! But even if that works, which isn't to be taken for granted, surely that's not what we were looking for. What we wanted was for Jack's *direct concern* for his daughter to be assigned some real moral weight, not for the calculations of the global consequences to turn out a bit differently. Utilitarianism treats people as units of happiness in an enormous utility calculation rather than seeing each of us as an individual person, separate from all the rest. And that's why it's objectionably impersonal. Indeed, it almost seems inhuman.

What about deontology? Here what governs our moral dealings with other people is duty and obligation. Where does this leave love and friendship? Many deontologists are likely to see these relations as merely relying on natural human sentiments, which need to be constrained by the moral law. Another option for a deontologist would be to account for the importance of personal concerns by portraying them as a form of obligation. To act out of friendship would then be to do what we're duty-bound to do by the moral law as it pertains to friendship. Again, while such a move might be successful, it doesn't seem to locate the significance of friendship in the right place. Imagine Jack trying desperately to save Kim, thinking to himself, "She's my daughter! I've got to save her! And under these circumstances duty requires me to save her!" As philosopher Bernard Williams has observed, the last sentence here seems to be "one thought too many."[5] Acting out of love and friendship just doesn't fit into the mold of obligation and duty. Deontology, like utilitarianism, doesn't seem to give a plausible and attractive account of the role of love and friendship in the moral life. If we take personal moral reasons seriously, we may have a reason to worry about whether either of these moral theories tells us the whole story.

Some People are More Comfortable in Hell

Jack himself is neither a utilitarian nor a deontologist. That he's no committed deontologist is relatively clear, for at some point he has broken nearly every plausible candidate for a deontological rule, even

5 Bernard Williams, "Persons, Character, and Morality," reprinted in his *Moral Luck* (Cambridge: Cambridge University Press, 1981).

if he regrets doing so. Jack is just not a "play by the rules" kind of guy, which suggests he's not a rule-utilitarian either. But he's clearly not an act-utilitarian, since he doesn't always relentlessly pursue the greatest good, no matter what. Sometimes he is swayed from that path by a deontological reason. He agrees with Audrey that they cannot sacrifice a mall full of innocent people in order to save even more innocent people. And in Season Six, he vehemently (and deontologically!) proclaims to Bill Buchanan that he's not trying to save Josh just because he's his nephew, but rather because he's an innocent kid and it's the right thing to do. However, Jack is often motivated by personal reasons when those he loves are at risk. He does not just pursue his mission and ignore their fate. But neither does he simply abandon his mission due to their plight. So what should we say about Jack Bauer and the things he does? And what can we learn about morality from watching him in action?

The difficulty we experience in categorizing Jack's behavior should provoke us to ask whether we want the kind of moral clarity our two theories offer us. Do we want our moral theory to try to eliminate the possibility of moral dilemmas as far as it can? It might seem so, for wouldn't a world without moral dilemmas be a more rational and morally superior world? And if there are moral dilemmas, then we have to abandon the idea that the claim that we *ought* to do something implies that we *can* do it. For in any bona fide moral dilemma there's going to be something that we ought to do but can't. Yet the "ought-implies-can" principle assures us that we won't ever be obligated to do anything that's beyond our grasp. That's reassuring.

But sometimes being reassured isn't a good thing. In at least some of Jack's dilemmas, we should be dissatisfied with any definitive moral solution. Why so? Because our world is messy, complicated, and tragic, and if that's the way things are, then our moral theory should see the world in that way rather than painting the world as a better place than it really is. In Season Four, Tony Almeida memorably says that Jack Bauer may be more comfortable in hell. Maybe we need our moral theory to be more comfortable there too. What we need, I submit, is a moral theory that recognizes the hellish and deeply problematic nature of human life. That is, we want a moral theory that refuses to work to eliminate moral dilemmas and instead accepts them as a necessary if terribly unfortunate part of the moral landscape: a messy theory for a messy and tragic world. Such is the world of *24*.

We can see Jack Bauer as a living example of such a moral outlook. He doesn't operate as if he is driven *only* by a concern for the greater good, or *only* by a concern to do what's right as a matter of principle, or *only* by a concern for those he loves. No, he's driven by *all* of these concerns. None of them takes pride of place in every situation. Sometimes Jack is nearly torn in half by competing concerns. When that happens, he often has no time to think and must react swiftly and decisively, as his training has taught him to do. But in the rare moments where Jack has the luxury of stopping to think about what he's doing and what he's done, the terrible moral toll life is taking on him shows itself. Think about the end of Season Three, when Jack sits in his SUV and sobs. Remember him staring out over the ocean as Season Six closes. Or look at Jack just after he's shot fellow agent and friend Curtis Manning in the beginning of Season Six. Of course, in each of these moments Jack is exhausted, both physically and emotionally. But while we can't really get at the interior of Jack Bauer, we detect in these moments a display of profound moral regret. And this regret isn't just a feeling to be excised because it's irrational. Instead, it's an emotional expression of Jack's moral judgment that some of what he did was morally wrong, maybe even deeply so. It isn't just that something turned out badly and Jack now wishes he had acted differently, which is no doubt the case at times. Even if Jack wouldn't have changed a single thing, he may regard some of what he did as deserving moral condemnation—even if not doing these things would also have deserved moral condemnation!

In the end, what does a day with Jack Bauer teach us about morality? Since we're not likely to face the situations he does, practically speaking, he can't be much of a moral role model. We probably don't approve of everything he does either. He isn't perfect. And his responses to difficult situations are varied enough that they resist any simple analysis. Indeed, they may very well seem inconsistent! But isn't that the point? Sometimes the world throws us a curve, presenting us with a situation where there's no morally correct response—a real, live moral dilemma, or a "moral blind alley," as Thomas Nagel has put it.[6] We'll have to decide what to do, of course, and we'll do that by weighing the various kinds of moral reasons that compete for

6 Thomas Nagel, "War and Massacre," reprinted in his *Mortal Questions* (Cambridge: Cambridge University Press, 1979).

our attention, without any simple formula that shows us the way. But if we've paid attention to 24's teachings, we won't assume we're guaranteed an option that will leave us with a clean conscience and without grounds for regret. Ironically, in the world of 24 it's the bad guys who often seem to have a crystal clear and uncompromising moral vision. But in living through the hardest days of Jack's life with him, we'll have learned that ambiguity, conflict, and dilemmas are part and parcel of the moral life.

Between Hero and Villain: Jack Bauer and the Problem of "Dirty Hands"

Stephen de Wijze

Jack Bauer: You are Marshall Goren?

Marshall Goren: Yes.

Jack Bauer: Eight counts kidnapping a minor, two counts child pornography.

Marshall Goren: Yeah, hey look I already made my deal. I testify against Wald and I walk.

[Jack pulls out his gun and fires a bullet through Goren's heart.]

George Mason: Oh God. Jack, are you out of your mind?!

Jack Bauer: You wanna find this bomb? This is what it's going to take!

George Mason: Killing a witness?

Jack Bauer: That's the thing about people like you George, you don't want to get your hands dirty. I'd start rolling up your sleeves . . . I'm gonna need a hacksaw.

Season Two, 8:00 AM–9:00 AM

No ethics in the world can dodge the fact that in numerous instances the attainment of "good" ends is bound to the fact that one must be willing to pay the price of using morally dubious means or at least dangerous ones—and facing the possibility or even the probability of evil ramifications.

Max Weber

Stephen de Wijze

Jack Bauer is the quintessential tragic hero. On the one hand, his limitless courage, obsessive single-mindedness, terrifying ruthlessness, self-sacrifice, and devotion to duty make him the most effective member of CTU in Los Angeles. Jack lives by what the German sociologist Max Weber (1864–1920) calls "an ethic of responsibility" rather than an "ethic of ultimate ends."[1] On the other hand, Jack's role as a CTU agent requires that he employ immoral means in order to achieve vitally important ends. As a result Jack has saved countless innocent civilians from horrific injury and death, prevented unnecessary wars, uncovered corruption at the highest level of government, and infiltrated the darkest recesses of the criminal underworld. But his accomplishments require him to engage in betrayal, deceit, torture, and even murder—activities that we ordinarily and rightly condemn as immoral (not to mention illegal). For Jack to succeed, he must do wrong in order to do right; he must get "dirty hands" in the process. What's more, in some important ways, Jack becomes like the very criminals and terrorists he loathes and detests and consequently suffers the moral opprobrium and internal torment that goes with it.

Does this mean that effective action by those in institutional roles, such as CTU operatives, are necessarily subject to a different (or even no) moral standard? Do concerns about achieving certain ends trump all moral considerations? In this chapter we'll explore the puzzling phenomenon of "dirty hands" and the notion of a "political morality" to which it gives rise. It seems that achieving noble ends sometimes requires immoral means. The standard moral theories, across both the consequentialist (right and wrong decided by consequences) and duty based ("deontological") spectrum, reject the possibility of getting dirty hands by either denying that immoral means can ever achieve good and worthwhile ends, or by insisting that the means used are not immoral. As we'll see, neither of these responses is persuasive, and an examination of the kind of situation Jack Bauer typically faces points to a better account of this moral puzzle and its solution.

24 offers vivid examples of moral dilemmas and the need, indeed obligation, for those who hold real power to get dirty hands. Jack and his colleagues, along with the President of the USA and his advisors,

1   Max Weber, "Politics as a Vocation" in *From Max Weber: Essays in Sociology*, trans. and ed. H. H. Gerth and C. Wright Mills (New York: Oxford University Press, 1958), p. 120. Page references to Weber are to this work.

face the most terrible choices imaginable. As philosopher Martha Nussbaum points out, drawing on insights from Greek tragedy, there is a fragility to goodness, since good persons can be morally ruined because of circumstances outside their control and what they are morally required to do to bring about the lesser of two terrible evils.[2] This chapter illustrates why an "ethic of responsibility" (what we shall call a "political morality") is possible, necessary, and desirable. We'll begin with a description of the phenomenon known as the "dirty hands" problem. This is the morally difficult and paradoxical situation where a good person is moved by moral considerations to commit serious moral wrongs due to the immoral or evil machinations of others. Typically, but not exclusively, this situation arises in politics where in order to achieve crucially important and worthwhile ends it is necessary to engage in immoral actions. We will use the term *politics* to refer to those activities that deal with matters that require the use of violence and coercion in order to succeed. To this extent, Jack Bauer fills an institutional role similar to that of a politician, as he has the responsibilities and power to confront threats to the citizens of the United States of America. We shall see that from the insights gained from a dirty hands analysis, the outlines of a political morality can be sketched: one that lays down the principles for a realistic middle path between the self-defeating moral poles of cynicism and naïvety.

An Important Warning

There have been some powerful and important criticisms made of *24*—with its depiction of torture and murder as legitimate means for government agents and politicians to pursue criminals and terrorists —especially post-9/11 and in the light of the Abu Ghraib scandal. *The New Yorker*[3] reported that the Dean of West Point, Brigadier General Patrick Finnegan, requested that the TV show's producers reduce and moderate its torture content. His particular worry is that

---

2   Martha C. Nussbaum, *The Fragility of Goodness: Luck and Ethics in Greek Tragedy and Philosophy* (Cambridge: Cambridge University Press, 1986).
3   Jane Mayer, "Whatever It Takes: The Politics of the Man Behind '24'," *The New Yorker*, February 19, 2007, available online at www.newyorker.com/printables/fact/070219fa_fact_mayer.

the depiction of torture is widespread, seen to be effective, and above all, the unambiguously right and patriotic thing to do when confronted with a terrorist threat. Such a view concerns Finnegan because it could have a deleterious influence on military cadets. It seems that the military rank and file (often avid followers of the series) question the validity of upholding the rule of law and human rights when facing ruthless and fanatical enemies, citing situations depicted in *24* as their reasons.

Other voices, such as the Slovenian political philosopher and cultural critic Slavoj Žižek, are concerned about another message implicit in *24*, one that indicates a sad and "deep change in our ethical and political standards."[4] Žižek argues that the program depicts torture in a way that is fundamentally dishonest and consequently deeply damaging to our moral and psychological well being. In all six seasons Jack's egregious and appalling acts of torture are committed in pursuit of his duties as an honest and virtuous person. This confers on him a particular "tragic-ethical grandeur." While it's clear that Jack's terrible actions trouble him, he nevertheless retains his humanity and emotional wholeness. Žižek and others point out that this is not what happens in reality. Torturers themselves very often develop into monsters and become the personification of the system's excess, ultimately destroying themselves and the very system that gave them legitimacy. The scandal of Abu Ghraib with the photos of the jailers clearly enjoying the torment of their prisoners is a recent reminder of this phenomenon.

While it is important to take such criticisms seriously this is not the place to respond to them. For present purposes, *24* offers a set of hypothetical situations which spur a discussion on the issue of dirty hands and a political morality. Although the cases are fictional and exaggerated, they offer a useful means of highlighting some key elements that make the problem of dirty hands so interesting from a philosophical perspective. *24*'s portrayals of clashes between fundamental values, the need to choose the least terrible option (rather than a choice between good and bad options), and the effect of institutional roles on our moral obligations and duties, nicely illustrate an

4   Slavoj Žižek, "The Depraved Heroes of *24* are the Himmlers of Hollywood," *Guardian Unlimited*, January 10, 2006, available online at www.guardian.co.uk/comment/story/0,3604,1682760,00.html.

aspect of our difficult moral reality and serves as a heuristic device to begin a serious philosophical analysis. At no point are terrible actions of murder or torture taken lightly or casually. On the contrary, the very purpose of a dirty hands analysis is to outline the appropriate moral boundaries for politicians and examine what follows when these limits need to be violated in extreme situations.

Dirty Hands Required

Jack acts in terrible ways as a CTU agent. He lies, kills, tortures, and if circumstances require it, even betrays his co-workers, family, and friends, neglecting them and/or subjecting them to monstrous treatment. (Jack's neglect of his daughter Kim, the interrogation of his lover Audrey Raines, and the torture of his brother Graem are cases in point.) Jack doesn't enjoy doing these things. Rather, he reluctantly and painfully accepts the need to commit these horrendous acts in order to protect the citizens of the United States. Failure on his part will result in catastrophic events. Jack forcefully points this out to CTU Director George Mason, who is taken aback when Jack murders Marshall Goren—a pedophile and kidnapper who has made a deal to turn state witness. Jack shoots Goren in cold blood and cuts off his head, not out of a sense of street justice, but as a necessary part of bluffing his way into the confidence of Joseph Wald, the leader of a criminal gang who possess information that can lead them to the terrorists who have nuclear weapons. Mason, appalled by the murder of a state witness, remonstrates with Jack, accusing him of losing his mind. Jack, in frustration, shouts at Mason: "*You wanna find this bomb? This is what it's going to take!*" and then adds, "That's the thing about people like you George, you don't want to get your hands dirty."

Jack is echoing a point made by many political theorists (and authors of fiction),[5] most famously Niccolò Machiavelli (1469–1527) but also more recently by eminent theorists such as Max Weber and Jean-Paul Sartre (1905–1980). Essentially the point is this: persons

---

5 The problem of dirty hands has also been the subject of many literary works. For a good sample of such works see Herman Melville's *Billy Budd*, Bertold Brecht's *The Measures Taken*, Albert Camus's play *The Just*, J. M. Coetzee's *Waiting for the Barbarians*, and William Styron's *Sophie's Choice*.

engaged in practical politics (realpolitik) are often forced to choose the lesser of two evils, using violence and other unpleasant means to achieve their goals. Consequently, morally upright persons cannot help but get their hands dirty in politics, and they are right to do so. As philosopher Michael Walzer enigmatically puts it, we want our politicians to be good enough for politics but not too good. If they are too good and keep their hands clean, they will fail to protect us; but if they have no qualms about committing such acts as murder and torture, they are persons that shouldn't be given power over us.

President David Palmer is this Walzerian type of politician. He is a good man who detests engaging in murder and torture, yet in extreme situations will authorize such actions when no alternative exists for protecting American citizens. By contrast, President Logan steps outside these boundaries because of weakness of character and unfettered driving personal ambition. He lacks the integrity and sound judgment required of those who are good enough for politics but not too good. Paradoxically, for morally good politicians to succeed in their fight against those who would harm us, they must at times, as Machiavelli famously reminds us, learn how not to be good. Sartre echoes this point in his play entitled *Les Mains sales* (Dirty Hands) where the main protagonist points out to his naïve idealist companion: "Well, I have dirty hands. Right up to the elbows. I've plunged them into filth and blood. So what? Do you think you can govern innocently?"

This is the crux of the problem facing good men and women in politics or similar social roles. Jack (and this applies equally to President Palmer and others) faces the kind of choices that ordinary people rarely, if ever, face in their day-to-day lives. This is not to say that such choices cannot occur in our private lives. However, the natural domain of terrible choices and the need to use violence is most often found in the sphere of politics, where individuals have specific and unique responsibilities because of their role and status. Politicians, for example, wield considerable power, which they are duty-bound to use to do good and combat evil. Dirty hands situations arise when the need to combat evil cannot be met without using methods, or indulging in actions, that are deeply repugnant to any civilized person. This point is well illustrated by the terrible and harrowing scene towards the end of Season Four in which Jack forces Dr. Basin (the CTU doctor) to stop operating on Paul Raines (who then dies as a result) in order to save the life of the badly injured informant, Lee Jong. Jack has to betray Paul (who recently saved his life) because Lee is the only lead he has for finding the evil Habib Marwan and the missing nuclear warhead.

This, then, is the problem of dirty hands, which Machiavelli and others have called the "ends-means problem in politics." Politicians who seek to bring about good in the face of evil, become, to some significant extent, mired and complicit with the very evil they seek to prevent. The successful politician in such circumstances must be prepared to use as everyday weapons of government "deceit and guile, unjust violence and sudden aggression, ingratitude in relations with allies and friends."[6] Dirty hands scenarios are distinguishable from moral dilemmas, tragic situations and simply immoral actions in that the agent's actions are morally justified, even obligatory, but still nevertheless wrong and shameful. This somewhat paradoxical moral position, where a person must do wrong to do right, arises when there is a justified betrayal of persons, values, or principles, due to the immoral or evil circumstances created by other persons or organizations. A good person is moved by moral considerations (the obligation to bring about the lesser evil) to commit moral violations (such as deceit, torture, and murder). Jack's choices in all the various seasons of *24* place him in just such situations.

Consider again the case where Jack forces Dr. Basin at gunpoint to let Paul Raines die in order to save Lee Jong. This situation is different from what we would ordinarily understand as a tragic dilemma scenario where a patient dies because a doctor is physically unable to attend two persons at the same time. In this dirty hands scenario, we have the added factors of betrayal and the immoral use of force to make the doctor abandon his patient for non-medical reasons. Remember though: Jack's enemies are ruthless, dedicated, and deadly. Time is against him, and stopping the terrorists is an overwhelming necessity. Consequently, he is justified in using coercion, torture, and even murder. Nevertheless he becomes morally polluted by doing so. Torture and murder, it must be stressed, always remain immoral and terrible acts even if special and rare circumstances also make them, all things

---

6   Stuart Hampshire, *Innocence and Experience* (Cambridge, MA: Harvard University Press, 1989), p. 163. Page references to Hampshire are to this work.

considered, the right thing to do. As the British philosopher Bernard Williams (1929–2003) points out, in such terrible moral conflict or dilemma situations, there can be no moral resolution of the conflict without some moral remainder or pollution adhering to the agent.[7] Given the choices Jack faces, he cannot act without becoming morally polluted. Again, paradoxically, Jack ought to be both praised for having the courage and fortitude for doing what had to be done but also condemned for committing terrible actions such as torture, deceit, and murder.

Dirty Politics

The phenomenon of dirty hands suggests that political action requires (both from a normative and prudential perspective) to do, or to tolerate, actions that would be regarded as wrong or evil if judged in terms of a personal morality. Furthermore, a successful leader, or anyone engaged in a difficult and demanding social role requiring decisive action, needs to know how not to be good if he or she intends to govern effectively in a world where so many people are not good. From an ethical point of view, what can be reasonably demanded from those engaged in such activities? What can we say about Jack Bauer's moral standing given his role as a CTU agent? Does the nature of his job render moral considerations otiose or irrelevant? Should we insist that morality is all of one piece, so that the standard moral boundaries and prohibitions apply to Jack despite the sizeable responsibilities he carries and the horrendous choices he must face? Or should we explore the possibility of a third option, one where Jack's role as a CTU agent enables him to operate in terms of a different ethic, one that at times embraces cunning, ruthlessness, and violence while abstaining from the values that good persons seek to promote; namely, justice, love, tolerance, gentleness, and charity? In short, does Jack operate according to what we shall call a "political morality"?

---

7 Bernard Williams, "Ethical Consistency," in his *Problems of the Self* (Cambridge: Cambridge University Press, 1973).

Is "Moral Politician" an Oxymoron?

The answers to the questions posed above depend on how we construe and understand the scope and importance of morality within human activities. And in turn, our decision on whether moral strictures apply to the domain of politics, as they do to other spheres of human activity, depends on our understanding of the nature of politics and what is required of those that partake in it. To this end, there are two fairly well developed paradigms for understanding the relationship between morality and politics.

The first, which we shall call the Anti-Morality view, denies that moral considerations have any place at all in the evaluation of political action. For example, Dean Acheson, President John F. Kennedy's secretary of state during the Cuban Missile Crisis, argued that when evaluating political action, prudential concerns must take precedence. Moral concerns, he insisted, simply do not bear on the problem. What lies behind the Anti-Morality view is the strong conviction that the stakes in politics are so high that it is results, and results alone, that matter.[8] Certainly, when we look at the choices facing Jack and the horrendous consequences that will obtain if he fails, the Anti-Morality view holds a certain attraction. Its fatal weakness, however, is that it allows politicians to act with impunity if they believe the stakes are high enough. This position throws the baby out with the bathwater, so to speak. It engenders a dangerous form of moral cynicism that ineluctably leads down a slippery slope where deceit, murder, and torture become acceptable and commonplace. Indeed, this cynical realist view and the consequent slide down an immoral slippery slope forms the background for all the key events of Season Five. Here we see the immoral and illegal actions and eventual demise of President Logan, Chief of Staff Walt Cummings, and defense contractor Christopher Henderson as they become more and more entangled in the actions of a shadowy group led by (as we later find out) Jack's brother Graem in order to secure oil interests in Central Asia. Their actions—unlike those taken by Jack in dirty hands scenarios—have no redeeming features.

8   The Realist School of International Relations follows this line of reasoning. See Michael Smith, *Realist Thought from Weber to Kissinger* (Baton Rouge: Louisiana State University Press, 1986).

Stephen de Wijze

The serious concerns with the Anti-Morality view lead to the second view on the relationship between politics and morality, the Morality as Seamless approach. This position argues that morality must apply seamlessly to all the spheres of human activity no matter how high the stakes involved or the importance of specific aims or goals. Civilized behavior demands this, and it prevents the descent into an attitude of anything goes among our politicians. The bulk of contemporary moral theorists share this view both from the duty-based and consequentialist perspectives. Some politicians who have held the highest office have explicitly endorsed this view. Jimmy Carter insisted: "A nation's domestic and foreign policy actions should be derived from the same standards of ethics, honesty, and morality which are characteristic of the individual citizens of the nation."[9]

The problem with this approach, however, is that it rejects the possibility that in some, albeit extremely rare, circumstances, insisting on only using moral means to combat evil could result in catastrophic consequences; consequences which could have been avoided but for this moral squeamishness. Certainly, Jack's task of stopping the detonation of nuclear bombs or preventing the release of lethal nerve gas in populated areas (just two among the many other horrendous possibilities) seem to be cases where we ought not to rest too heavily on moral niceties. In these extreme situations, the Morality as Seamless approach requires politicians to sacrifice the lives and well being of innocent citizens for the sake of moral rectitude. If this is correct, the Morality as Seamless approach engenders a form of political naïvety that is dangerous in a world where the evil aims of others place us in considerable danger. It's one thing to choose to sacrifice one's own well being and life for moral considerations (to embrace a doctrine of pacifism, for example), but quite another to do this when one has a specific responsibility for the lives and well being of others.

Where both the Anti-Morality and the Morality as Seamless perspectives make a fundamental error is in seeking to make our complex and messy moral reality one all encompassing and simplifying relationship between moral theory and the practice of politics on the ground. In both cases, this results in distorted moral judgments by

9 Quoted in Stephen A. Garrett, "Political Leadership and the Problem of 'Dirty Hands'," *Ethics & International Affairs* 8 (1994): 162.

insisting on situations which are either politically naïve ("no matter what always use moral means") or unnecessarily cynical ("no moral strictures whatever are necessary in politics"). Consequently, a third view, one that advocates a "political morality" seeks to rectify these faults and offer an account that better resonates with our moral reality. The third view offers a more nuanced and realistic account of how good persons ought to act (and feel about themselves) when engaged in realpolitik. To promote the public good, this view seeks a moral code that allows (and sometimes even requires) the violation of moral prohibitions that would apply in our personal lives.

Living in the World of Realpolitik

Let's first examine the nature of politics using an insight from Machiavelli, who argues that politics is a *sui generis*, or unique, activity because in such a profession a "man who wants to act virtuously in every way necessarily comes to grief among many who are not virtuous."[10] The responsibility of a person like Jack is immense; the lives and well being of a great many people rest upon him. Consequently, it is appropriate that Jack should put aside any qualms he may have from a personal moral perspective and, as Machiavelli insists, "learn how not to be virtuous, and to make use of this or not according to need" (91). The effective use of political power demands a ruthless pursuit of collective goals for the general good. Generosity, charity, and "turning the other cheek" will result in failure. Too many persons, organizations, and states will take advantage of such virtues, which they conceive as cowardice and moral squeamishness. Jack's success arises from his particular virtues, namely, his courage, decisiveness, clear-headedness, unbounded energy, ability to command, and his single-mindedness in the pursuit of his enemies. We admire him for these virtues and also feel trepidation at his ability to maneuver so successfully in a world of violence, deceit, and chaos. But the world of realpolitik often demands a certain orientation that isn't always compatible with the values we cherish in our personal lives.

10 Niccolò Machiavelli, *The Prince*, trans. George Bull (London: Penguin Books, 1981), p. 91. Page references to Machiavelli are to this work.

It would be a mistake to think that the violent and turbulent world of realpolitik is simply a response to the societies of the past and that the Machiavellian insights no longer apply to the stable and benign milieu of liberal democracies. Jack's predicaments in *24*, albeit exaggerated, are not impossible, and liberal democratic societies face threats to their existence no less dire than those faced by the city-states in Machiavelli's time. We still need men and women who are prepared to commit violence on our behalf to keep us safe. The main difference from medieval times is that liberal democracies rightly expect their politicians to act within moral boundaries and behave in a manner that distinguishes them from those who clearly reject any moral constraints on their behavior. We also want our political systems to be sufficiently transparent so that we can properly judge the behavior of our politicians. Morality matters, even if in the realm of politics its application is more complicated than in other realms.

The Morality of Politics

So what makes the domain of politics significantly different from other social spheres thus requiring a specific political morality? Let's highlight three important factors. Firstly, the world of politics differs from other domains in that the aim and nature of politics itself are special. In its proper role, politics is the use of coercive power in the pursuit of justice and the general good. Realpolitik is the continual battle over scarce resources and the attempt to ensure security and stability in a chaotic world with limited powers. The realization of realpolitik is that, at best, solutions to problems will be shabby compromises, shaky alliances, and the acceptance of the least bad option. As Stuart Hampshire points out, politicians must be able to live with "expectation of unavoidable squalor and imperfection, of necessary disappointments and mixed results, of half success and half failure" (170). All of these factors are plainly evident in Jack's world of terrorism, espionage, spying, and brutal politics.

Secondly, the role of the politician requires an acceptance of additional moral duties and obligations, primarily to always act to protect the reasonable interests of innocent fellow citizens. This task must at times take precedence over their own moral scruples and personal well being. There can be no doubt that Jack suffers terrible personal and moral loss due to his job. He continually has to neglect and place in danger those nearest and dearest to him. What's more, his moral goodness and sense of self-worth are constantly at risk due to the things he has to do in order to succeed. Weber emphasizes this point. Whoever engages in realpolitik "must know that he is responsible for what may become of himself under the impact of these paradoxes" (125). "He who seeks the salvation of the soul, of his own and others, should not seek it along the avenue of politics, for the quite different task of politics can only be resolved by violence" (126).

The third reason why the practice of politics requires a political morality is that the particular structural and functional features of political office change our moral judgments. The sheer numbers of people affected by political decisions, the largely impersonal and bureaucratic administration of the law, and the need to make decisions which will always benefit some groups over others, necessitate a far greater emphasis on consequentialist reasoning in public affairs. This is coupled with the fact that very often politics requires choosing between least bad options rather than between clearly good and bad ones. Politics is that sphere where the unceasing power struggle between states and parties takes place. The primary task of those with power is to battle anarchy and uncontrolled violence and to ensure as far as possible stability in order to promote justice and peace for the vast majority of innocent citizens. In carrying out this task those exercising real power will, all things considered, sometimes get their hands dirty. This view does not claim that morality has no place in politics. On the contrary, unlike the advocates of the Anti-morality view, a political morality seeks to find the realistic and appropriate moral yardstick by which to judge politicians. Even when they are forced to get dirty hands, the moral pollution that results is not easily removed. It serves to remind politicians and others that even when acting for the general good, some actions, which are on balance justified, still leave a moral remainder that rightly evokes a sense of horror and disgust.

What then can we reasonably demand of those who, like Jack, incur the responsibilities of political power, and in order to succeed partake in immoral and violent actions? Again following Stuart Hampshire, we can ask that they recognize the weight of peculiar responsibility in disposing of the lives of others. Secondly, politicians must be clearheaded and not divided in mind about their obligations to protect the reasonable interests of their innocent fellow citizens. Finally, we can expect that persons engaged in realpolitik should be prepared at all times for the occurrence of uncontrolled conflict of duties. This will involve situations that exclude the possibility of a decent outcome, where all the lines of action seem dishonorable and blameworthy, and there will be no possibility of avoiding dirty hands and the deleterious moral consequences.

Jack Bauer: Heroic Villain

In conclusion, what moral judgments can we properly make about Jack's terrible actions? We need to find a third way between outright condemnation and complete silence. We need to both praise Jack for his courage, sacrifices, and devotion to duty, and yet to condemn un-equivocally acts of murder and torture. Paradoxically, in such cases we need to both praise and chastise him. Furthermore, we need to recognize that persons like Jack are between hero and villain. They dirty their hands and destroy their own moral goodness by their actions, but they do this for the best of reasons. So we need to both admire and deride them for what they have done, both praise and blame them for their (necessary) actions on our behalf. It is appropriate that at the end of each season, after Jack has saved the day and is a hero for doing so, we are left with him dealing with the fallout of his job—betrayed, hunted, burnt-out, and bereft. Although our well being relies on the Jack Bauers of the world to do our dirty work, very few of us are willing to lead this kind of life, the life of a tragic hero.[11]

---

11 Thanks to Jeremy Barris for his insightful and incisive comments on an earlier draft.

Beyond the Call of Duty

Richard Davis

You are mistaken if you think that a man who is good for anything at all ought to consider the risks of life or death.
Plato, Apology

Do you understand the difference between dying for something and dying for nothing?
Jack Bauer, Season Six

In April, 2007, 15 Royal Navy sailors and marines were taken prisoner and held hostage for nearly two weeks by Iran's Revolutionary Guard. Their crime? Allegedly crossing over into Iranian waters. Within 48 hours a British sailor was plastered all over Iranian TV publicly confessing that the Britons were entirely at fault in the matter. Another sailor wrote a letter—no doubt under some duress—calling for the UK to withdraw all of its troops from Iraq. Then to cap things off, the British soldiers were paraded in front of the Iranian President, where they gave him a big "thumbs up" before being allowed to go home. If you were one of the captives, what would you have done? Would you have cooperated with your captors? Or would you have resisted them, possibly putting your own life at risk?

Not surprisingly, the British people recoiled in shame. As one commentator put it, "The honorable thing would have been to renounce their coerced behavior, denounce the Iranians' use of them for propaganda, and acknowledge that anything they endured was nothing compared to the sacrifices others have made." Sadly, for the Tehran 15, "their personal desires took precedence over their obligations."[1]

In far more dramatic fashion, *24* routinely confronts its viewers with life and death scenarios in which the show's characters must put themselves in serious danger, risk death, and in some cases make the ultimate sacrifice. Ryan Chappelle must agree to Stephen Saunders' demand for his execution, otherwise there will be further virus attacks on the public. If Lynn McGill doesn't shut down a remotely inaccessible computer program in a room full of deadly Sentox nerve gas, Chloe won't be able to use the A/C to flush the contaminated areas, and everyone in CTU will die. When Cheng's men demand to know who the Director of CTU is, Nadia Yasir hesitates and Milo Pressman steps forward in her place. He is killed at once.

Without a doubt, however, it is Jack Bauer who is most often called upon to engage in acts of extreme self-sacrifice. Indeed, if it weren't for Jack's personal sacrifices, the city of Los Angeles would have long since ceased to exist! An atomic bomb must be flown out into the desert and detonated. Jack volunteers to pilot the plane. He lets Kingsley's men torture him rather than reveal the location of the chip containing the source files for the Cyprus audio recording—files that show the recording to be a forgery and therefore no basis at all for President Palmer's launching the planned nuclear retaliation.

But isn't it asking too much to require anyone, even Jack Bauer, to give up his life for others? Isn't it precisely because Jack goes "beyond the call of duty" that we consider his actions praiseworthy and his character heroic? He does what duty does not require, and we love and admire him for it. Still, this can seem paradoxical. If what Jack does is good, then why isn't it something he ought to do, something we could blame him for not doing? If we answer, "It's his job," then that seems to diminish the merit of his actions. We don't normally call someone a hero if they're just doing their job. Moreover, if death puts an absolute end to us, blots us out of existence, how could anyone be morally obligated to give up their brief fling with existence for the sake of others—especially those they don't even know?

1   Robert Sibley, "The Ugly Consequence of Our Narcissism," *The Ottawa Citizen*, April 11, 2007.

Soldiers, Grenades, and Heroes

To consider these questions, let's take a look at how philosophers typically divide up moral actions. An action is said to be morally obligatory if it's something one ought to do; it's a good thing to do and bad not to do. For example, if Jack promises Wayne Palmer he won't give the Chinese an FB subcircuit board—yes, the one containing details on the entire Russian defense system—in exchange for Audrey Raines, then Jack has a moral obligation to follow through. He has a duty to the president to keep his word. If he doesn't, he is subject to our moral censure or disapproval.

A moral prohibition is the flipside of a moral obligation. It is something one mustn't do; not only is it good not to do it, it's strictly forbidden. Of course this is what makes Nina Myers one of *24*'s most shadowy and intriguing moral figures. She is inexplicably drawn to doing what is prohibited. She manipulates CTU security clearances, sells state secrets to terrorists, and when Teri Bauer finds out too much, Nina murders her. She does what she shouldn't, and in the end she pays for it with her life.

Philosophers also recognize an "in between" class of moral actions. If an action is neither obligatory nor prohibited, we say that it's morally permissible: morally okay to do but also morally okay not to do. It's neither praiseworthy nor blameworthy. It's just neutral. Jack's decision to earn his living working on an oil rig (as opposed to working as a professional cowboy) while in hiding from the Chinese falls into this category. Perhaps the greater part of the actions we perform in the moral realm are of this nature.

So we have this threefold moral division: the obligatory, the prohibited, and the permitted. However, in a highly influential article "Saints and Heroes,"[2] the philosopher J. O. Urmson has disputed this classification. There is a missing fourth category, he says: the supererogatory.[3] This is just a fancy philosopher's word that means "going beyond what duty requires." To illustrate this concept, Urmson

---

2   J. O. Urmson, "Saints and Heroes," in *Moral Concepts*, ed. Joel Feinberg (Oxford: Oxford University Press, 1969). Page references to Urmson are to this work.
3   Urmson doesn't actually use this term to describe his category, but it has become a favorite among philosophers.

asks us to imagine a soldier who throws himself on a live hand grenade to save his comrades. The question arises, he says:

> if the soldier had not thrown himself on the grenade, would he have failed in his duty? Though clearly he is superior in some way to his comrades, can we possibly say that they failed in their duty by not trying to be the one who sacrificed himself? If he had not done so, could anyone have said to him, "You ought to have thrown yourself on that grenade"? . . . The answer to all these questions is plainly negative. (63)

What Urmson is saying is that a supererogatory act isn't something you're obligated to do; nor can we blame you if you choose not to do it. However, it is both permissible and highly praiseworthy.

Must Chappelle Die?

This has the effect of shedding new light on Ryan Chappelle's character—generally thought to be wanting in important respects. When Stephen Saunders discovers that Chappelle's expertise at following "money trails" has led to Saunders' Cayman bank account, he knows it's only a matter of time before Chappelle tracks him down. Accordingly, Saunders demands Chappelle's execution (within the hour) on threat of releasing the virus—already wreaking havoc at the Chandler Plaza Hotel—at hundreds of locations across the country. It's a race against time to find Saunders before the deadline, and a distraught Chappelle knows it's not going to happen. Caught trying to leave CTU, Chappelle has to be placed under surveillance. Then moments before Jack kills him, Chappelle confesses, "You were right back at CTU to put me under watch. I wasn't going out for a cigarette, I was trying to bolt. But I know this has to happen."

But give the guy a break! If Urmson is right, we really shouldn't blame Chappelle. The poor guy is being driven to do something that isn't actually his duty. To be sure, it has to happen, but arguably all that means is that Chappelle must be killed (with or without his consent) or operational objectives won't be achieved. They're just buying more time for the purpose of locating Saunders before he makes good on his threats. So Chappelle's done. You might object that Chappelle has a duty to sacrifice his life in this case; after all, Division has placed him in charge of CTU. Consider, for example, the Homeland Security Act of 2002. Section 101 states that the US Department of Homeland Security exists to "prevent terrorist attacks within the United States." Surely then, its employees—and, by extension, those in CTU—must be under some sort of obligation to be prepared to give their lives for that purpose.[4]

Well, perhaps so. But all that shows is that Chappelle should know up front that he could be killed in the line of duty. You might think you're just following up on a promising new lead. The next thing you know, however, you're standing in a room aglow with hazy radioactive plutonium! (If you're not Field Ops, stay out of the field!) Hiding under the desk in your glass office might not help either—not if members of Joseph Wald's paramilitary operation have disguised themselves as phone line technicians in order to plant explosives inside the bowels of CTU, or Cheng's mercenaries are making their way through an underground sewer system and are about to launch an armed assault on the facility.

So perhaps there is a general obligation here to perform one's duties, knowing that they might result in one's death. It hardly follows that Chappelle has a specific duty to take his own life or to allow Jack to shoot him in the back of the head—executioner style. Even Jack seems to realize this. If Chappelle is duty-bound to die and Jack to kill him, then why plead "God, forgive me" before pulling the trigger? If everyone is simply doing his duty, what's to forgive? At any rate, what if it had been Kim Bauer who discovered Saunders' Cayman account? And suppose Saunders had therefore asked for her execution? Would she have had a duty to do that as a CTU employee? This is far from clear. And would Jack have agreed that a bullet needed to be put through her head as well? Well, we all know the answer to that one. The point is: on the surface, it is somewhat difficult to see how anyone could be morally required to give up his or her life for others. Sacrificing one's life seems, for all the world, to go well beyond the call of duty.

---

4   Compare the US Army *Code of Conduct* established by Eisenhower in 1955: "I am an American fighting in the forces that guard my country and our way of life, I am prepared to give my life in their defense."

The Duty to Die

Like anything else in philosophy, however, this conclusion has not gone unchallenged. According to the distinguished Cambridge philosopher G. E. Moore (1873–1958), when we are trying to decide between alternate courses of action, what duty requires of us is clear: to perform that action "which will cause more good to exist in the Universe than any possible alternative."[5] Moore sees a logical "hook up" between the goodness of an action and our duty to perform it. But here we strike a problem. For of the soldier who sacrifices himself by falling on the grenade, Urmson says, "clearly he is superior . . . to his comrades." And this suggests that the soldier's action has made the world a better place than it would have been had no one fallen on the grenade and all died. He has done what is best. Now since failing to do what is best (and within one's power) is normally considered blameworthy, it follows that doing what is best is obligatory. Hence there is no such thing as a supererogatory act.

If we think about this argument carefully, though, we can see that it doesn't really show there is always a duty to sacrifice one's life for others. To see this, let's simplify the argument as follows:

1   It is better to sacrifice one's life for others rather than not.
2   Duty requires that we do what is best provided that it is within our power to do so.
    Therefore,
3   Sacrificing one's life for others rather than not is a duty provided that it is within our power to do so.

The problem lies with step (1). How are we to understand it? Should we read (1) as saying that it is always better to sacrifice one's life for others, or just that it is sometimes better? Let's call the first way of reading (1) the Always Better Principle. Now the fact is: our little argument works only if this principle holds true. Otherwise, our conclusion at step (3) cannot rule out the possibility that there are some acts of self-sacrifice that go beyond the call of duty.

5   G. E. Moore, *Principia Ethica* (Cambridge: Cambridge University Press, 1948), Sec. 89.

How to Dismantle an Atomic Bomb—Or Not!

The question facing us, therefore, is whether the Always Better Principle is true. There is reason to think not. Think back for a moment to those far off, fabulous hours of Season Two. A string of tension-filled torture sessions (of NSA Director Roger Stanton, Islamic terrorist Syed Ali, and the brainwashed Marie Warner) finally yields the location of the atomic bomb set to go off that day—Norton Airfield. That's the good news. The bad news is: the bomb's trigger is tamper-proof; if it's dismantled, it will detonate on the spot, and that's going to happen in 55 minutes anyway.

Given these constraints, there's only one workable solution. The bomb has to be loaded onto the fastest, most reliable plane at the airfield, and then flown into the Mojave Desert. But that's not the worst of it. It also has to be dropped in a very precise location: a depression below sea level but also surrounded by mountains to contain the radioactive fallout. Unfortunately, the only available plane is a Cessna. So it doesn't have the on-board equipment to deliver its payload with the needed degree of accuracy. The pilot will have to go down with the plane.

What happens next is remarkable. Jack makes the unilateral decision that he alone will fly the plane. Then when the president inquires about the identity of the pilot, Jack actually lies to him: "We have a few volunteers, sir. All of them good men." In fact, there are no volunteers. Jack hasn't made the slightest effort to find any. Even Tony Almeida can't believe it: "Jack, there's gotta be somebody else who can fly that plane, somebody who doesn't have a family or at least doesn't have kids. C'mon." Jack's reply is a complete red herring: "I didn't have time to take a census, and I can't order anyone else to do this." Tell that to Kim Bauer. At any rate, there was time—except that Jack wasted it all jawing on the phone with Tony about Kim's whereabouts, and about some safe in his apartment containing a will, a letter for Kim, and so on. Tick, tock. Tick, tock. Talk about wasting time.

What's going on here? Ask George Mason. He gets it. Emerging from his place of hiding at the back of the Cessna, George tries to convince Jack to let him fly the plane; all he gets is grief. After some back-and-forth, however, George manages to expose the true intent behind Jack's actions:

> You still have a life, Jack. You wanna be a real hero, here's what you do. You get back down there and you put the pieces together. You find a way to forgive yourself for what happened to your wife. You make things right with your daughter, and you go on serving your country. That'd take some real guts.

All Jack can do is sheepishly hang his head. George has his number. Jack's primary intent isn't really saving lives, though that operational objective will no doubt be secured as well. Jack is trying to escape, to get relief: from his guilt, his personal pain, and his fractured relationships. Let's face it: it's an attempted suicide with some happy consequences for LA tacked on.

There is a lesson to be learned here. The Always Better Principle simply isn't true: it's not always better to sacrifice your life for others rather than not. It's not better, for example, when doing so is an act of suicide that will orphan your daughter, rob the country of someone widely recognized to be its single most effective weapon against terrorism (yourself), and when you know very well that others are better positioned to make the sacrifice—that is, willing to make it and with far less to lose. In such a case, self-sacrifice is neither permissible nor praiseworthy; it's downright immoral.

Sentox Can Really Get On Your Nerves

Clearly then, we can't simply assume that anyone who gives his or her life on behalf of others is automatically to be praised for having gone beyond the call of duty. As we've just seen, a self-sacrificial act might well be contrary to duty. But neither can we assume that it is never our duty to make the ultimate sacrifice. For consider what Mike Novick says to David Palmer to justify the idea of a pilot going down with the plane: "One man dies, Mr. President, to ensure the safety of millions." This One for Many Principle, as we might call it, seems to underwrite someone's having a duty here. But which "someone"?

Once again, *24* presents us with valuable material for philosophical reflection. Anyone who knows anything recognizes that when Division sends someone over to take control of the chain of command, there's going to be a few speed bumps. Transitions like this have to be managed with tact and delicacy. Kicking Bill Buchanan out of his office, and requiring that everyone call you Mr. McGill, is probably not what Dale Carnegie would recommend for your first day on the job. But then of course you're not Lynn McGill. This guy is a self-fulfilling prophecy on wheels. He's paranoid that no one respects him, and so of course acts in such a way that no one can. He's sure that everyone is working behind his back; so he monitors their calls and requires all their work to be mirrored to his system. Not surprisingly, this spawns secret meetings and conversations wherever he looks. Eventually, his judgment becomes so impaired that he devotes all of CTU's resources to apprehending Jack Bauer instead of finding the Sentox nerve gas.

The pressures on McGill continue to build when his drug addicted sister starts begging him for money. When he meets with her, he is promptly robbed not only of his cash but his CTU key card as well. Embarrassed, he never reports it. Finally, McGill snaps and has to be put in holding. Well, you can guess what happens next. Terrorists use his key card to gain entrance to CTU and release a canister of Sentox into the air duct system. A number of people are killed, including the much beloved Edgar Stiles.

Fortunately, our favorite characters manage to get themselves (or find themselves) in barrier-sealed rooms. But a corrosive agent in the Sentox is quickly eating away at the barriers. Chloe's attempt to flush the Sentox out of the contaminated areas fails because of a computer interrupt on the A/C control unit. The only glitch is that the unit is located in a contaminated area. Wait a second! Jack's pretty good at holding his breath. Let's get him to shut it down. Sorry, no can do. He's already tried; he's too far away. The only one close enough is Lynn McGill, who is in a room right beneath the A/C unit.

Here's a question for you. Does McGill have a duty to sacrifice his life for Jack and friends? Turning to the security officer assigned to guard him, McGill says: "We have to do this, Harry. We're going to die anyway. If we don't, so will everyone in CTU. We have to do this." There it is again, that One for Many Principle. Here the "have to" isn't like the one Chappelle faced, namely, the "have to" of operational objectives and forced self-sacrifice.[6] Jack can't enforce

---

6   In Scott Calef's chapter, he argues that McGill's decision *is* forced. However, by a "forced" decision, Calef simply means one in which the consequences are the same regardless of whether the decision is made. I don't dispute that. My claim is quite different: namely, that McGill's decision isn't forced in the sense of being causally constrained or determined.

anything here. He's in another room separated by a corridor of deadly Sentox. This is McGill's decision; it's entirely up to him. The "have to" in play, rather, is that of moral obligation. With the terrible consequences of his actions before him, the clear light of reason returns to McGill, and he calmly applies the One for Many Principle to himself. It's no longer "Someone must die to save the many," it's "I must die to save the many." It's the right thing to do. For if he does nothing, he'll be dead in minutes anyway—along with everyone else. Besides, this is all his fault; he alone has put them in this fix. And only he is in a position to shut down the program.

For all the world then, and as strange as it may sound, there are these cases in which there appears to be an actual duty to sacrifice oneself for others. Even so, this conclusion has troubled some thinkers. For example, according to philosopher David Heyd, "Doing one's duty does not win the agent any credit. She only did what she had to."[7] You'd better go that extra mile, or we'll not praise you at all. Well, here I can only reply, "Nuts!" McGill's actions are indeed praiseworthy—and objectively so. They're not forced; they're free. They spring from a good intent: to save lives. There's not the slightest hint that McGill is merely trying to appease his own sense of guilt or to atone for past wrongs. Not that there's anything wrong with that! Moreover, unlike Harry Swinton, the security officer, there's no hand waving or back peddling over Jack's assessment of the situation, no retaliation for his "treasonous" removal as acting director of CTU, no shrinking from duty out of fear or panic. This guy is made of sterner stuff than that. As McGill slouches to the floor, the Sentox only a breath away, Jack's voice is heard over the loud speaker: "I want you to know what you did was successful. The seals are holding. I will personally notify your families and tell them of the sacrifice you made." McGill goes out a hero. No question.

Going Beyond the Call

It's no secret that if you want to learn how to interrogate a witness, rescue hostages, or lead an assault team, Jack Bauer is your "go to"

---

7   David Heyd, "Supererogation," in *The Stanford Encyclopedia of Philosophy (Fall 2006 Edition)*, ed. Edward N. Zalta, available online at www.plato.stanford.edu/archives/fall2006/entries/supererogation/.

guy. Believe it or not: he can also teach us a thing or two about the moral life. Jack's moral life isn't perfect of course, but it's on the move, expanding in both breadth and subtlety. Jack learns from his past mistakes—even in the area of self-sacrifice. In the world of *24*, there is constant pressure to adopt the self-serving, political agendas of presidents, chiefs of staff, handlers, and the like. If you're not careful, you'll be dying for those agendas. Jack's polygraph-like insight into human nature enables him to see through the flawed, self-interested plans of those around him. A fed up Bauer eventually declares: "I'm tired of putting my ass on the line for nothing. I'm done putting my ass on the line for nothing." Some things are just not worth dying for. Frequent contact with death has a way of sharpening one's focus on what really matters. Thus Jack refuses to offer himself up to the Chinese just to help President Logan save political face— "the idle business of show"[8] as one Stoic sage puts it. Instead, Jack wisely goes into hiding.

Jack's question to us is: "Do you understand the difference between dying for something and dying for nothing?" Is there really anything worth dying for? Not surprisingly, Jack points the way. Without a moment's hesitation, he sets up the planned exchange with the Chinese: the subcircuit board for Audrey. Of course, he can't actually give the component to Cheng, for that would compromise Russia's defensive capabilities, and then President Suvarov would have no choice but to retaliate against the US, thereby triggering a global military conflict. Jack isn't about to pull a "McGill" either, putting the lives of the many at risk. Absolutely not. Jack knows he has rare expertise.[9] After Audrey has been safely returned, he will ensure that enough C4 explosive detonates that both he and the subcircuit board are destroyed.

In one way, then, his planned death is for all—all those who would lose their lives in the military devastation to follow were Cheng to obtain his subcircuit prize. No doubt Jack has a duty to prevent that from happening. Yet this doesn't exhaust the moral complexities of the plan. For Jack's main intent is to offer his life as a ransom for one person, Audrey—to buy her back from torture and imprisonment at

---

8   Marcus Aurelius, *Meditations* (Mineola, NY: Dover Publications, 1997), p. 47.
9   I thank Doug Geivett for drawing this to my attention.

the hands of the Chinese, something he himself has experienced first hand. The sacrifice for Audrey is gratuitous. It follows neither from the One for Many Principle,[10] nor from some specific duty Jack has towards Audrey. Sure Jack says, "Audrey Raines was willing to give up her life to save mine. I cannot and will not do anything less for her." But this is said to Wayne Palmer, and is nothing but dramatic overstatement designed to stir up the president's emotions and pry that subcircuit board out of his tightly clenched fist. The reality is: Audrey only went to look for Jack. She didn't risk her life, leading an assault team to spring him from captivity. Jack intends to keep his duty (to the many) but then go beyond that, personally sacrificing himself that Audrey (the one) might live. Thanks to some CTU bungling, Jack's plan falls apart and he's spared from paying that heavy price. It hardly matters though; he's got "hero" written all over him.[11]

Leaders of the cult-like religion Scientology once described actor Tom Cruise as their "Christ." "Like Christ," they noted, Cruise has "been criticized for his views."[12] Good heavens. At one time or another, we've all been criticized for that. That's not what makes someone Christ-like. Better to ask yourself: Have I ever been willing to sacrifice my life that others might live? That even one might live? I'm sorry. When it comes to the answers to these questions, I'll take Jack Bauer over Tom Cruise any day.[13]

10 For the purists out there: this would constitute a fallacy of division. Even if I have a duty to sacrifice my life for a certain group *as a whole*, it doesn't follow that I owe that duty to *each part* of that whole in and of themselves.
11 In his chapter, Rob Lawlor argues that since Jack couldn't provide a "100 percent guarantee" that his actions here would succeed, we should consider him a "liability" and not a hero. But that strikes me as a bit strong; it would imply, for example, that there are no heroes. For if you think about it: none of our actions comes with *that* sort of guarantee— not up front anyway. It's always possible that some event (however unlikely) will thwart our action plans.
12 Emily Smith, "Cruise 'is Christ' of Scientology," *The Sun*, January 23, 2007.
13 Special thanks are due to Glen Meyer for all those "sacrificial" conversations, and to Caroline Davis for her many helpful suggestions on early drafts.

Truth and Illusion in *24*: Jack Bauer, Dionysus in the World of Apollo

Stephen Snyder

It's impossible for words to describe what is necessary to those who do not know what horror means. Horror. Horror has a face . . . And you must make a friend of horror. Horror and moral terror are your friends. If they are not then they are enemies to be feared. They are truly enemies . . . You have to have men who are moral . . . and at the same time who are able to utilize their primordial instincts to kill without feeling . . . without passion . . . without judgment. Because it's judgment that defeats us.
Colonel Kurtz, Apocalypse Now

We have need of lies in order to conquer this reality, this "truth," that is, in order to live.—That lies are necessary in order to live is itself part of the terrifying and questionable character of existence.
Friedrich Nietzsche, The Will to Power §853

Jack Bauer knows the face of horror, the lie that is needed to face the troubled nature of our post-9/11 existence in which security has become the highest national priority. On the one hand, the security apparatus designed to protect us from terror cannot become synonymous with that terror. On the other hand, there are days, perhaps just a few, when terror must be unleashed for the survival of Western civilization. These temporary measures require the sacrifice of a person who can act without judgment, lest it "be judgment that

43

defeats us." But this provisional suspension of judgment also constitutes a lie, a lie that lurks below the surface of the Western world. The truth behind the illusion—the torture, the deception, betting an individual's life like a chip in a game—is the terrible price we pay to carry the illusion forward.

From its inception, the mercurial relationship of truth and illusion is manifest in the plot of *24*. The first fissure appears in episode one when Richard Walsh informs Jack of a security breach detected within the ranks of the CTU. The breach may be related to an attempt on presidential candidate David Palmer's life. If the plot succeeds, the country will be thrown into great turmoil. After years of apparent progress on the front of racial equality, the assassination of the African-American candidate would release enormous unrest. Walsh makes it clear that the source of the leak is unknown: Jack is the only one he can trust. *Trust no one with this information; let no one know you are aware of the compromise.* To find the truth, the illusion of the status quo must be maintained: the integrity of CTU—America's front line against terror—must appear intact. At the same time, the mole threatens to turn the resources of the unit against itself and the American people. As if it were an autoimmune response, the checks and balances of CTU work against Jack in his attempt to repair the damage. In order to prevent the infiltrator's plans from being carried out, Jack must circumvent the bureaucratic mechanisms intended to prevent abuse of the power allotted to the security establishment. Thus while maintaining the illusion of order, Jack initiates a process of trial and error testing aimed at purging CTU of malignant operatives. Jack's actions require him not only to disregard CTU protocol, but to disregard many of the rules of humanity. Jack is the terror behind the mask of procedure—the inhumanity required to further humanity.

Duality

In *The Birth of Tragedy*, Friedrich Nietzsche (1844–1900) presents the mythical duality of Apollo and Dionysus.[1] Apollo is the god of

---

1 See Julian Young, *Nietzsche's Philosophy of Art* (Cambridge: Cambridge University Press, 1992).

the sun, for Nietzsche, the god of the visual arts. (Let's forget for the moment that Apollo is usually depicted holding a harp.) Dionysus is the god of music and intoxication. Apollo represents beauty, but for Nietzsche, this aspect of Apollo is manifested through sustaining life's illusions. Dionysus is the god of what is not seen. Opposed to the light of Apollo, the experience of Dionysus takes one beyond the notion of the self and the illusion of individuation. Nietzsche uses the classic opposition of Apollo and Dionysus as a metaphor for everyday appearance and the forgotten secret that lies below the surface. Under this pretext, the layered realities of truth and illusion find expression in his philosophy.

Nietzsche articulates the dualism of Dionysus and Apollo in two ways, metaphysically and aesthetically. The threads of this duality are woven into the plot of *24*. The metaphor for the illusion of order in which we live forms *24*'s metaphysical layer. The Apollonian represents the overarching support system supplying society with the mechanism, and the illusion, for maintaining a well ordered life. This system provides the citizenry of *24* with the confidence needed to face quotidian existence. The CTU director, perched in his office above the team, and the institution of the presidency are emblems of the process intended to guarantee the legitimate implementation of national security policy and the just function of government. Despite their officious presence, these icons of the Apollonian framework are insufficient. The optimistic belief that their order holds the key to lasting stability yields a false sense of satisfaction. Faced with crises that threaten the Apollonian order, the promise of lasting stability, the processes in which we place so much trust cannot be fulfilled on their own terms. Dionysus, manifested in Bauer's brutal practicality, cuts through the Apollonian limitations, revealing its illusion.

The Apollonian illusion, for contemporary American culture, is manifest in the faith in progress and the institutions legitimized through the democratic process. These institutions provide the backbone of Western civilization, providing a secure foundation on which to carry a civilization forward. But they also provide a moral grounding for our culture. Follow these procedures and the outcome will be just. However, when the functional and moral procedures necessary for maintaining law and order become an obstacle to institutional survival, Bauer's terrible acts allow the layered bureaucracies of the Western world's security apparatus to function. There is no protocol or law he will not break in the name of deterrence. Even the moral codes of Western society, codes Jack holds dear, are broken to uphold the firmament of the Western world. Clearly, founding a well ordered society on the terrible "Dionysian" truth of Bauer is impossible, yet the Apollonian is inadequate. Without Bauer, there is no "saving illusion." Thus, within the framework of Apollo, the terror of Dionysus saves us, even if for a short time. The lesson is not to forsake the role Bauer must play in our world.

Nietzsche's juxtaposition of Dionysus and Apollo finds an aesthetic parallel in the culture of myth that surrounds effective dramatic portrayal. In the post-9/11 era, the role of the Special Forces operative and the covert agent has a tangible presence in the popular imagination. This facet of the culture of myth provides the necessary ingredient that allows the drama to become real to the viewer. Within the span of each season's 24 episodes, the unfolding plot of *24* draws the willing viewer into a world of suspense, fear, and perhaps the acceptance that horrible action must be taken to deliver our salvation.

The World of Appearance

Apollo, the sun god, is opposed to Dionysus as the god who dispels darkness. It is Apollo who brings clarity to thought through expulsion of what is irrational.[2] In this sense, the security apparatuses of CTU and the Western world signify the Apollonian illusion: the appearance of security and truth. We trust in the institutions that protect us. Without them, society would not progress, for fear and mistrust would mark our every step.[3] But, as Nietzsche noted, there is an optimism in this appearance that will lead to decline, for the promise cannot be kept on its own terms. When the system of appearances, the illusion of law and order's efficacy, is threatened, then Jack is called forth to set the system right. The system of order cannot function without Bauer, yet it cannot openly acknowledge the necessity of his service. Consider, for example, Vice President Daniel's decision not to prosecute Karen Hayes and Bill Buchanan for

2   See Carl Kerényi, *Dionysos: Archetypal Image of Indestructible Life*, trans. Ralph Manheim (Princeton: Princeton University Press, 1976), p. 209.

disobeying his orders in the conclusion of Season Six. Their prosecution would show the public the weakness of the presidency while in crisis, for their disobedience allowed Jack, once again, to avert catastrophe. Apollo's clarity could not exist without the dark contradictions manifest in Dionysus. Yet, at the same time, to acknowledge the contradictions would dispel the clarity. Season Two opens with Jason Park's tortured utterance: "Today." The message is passed on to the NSA: today terrorists plan to detonate a nuclear device on US soil. This information is vital; the lives of tens of thousands of Americans depend on it. No set of procedures that govern a people would deny that acquiring such information is essential. But herein lies the contradiction, for the procedures would disallow the method of acquisition. Jack Bauer procures the leads and facts vital to CTU's mission, but Jack's dark methods cannot be acknowledged in the specious light of appearance.

Jack as Dionysus

Dionysus is commonly known as the god of the vine, an elusive figure, associated with intoxication. Outside of being elusive, Jack Bauer couldn't be further from this Bacchanalian figure.[4] But this is just one face of Dionysus. The most ancient manifestations of Dionysus equate him with Hades, the god of the underworld.[5] Dionysus ruled over darkness, while Apollo, the sun god, held dominion over light. But Dionysus' relationship to Apollo is not mutually exclusive, for Dionysus represents the life that springs from darkness. Dionysus was a god of the crops; a sacrifice to Dionysus ensured the next year's harvest. Dionysus' power of intoxication, though at times associated

3 The question of whether anyone in the world of 24 can be trusted is taken up in the chapter by Eric M. Rovie.
4 In Season Three, Jack succumbs to heroin addiction while working undercover with the Salazars. Jack kicks the habit, but his addiction becomes a metaphor within the metaphor, for it is clear that Jack used heroin to mask the pains incurred from the loss of his wife.
5 Carl Kerényi, *The Religion of the Greeks and Romans*, trans. Christopher Holme (New York: E. P. Dutton, 1962), pp. 227, 265. *The Religion of the Greeks and Romans* will be referred to herein as RGR.

with mere drunkenness, in a deeper sense is linked to his powers of ecstatic release. Lastly, Dionysus was a god who released his wrath upon those who refused to recognize his divine power, for he was born of Zeus and a mortal woman. Because of this, some denied his divinity and suffered a terrible fate.

Zeus put Dionysus on the throne as an infant, making his wife Hera jealous.[6] Hera commanded the Titans to kill Dionysus and they obeyed. As Titans pursued the infant Dionysus, he eluded them by changing forms. The last form he took was the Bull. In this mortal form, the infant god was torn to pieces (GB 451). Zeus saved Dionysus by keeping a part of the infant's body, which, according to some accounts, he regenerated by sewing the god child into his groin. The resurrection, which followed upon his terrible dismemberment, makes Dionysus a symbol of the indestructibility of life. This notion of Dionysus as an unyielding force of nature, a god that takes mortal form, capable of setting one free or of wreaking a horrible vengeance, is in the character of Jack Bauer.

Why a God?

Bauer is just an agent doing his duty; he acts according to the greatest good for the greatest number. In how many episodes is this utilitarian equation invoked? If we don't commit this act of torture, if we don't suspend these rights, how many deaths will result from a nuclear explosion, a nuclear power plant meltdown, the release of nerve gas, or a weaponized biohazard? The logic is cold and clear: the pain and injustice imparted on the few cannot stand in the way of the tens of thousands who could be saved. The utilitarian logic, however, is merely the backdrop for 24. It provides the classic tragic collisions between conflicting levels of social obligation. Bauer is at the center of these collisions. His actions and decisions are his sacrifice, which over the years exact their toll. Nowhere is this more evident than in the condition and demeanor of Jack upon return from captivity in China. The signs of physical torture are apparent. Jack's hands

6 George Frazer, *The Golden Bough: A Study in Magic and Religion* (New York: MacMillan, 1951), pp. 450–451. *The Golden Bough* will be referred to herein as GB.

are scarred from burning. One senses, however, that though Jack's body was tortured, his psyche is also deeply scarred—both by Cheng's torture and reflection on his own actions performed in the state's service.

Sacrifice

Shortly before the Titans ripped Dionysus to shreds, Zeus placed the infant Dionysus on the throne. This, in some accounts, was a symbolic gesture made before the demise of a child king who was sacrificed in place of his father (GB 451). Thus, Jack is put on the throne and is given the power of a god. But through his actions he is sacrificed, for though the Apollonian system must have Jack to succeed, those who manage the bureaucracies are always willing to relinquish him in their struggle to maintain the appearance of order.

Jack's task is superhuman, but his form remains human, and his actions, which serve to unify the illusion of state, slowly chip away at his humanity. Season One begins with a collision of duties. Subversive operatives hold Jack's wife and daughter hostage; they will not be released unless Jack aids them with the assassination of David Palmer. Jack must simultaneously work with the assassins, to save his family, and fulfill his duty to the state. The assassination is averted and Jack's family is narrowly rescued, but the internalization of opposing roles causes his wife and daughter to question his abilities as a father and husband. In the final moments of Season One, Nina Myers, Jack's heretofore most trusted agent and ex-lover, kills his wife. The sacrifice is made, the Western world is safe for another season, but Jack has paid the price.

As Season Two begins, Jack has been inactive for 18 months, unable to deal with the loss his sacrifice required. Once on board, however, Jack again invokes the darkness of Dionysus. A group called Second Wave is in possession of a nuclear weapon, which it plans to detonate in Los Angeles. Following a lead, Jack interrogates federal witness Marshall Goren. As CTU's exasperated director George Mason looks on, Jack shoots him. Jack asks Mason to bring him a saw, and he proceeds to remove Goren's head, tucking it in a duffel bag. The "head in the bag" is Jack's ticket to the inner circle of those coordinating with Second Wave. Goren's head is a gift for the man against whom Goren would have testified. Moral judgment clouds reason. Under extraordinary duress, Jack is able to provide CTU with the necessary leads, leads unavailable by other means. With no room for optimism, Jack possesses the clarity to examine the brutal facts of the situation. Following CTU protocol would have left them with no leads on the nuclear device. CTU needed Jack's dark logic. Yet the establishment can never forgive Jack for his ability to bring clarity of action to the situation at hand. His success is bought at the cost of losing the support of those who run the security apparatus when it ceases to be in crisis mode. The expectations of the establishment are oriented toward maintaining the quotidian illusion, yet, as bureaucrats, they cannot accept measures that go beyond the standard play book, even if these measures are their reason for existence. Because of this, Jack's life is bartered away, again and again. In Season Two, President David Palmer grants Nina Myers immunity in advance for the murder of Jack, in exchange for the promise of aiding CTU in finding the nuclear device intended for Los Angeles. In Season Six, Jack's freedom is purchased from his Chinese captors by President Wayne Palmer only to be given over to terrorists to be tortured and killed, for the promise of handing over Assad, one of the world's most notorious terrorists.

Bulls were often sacrificed to Dionysus because he was in the form of a bull when the Titans slew him. In a throw back to the most archaic forms of Greek ritual, Dionysus the god would appear in the mortal form of the "Bull-son" (RGR 69). In an unholy act of murder, the god manifest as a bull would be sacrificed. The ritual of *Bouphonia* was performed to ensure the harvest would not be destroyed by drought. Sacrificing the bull was seen as a religious necessity. But killing the sacred bull was also murder. Thus, a ritual trial ensued, over which the king presided. During the mock trial, a chain of blame was established. Blame shifted from those who sharpened the instruments of death, to the maidens who delivered them, to the butchers who actually used the knife and the axe to slaughter the bull. In the end, the blame is passed on to the instruments of death. The axe is exonerated; the knife is found guilty and thrown into the sea (GB 540). Analogously, Jack is sacrificed to avert disaster. The presidents each sanction the unholy acts, blaming the knife, so to speak, for the situation demanding Jack's sacrifice is beyond the control of an individual.

Resurrection

Jack, the force of nature, is even reborn out of death. Pursued by the henchmen allied with the remnants of the Coral Snake unit, Jack is subdued and hung by his bound hands. In the famous pose of Marsyas, who was flayed by Apollo for having lost a challenge,[7] Jack is flayed by Stark, an operative of a powerful coalition intent on initiating a Middle East war to profit from the rise in the price of Caspian Sea oil. The war is to be instigated based on fabricated evidence— a series of recorded calls linking the explosion of a nuclear device on US soil to three Middle Eastern governments. A chip, in the possession of agents working with Jack, stores the evidence of how the calls were constructed. Finding the chip would expose the illusion used to justify war. Jack is tortured, and, in the process, his heart stops. Intent on recovering the chip, the captors resurrect Jack. His return to the world of the living allows Jack to resolve the collision created by those who would profit from a war born out of deceit.

We have a series of coincidences paralleling the character of Jack Bauer with the myth of Dionysus. Perhaps the authors of 24 read Greek myths. So what? The answer is seen in the more practically oriented aesthetic perspective employed with Nietzsche's analogy of Apollo and Dionysus. The theme of truth and illusion dominates 24. According to Nietzsche, it should dominate our lives. If it does not, we falsely assimilate one into the other, leaving our view of reality suspect, manifesting the specious optimism that leads to despair. Nietzsche writes that the pre-Socratic Greeks recognized a terrible dualism in the fabric of the universe. The Dionysian terror that lurked below the surface of existence could not be confronted

---

7 According to legend, Marsyas found a flute made by Athena. Athena was not happy with her creation and discarded it. Marsyas was able to play the instrument with such skill that he challenged Apollo to a musical contest, wagering he could play better on his flute than Apollo on his harp. The first round of the challenge ended in a draw, but Apollo asked for a second round. In the second round, Apollo played the harp upside-down, a feat Marsyas could not duplicate. The wager allowed the winner to treat the loser in any manner he chose. Apollo chose to tie Marsyas to a tree and flay him alive. The tale of Marsyas' inauspicious gamble is viewed as symbolic of the opposition between Apollo and Dionysus.

directly, but through the veil of Apollonian art it could be glimpsed. Its mere recognition would temper the optimism of Apollo enough to make the myth viable as a guide for how to live. The plot of the tragedy, the effective work of art, must reflect the kernel of the world's metaphysical dualism. But to effectively present this dualism, the plot must have a medium for presenting the Dionysian elements. For Nietzsche, there must exist a culture of myth real enough to the audience such that the dramatic plot can become the viewer's reality. The fear created through the 9/11 attacks and its politicization has created fertile ground for a new myth. The agents of "good," who must selflessly do what is necessary to prevent the heinous aims of the terrorist, are the ideal protagonists for this new myth.

Terror

Terror pervades the plot of *24*. While CTU pursues its aims, the methods of the terrorists become those of CTU: the means of one are the means of the other. This becomes explicit when Stephen Saunders, a British MI-6 agent thought to be dead, resurfaces, threatening to release the deadly Cordilla virus into densely populated American cities if his demands are not met. Saunders wants the list of foreign nationals working for the US as covert operatives. The publication of this information would devastate America's intelligence network, leaving the country virtually defenseless against espionage. Having faced the trauma of his family's kidnapping, Jack oversees the abduction of Saunders' daughter, threatening to expose her to the Cordilla virus if Saunders will not reveal the last deadly canister's location. Saunders complies, but the coercive act, when employed by the terrorists, is heinous; the same action, carried out by CTU, is for the greater good.

Truth and illusion in *24* depends on information. Torture is used to get the truth. According to the myths of antiquity, the power of seeing the truth was gained by breaking a fundamental law. Nature reveals its secrets through its violation. A clairvoyant, for example, is the product of incest. Breaking nature's rules revokes the laws of nature. Nietzsche argued that Dionysian "wisdom . . . is an abominable crime against nature; that anyone who, through his knowledge, casts nature into the abyss of destruction, must himself experience the dissolution of nature."[8] In *24*, breaking the most fundamental laws of our country, violating the individual's rights in a manner compatible with the very foes CTU seeks to vanquish, constitutes the contemporary American version of this dark myth: a price that must be paid for the truth of survival.

Many of *24*'s viewers abhor torture. Some would argue that its use undermines America's moral standard and its authority as a moral force in world affairs. In addition, most experts agree that it does not provide reliable information. So why bother with it? The answer to this question, as far as policy is concerned, goes beyond the scope of this chapter, and, I contend, is irrelevant to the plot of *24*. In *24*, the use of terror is not to be taken as a political endorsement of torture. Terror is a dramatic tool employed to make the plotline real. The fact that *24* draws a devoted audience from the entire political spectrum confirms this. If terror had been used for explicit political purposes, it would not have been an effective element of plot. If the audience follows Jack in his first application of torture, even if they find it repugnant, then they will follow the plot almost anywhere. They will even accept that Jack can cross Los Angeles by car in three minutes. Terror is the link between the metaphysical or symbolic essence of the world and the aesthetics of the theatrical. It makes the plot realistic, without being real. The dramatic format of *24* gives the viewers a glimpse of the Dionysian terror, without its direct experience. This is what gives a great plot its power. It is also what gives myth, drama, and art the power to convey a truth one cannot rationally express.

Only through the dramatic veil can we safely view the dismantling terror of Dionysus. Only in tragedy—and *24 is* a tragedy, for Bauer is a tragic figure—can we delight in the destruction of the individual. Jack's acts are not utilitarian; they are a form of altruism. We often think of altruism as selfless giving, along the lines of St. Francis, renouncing self-interest and acting charitably toward others. Arthur Schopenhauer (1788–1860) saw the answer to the universe's metaphysical poverty in altruism—an ascetic denial of the individual, a selflessness that would circumvent the contradictory drives of *Will* through its renunciation. Nietzsche was not so sanguine about

---

8 Friedrich Nietzsche, *The Birth of Tragedy: Out of the Spirit of Music*, trans. Shaun Whiteside (New York: Penguin Books, 1993), §9:47.

selflessness. Rolling back the bounds of individuality could lead to a "witch's brew" of horrors. The Dionysian denial of individuality is like a poison that is part of a medicine. Too much will kill; just enough will cure. So on the tragic stage, Jack sacrifices his individuality and acts according to the primal *Will* of the Western world, *without judgment*, in order to bring about redemption for the next hour, day, or season.

Jack's achievements in the realm of counter-espionage are matched by a curse in the realm of relationships. Audrey Raines, the one-time lover of Bauer thought dead, resurfaces in Season Six. Searching for Jack in China, she was imprisoned and psychologically impaired. Recognizing her symptoms, Jack feels it imperative to aid the only person who sacrificed for him. But when her father, Secretary of Defense Heller, comes to CTU to take custody of his daughter, he orders Jack never to see Audrey again. "You're cursed, Jack. Everything you touch, one way or another, ends up dead." Like the Midas touch, the deathly currency Jack compiled through his service to the State is irredeemable in the realm of interpersonal relationships. As Season Six closes, Jack points a gun at Heller, demanding, "I want my life back." Heller tells him the cold truth: Jack can never return to the life of the mere mortal, for he has crossed a line from which there is no return. All Jack had ever done was serve Heller and people like him. Jack Bauer lives as the savior of the state, but as a man, he has no future.

The truth in the illusion that the system has prevailed, that good has triumphed over evil, lies in the sacrifice of Jack. The weight of the world rests squarely on his shoulders, and like Atlas he does not shudder. Without judgment, he "makes a friend of moral terror," to prevent it from becoming an even more terrible foe. In the act, Jack sacrifices what is most human, the opportunity to love, to have family and share in a community of friends. But this is the dark superhero that is needed in post-modern society. The posturing surety of a bulletproof Superman, representing the very best that humanity can be, cannot capture the imagination of a post-metaphysical culture which needs the Dionysian illusion in order to glimpse the terrible truth of existence.

9:00 AM–12:00 PM

THE OVAL OFFICE AND THE HALLS OF POWER___

President Palmer and the Invasion of China: The Beginning of a Just War?

Jennifer Hart Weed

September 11, 2001 struck fear in the hearts of Americans around the world. The destruction of the World Trade Center's twin towers by terrorists heralded a new era in human history, one marked by debates concerning the justice of "the war on terror" and the ways in which the United States and its allies should prevent further attacks. While these debates occur in the real world, similar debates take place within the "real time" of *24*. Although it's common to hear talk about the justice or injustice of the war(s) on terror in both *24* and the real world, the specifics of what would make a war just are not commonly discussed. In this chapter, we'll discuss the conditions of just war theory and apply them to the covert invasion of the Chinese consulate in Season Four of *24*, in order to determine whether or not former President David Palmer's order to invade the consulate was the beginning of a just war.

The Invasion of the Chinese Consulate

In Season Four, a terrorist named Habib Marwan steals the nuclear "football," which contains the locations and codes for all of the weapons in the American nuclear arsenal, by felling Air Force One, injuring current President Keeler in the process. Due to the serious injuries inflicted on the president, Vice-President Logan is sworn in as his replacement. Logan realizes eventually that he is ill equipped to deal with all of the crises emerging throughout the day and so brings in former President David Palmer to act as an advisor, just until those crises are averted.

As Season Four progresses, it is revealed that Marwan has gained control of a nuclear warhead, which he will reprogram to attack an American city. Jack Bauer tells Palmer that the only chance to save the country from a nuclear bomb is to find Lee Jong—a Chinese citizen living in Los Angeles—and interrogate him about Marwan's location.

Lee is traced to the Chinese consulate in Los Angeles. So Palmer telephones the consul to request that Lee be handed over to the United States for interrogation. If the allegations of a connection between Marwan and Lee are true, then Lee is guilty of aiding terrorists in the United States and would be subject to arrest and prosecution. The consul refuses to produce Lee without authorization from the ambassador, who is out of touch. The consul also raises questions about the nature of the evidence that is alleged to link Lee with Marwan. Because time is of the essence, as is always the case on *24*, Palmer authorizes a covert operation in which CTU agents, led by Jack, invade the consulate and kidnap Lee. Unfortunately, the consul is shot and killed by one of his own men during the invasion. Lee is also shot, but he survives his injuries.

Since the Chinese consulate is considered Chinese soil, Palmer in effect authorized a covert invasion of China. Although no shots were fired by CTU, their actions nonetheless constituted an aggressive military action that violated the boundaries and sovereignty of Chinese territory. Although Palmer and CTU subsequently deny that they had anything to do with the invasion, they admit (hypothetically) that an invasion by American operatives would have constituted an act of war. In so doing, they invoke the commonsense view that the violation of a nation's territory by a foreign force is an act of aggression, which is in turn an act of war.[1] So given that the invasion of the consulate by CTU operatives was an act of war, we can ask whether it was just.

---

1 Michael Walzer, *Just and Unjust Wars*, 2nd edn. (New York: Basic Books, 1977), pp. 51–52. Page references to Walzer are to this work.

Just War Theory: A Tale of Two Thomases

Just war theory has its roots in classical and medieval thought. One of the key figures in this tradition, St. Thomas Aquinas (1225–1274), asks in his *Summa theologiae* whether it is always sinful to wage war. In framing the question in this way, Aquinas acknowledges that many Christians assume that Christianity *requires* a commitment to pacifism. Aquinas agrees that at least some cases of war are sinful, but he argues that it is not always sinful to wage war; some wars are just. In order for a war to be just, however, the following three conditions must be met:

1   The sovereign or leader of the group who will be waging war must have the authority to wage war.[2]
2   The war must be waged for a just cause, i.e., "those who are attacked should be attacked because they deserve it on account of some fault" (Aquinas, IIa–IIae.40.1).
3   Those waging war must have the correct intention, that is, they must intend to advance the good or to avoid evil or both (IIa–IIae.40.1).

Many contemporary discussions of war focus on a fourth condition, which Thomas Hurka describes in the following way:

4   That the destructiveness of war must be proportional to the relevant good that the war will bring about.[3]

Although Aquinas does not include the proportionality condition in this discussion, he would have accepted it because it is in keeping with his commitment to justice and the advancement of goodness. Taken as a whole then, if a war violates any of the four conditions, then that war is unjust (Hurka, 35). However, a war can be more or less unjust, and so it is helpful to remember that some unjust wars

---

2   St. Thomas Aquinas, *Summa theologiae*, trans. Fathers of the English Dominican Province (Notre Dame, IN: Ave Maria Press, 1948), IIa–IIae.40.1.
3   Thomas Hurka, "Proportionality and the Morality of War," *Philosophy and Public Affairs* 33 (2005): 34–66. Page references to Hurka are to this work.

can be better than others, which will become relevant to our discussion of the invasion of the Chinese consulate.

Hurka points out an additional consideration that arises in the just war tradition with respect to the proportionality condition: the distinction is between *jus ad bellum* and *jus in bello*. *Jus ad bellum* refers to "the resort to war," and takes into account the justice of going to war (35). *Jus in bello* refers to "the means used to wage war," and it takes into account the justice in the waging of war (35). So in reference to the fourth condition, one must take into account the proportion of relevant goods and evils in both the act of going to war and in waging war. For example, with regard to *jus ad bellum*, a state should not go to war to promote goods that could be brought about via diplomacy (37). President David Palmer gave considerable attention to this condition in both Season Two and Season Four, as he engaged in diplomatic discussions in an attempt to avoid armed conflict with other nations. To ignore diplomatic solutions or to short-circuit diplomatic solutions in the rush to war would be to violate the proportionality condition and thus a war waged in those circumstances would not be just. In contrast, the proportionality condition with regard to *jus in bello*, for example, would militate against using nuclear weapons when conventional weapons could be used effectively to win a war because the destructiveness of nuclear weapons far outweighs those of conventional weapons, without bringing about a countervailing good. So Marwan's use of a nuclear device in Season Four, and the Russians' use of multiple nuclear devices in Season Six, would violate the proportionality condition with regard to *jus in bello*. In both cases, they had no reason to "go nuclear" as a first option when conventional weaponry is widely available and effective.

Condition 1: Former President David Palmer and the Invasion of China

Now that we've looked at the four conditions of a just war, we can apply those conditions to the invasion of the Chinese consulate in Season Four. Recall the first condition,

1   The sovereign or leader of the group who will be waging war must have the authority to wage war (Aquinas, IIa–IIae.40.1).

Aquinas' first condition is meant to point out that a just war is waged by a head of state or a body of persons who function as the head of state; just wars can't be waged by private citizens, civil servants, or Division creeps like Ryan Chappelle. In Season Four, former President Palmer orders the invasion, but he is not the head of state at that moment. Although he is brought in by Logan to be a special advisor, Palmer is given limited authority over the efforts to combat terrorism. He was not authorized by the Congress to wage a war with the Chinese, or to order an invasion of China. Although we might be sympathetic with Jack's argument that the invasion was necessary in order to stave off a nuclear holocaust on American soil, Palmer's actions do not meet the first condition for just war. Palmer did not have the authority to involve the United States in a war with China or to order an aggressive act against the nation of China.

But what about the real head of state, President Logan? Logan seems to be the ultimate cause of this unjust war because it was his responsibility to handle the terrorism crisis or to resign. He was the only one who could have authorized the invasion of the Chinese consulate, once he had gone through the appropriate political channels. We all cheered when Logan brought Palmer in as an advisor, because Logan lacked decision-making abilities and leadership qualities. He should bear the ultimate responsibility of the unjust war.

Those who take a "lesser evil" approach to politics would argue that a democratic state is justified in performing or permitting some evil actions in order to prevent a greater evil from coming about.[4] This is precisely the line of thought that Palmer and Jack frequently follow. One might argue that Palmer is justified in breaking certain rules and conditions in order to protect the American people, but one cannot call this invasion a just war. Any justification of Palmer's actions after the fact should admit this. Since the first condition for a just war was not met, Palmer's invasion was not part of a just war. However, it is still helpful to analyze the other three conditions in order to determine *how unjust* the invasion was. As Hurka points out, unjust wars can be waged more or less justly (35).

---

4 For example, see Michael Ignatieff, *The Lesser Evil: Political Ethics in an Age of Terror* (Edinburgh: Edinburgh University Press, 2005), pp. 2–8. Page references to Ignatieff are to this work.

Condition 2: The Just Cause

2   The war must be waged for a just cause; "those who are attacked
    should be attacked because they deserve it on account of some
    fault" (IIa–IIae.40.1).

According to this condition, the just war must be waged for a just
reason or on account of a just cause. So those having war waged
against them must deserve the war in some respect. The standard
examples given of a just cause for war include the resistance of
aggression (which could include invasion), the response to a sufficient
threat that would include a "manifest intent to injure," and a situation
in which failing to act increases the risk of injury (Walzer, 80–81).

   As we know, Palmer and Jack would argue that the invasion was
justified because the Chinese were harboring a terrorist, who was a
co-conspirator with a terrorist group that was planning an imminent
attack on the United States. Harboring Lee Jong would be analogous
to harboring terrorist training camps within the borders of another
country. China's decision to harbor someone with terrorist connections seems to provide the basis for an aggressive action, but only
after diplomatic solutions have been exhausted. Palmer recognizes
this, and so he tries to persuade the consul to deliver Lee voluntarily.
But the consul resists, citing doubts about the validity of the evidence
used to demonstrate Lee's connection with Marwan and reasserting
Chinese sovereignty over the citizens in its territory. The consul could
have offered a diplomatic solution by suggesting that Lee be interrogated in the consulate by Chinese or American agents. Even if the
consul chose to invoke diplomatic immunity for Lee, who was not
a member of the consulate staff, the consulate would have been
expected to cooperate with the Americans in their investigation of
Lee's criminal wrongdoing. But the Chinese were unwilling to agree
to a diplomatic solution to the conflict; they wouldn't even cooperate
at a minimal level.

   Once diplomatic solutions are exhausted, Palmer weighs the
respect for Chinese sovereignty against the imminent detonation of
a nuclear bomb in the United States, deciding to act aggressively for
the purpose of preserving American lives. He makes the judgment
that the lives of those living on American soil, which would include
both citizens and non-citizens alike, outweigh the civil rights of one

Chinese citizen and the respect for Chinese sovereignty. Based upon the requirement of the just cause condition, it looks as if the threat posed by Marwan and Lee Jong satisfies this condition.

As Michael Ignatieff points out, when one is threatened by terrorists one must act in such a way as to balance a whole host of important values and ethical principles, such as national security, the respect for persons, international relations, and so forth (9). But if the nation does not survive, then all of these values and principles are effectively lost. So the preservation of a nation, along with its values, is something worth defending (10–11). Michael Walzer argues explicitly that the use of nuclear weapons "explodes" the theory of just war, because it would bring a nation under "the rules of necessity" rather than the rules of just war (252–253). In other words, the leader of a state under imminent threat of a nuclear attack would be justified in responding to that danger beyond all proportionality. In the *24* scenario, in the absence of Chinese cooperation with a diplomatic solution, Palmer chose to respond to an imminent nuclear threat at the cost of Chinese sovereignty. In so doing, he meets the second condition for a just war.

Condition 3: The Just Intention

3 Those waging war must have the correct intention, that is, they must intend to advance the good or to avoid evil or both (IIa–IIae.40.1).

The third condition for just war argues that the war must have a just intended outcome that would promote the good, or limit evil, or both. This seems very straightforward, but is actually quite complicated. It's very easy to think that one is on the side of good, but it's much more difficult to actually be on the side of good.[5] One could be wrong about which side one is on, especially in the scenarios of *24* in which there are moles, triple-agents, political intrigues in the White House, blackmailing plots, and so on. Moreover, one could have a

---

5 James Turner Johnson, "Threats, Values, and Defenses: Does the Defense of Values by Force Remain a Moral Possibility?" in *Just War Theory*, ed. Jean Bethke Elshtain (Oxford: Blackwell, 1992), p. 59.

correct intention such as disarming Russian terrorists, but be ignorant of a piece of crucial information such as that President Logan is involved in bolstering terrorism for the purpose of manufacturing a conflict.

In Season Four, Palmer's stated intention is to kidnap Lee Jong and to bring him out of the consulate unharmed. Palmer did not intend to injure any of the Chinese citizens in the consulate or to damage the consulate. In fact, Jack told his operatives not to fire their weapons, and they didn't. Both the consul and Lee were shot by Chinese officers in the ensuing struggle. Palmer's intention seems to be good, since the goal of the operation is to interrogate Lee in order to find out what he knows about Marwan and the location of the nuclear device. It is not his intention to have a protracted conflict with China; it is not his intention to kill Lee. Palmer's ultimate goal is to prevent the detonation of a nuclear device on American soil, which would potentially kill Lee and all of the inhabitants of the Chinese consulate in addition to other persons living within the radius of the blast. So one could say that Palmer intends to save the lives of the Chinese citizens living in the consulate, as well as the lives of Americans and non-Americans who are living within the blast radius. Palmer's intention seems to be just, satisfying the third condition. A horrifying illustration of what might have happened should the device have been detonated takes place in Season Six, when a device is detonated in Valencia, California. Buildings explode into flame, a helicopter drops from the sky, and thousands are instantly killed. This is the kind of evil that Palmer was trying to avoid by invading the consulate to capture Lee Jong.

Condition 4: The Proportionality Condition

4   That the destructiveness of war must be proportional to the relevant good that the war will bring about (Hurka, 35).

The fourth condition for just war argues that the destruction brought about by war must be proportional to the goodness of the outcome brought about by that same war. As we have already discussed, foregoing diplomacy in a rush to war would violate the proportionality condition as regards *jus ad bellum*. Moreover, the proportionality as regards *jus in bello* must also be considered.

With respect to *jus ad bellum* in Season Four, it would have been better if a diplomatic solution to the conflict between the Chinese and the Americans had been reached. But a contributing factor in this scenario, as in many scenarios in *24*, is the timeframe. The timeframe is almost a character in the show in that it exercises considerable influence over how decisions are made and what decisions are made. In the invasion scenario, Palmer's knowledge that the bomb will go off soon eliminates his ability to give the Chinese consul unlimited time to find the ambassador, sift through the evidence against Lee, and make a determination as to whether or not they will allow the Americans to interrogate Lee. Once again, the Chinese could have brokered a compromise here, by offering to expedite the decision-making process, or by inviting representatives of CTU to interrogate Lee on Chinese soil. They could have offered to interrogate Lee themselves, but they refused to compromise. So the failure of diplomacy is not solely the fault of the Americans, nor did they act entirely pre-emptively. The Chinese bear some responsibility for the break down of diplomatic talks. Moreover, as both Walzer and Ignatieff point out, an imminent nuclear threat forces a response from the nation under attack beyond all normal proportionality. Despite the danger of the attack, Palmer still respects the proportionality condition by attempting to broker a diplomatic solution to the conflict with China. He goes beyond what would normally be expected or required in the case of an imminent nuclear threat. Thus, the proportionality condition as regards *jus ad bellum* is not violated by the Americans.

With respect to *jus in bello*, since the consul is shot and killed this element of destruction must be taken into account against the backdrop of the armed conflict. Even though the death of the consul was not caused by Jack's operatives, it was the invasion that prompted the use of military force on behalf of the Chinese and so the act of war contributed significantly to the consul's death. But since Jack had ordered his men not to fire their weapons, the death of the consul was clearly unintended. Moreover, as Hurka points out, the moral responsibility for a resultant evil can be diminished by another individual's "intervening choice" (50). So although it was the invasion of the consulate that brought about the situation in which the consul was shot and killed, it was the intervening decision of the consul to offer armed resistance that brought about the actual death of the consul. Since the invading force did not shoot at the consulate defense force, the defense force was not obligated to shoot back. They responded with more force than was being directed at them during the invasion, and so they bear some moral responsibility for the death of the consul.

When one weighs the death of the consul against the death of millions of Americans, particularly in light of the destruction seen in Valencia in Season Six, it seems to be a much lesser evil. Similarly, the lives of all human beings living within the radius of the nuclear blast, including the inhabitants of the Chinese consulate, constitute a greater good than the unfortunate death of the consul. So as regards the proportionality condition *jus in bello*, the destructiveness of the conflict and the death of the consul seem to be outweighed by the preservation of life of millions of Americans and non-Americans living within the radius of the nuclear blast. With respect to both *jus ad bellum* and *jus in bello*, former President Palmer appears to act justly.

Praise for Palmer

Just war theory articulates four important conditions that must be met in order for a war to be just. These conditions prompt us to look closely at any armed incursion in order to see who ordered the incursion, why it was ordered and how it is conducted. Since the invasion of the Chinese consulate was ordered by former President Palmer, this incursion is not an act of a just war. However, as regards the other conditions for just war, it seems clear that President Palmer waged an unjust war somewhat justly. While he doesn't accrue moral credit for waging a just war, he could be praised somewhat for exhausting diplomatic solutions prior to the conflict as well as consciously limiting the destructiveness of the invasion. As is frequently the case in *24*, good people frequently commit unjust acts in the pursuit of national security. But Palmer does not "override the rules of war" just because his nation is faced with an imminent nuclear attack. He takes into account proportionality with respect to both the recourse to war and the waging of the war. As a result, Palmer attempted to minimize the death and destruction that resulted from the conflict, while attempting to preserve millions of human lives. When it comes to having confidence in the leadership of President David Palmer over and against other alternatives, one *24* fan put it best: "I'd vote for David Palmer any day."

10:00 AM–11:00 AM

Jack Bauer as Anti-Eichmann and Scourge of Political Liberalism

Brandon Claycomb and Greig Mulberry

[Jack Bauer has organized the kidnapping of bio-terrorist Stephen Saunders' daughter, Jane. He is questioning her about her father.]

Jane: First of all, I hardly know my father; and whatever this is, I know it's illegal. You have no right to keep me here. Release me now, I haven't done anything wrong.

Jack: You better listen to me very carefully Jane. Right now your father is engaged in terrorist activity against the United States of America; this morning he killed hundreds of people and has threatened to kill thousands more. Now I can only imagine how difficult this must be for you to believe, but trust me: you're going to cooperate with us. There's a lot at stake and there's not a lot of time.

Jane: I'm not going to do anything, I want to talk to a lawyer.

[Jack, standing several feet away and sideways to Jane, turns to look briefly at her to size up her demand and this moment. He gives a calm, dismissive exhalation, takes a drink, then moves slowly toward her.]

Jack: There's no lawyer. There's just you and me.

At What Cost?

Jack Bauer doesn't give a damn about anyone's Constitutional rights. Dedicated *24* viewers, long since past sharing Jane's naïveté, instantly understand his dismissive exhalation, and know how far Jack is willing to go to acquire her cooperation. Her demands for legal counsel, her declaration that Jack has no right to kidnap her and keep her locked up, and her insistence that she doesn't have to tell him anything come across almost as dark comedy in light of Jack's willingness to disregard nearly any barrier, legal or otherwise, that might stand between him and his goal.

Fans of *24*, the authors included, surely relish not just the show's constant, complex action, but Jack Bauer's capacity to bend that action to his will. A man of action, Bauer appears to have written no tracts on political philosophy. We discern in his words and deeds, however, a consistent perspective that indicates Jack's curious blend of anti-authoritarianism and anti-liberalism. What happens when a federal super-agent rejects both his obligation to obey orders he doesn't accept and the laws and guidelines of the American tradition of political liberalism? At least on *24*, the world gets saved—a lot. At what cost? Looking at Jack's similarities and dissimilarities to two other arch-antiliberals will help us answer this question.

Eichmann

Political liberalism, as we'll be concerned with it in this chapter, is defined by its commitment to the rule of law and to the fair debate between differing conceptions of the good. (Liberalism in this sense is not to be confused with liberal as opposed to conservative as the terms are used in contemporary American politics. Both liberals and conservatives in that sense are advocates of liberalism in the sense we'll be discussing here.) At its core, liberalism consists in providing a space in which people can argue about what should be done. Jack Bauer's rejection of this philosophy recalls the work of the twentieth-century political philosopher Carl Schmitt. According to Schmitt the essence of political action is the discrimination of friends from foes. By taking political positions one necessarily takes other actors as supporting or opposing one's way of life. For Schmitt, there is no escape from this fact of human existence; one can only obscure it by pretending, as he thinks liberals do, that compromise is always possible, that debate is always potentially productive.

We'll explore the parallels between Schmitt's and Bauer's views shortly, but the connection should already be clear. Jack has no patience for any of the restrictions set by the law on his plans to save American innocents. To challenges that would lead to real discussions about what the heroes of *24* should be trying to achieve he typically responds with the show's recurring moral refrain: "We don't have a choice." At least in a crisis, Jack Bauer is as illiberal as they come.

We can appreciate Jack's illiberalism further by comparing him with Adolf Eichmann. Eichmann was the officer in charge of the Nazi's final solution to "the Jewish problem." The political philosopher Hannah Arendt made a study of his 1961 trial in Israel that articulated her new conception of evil. Eichmann defended himself by claiming that in arranging the deportation and mass killing of Jews he was simply doing his duty by following orders. Whereas the prosecution sought to undermine Eichmann's defense by showing that he was a more active and engaged agent of the final solution than he admitted, Arendt condemned the accused on the basis of his own defense. Taking him at his word, Arendt argued that Eichmann exemplified what she termed "banal" evil. By being thoughtless, refusing to see his situation from the perspective of others or to take responsibility for the orders he carried out, Eichmann abdicated his role as an ethical being. By serving as a cog in an enormous bureaucratic machine, by telling himself that he did not have a choice, Eichmann facilitated great evil.

Eichmann's obedience and refusal to think for himself meshes with Schmitt's account of the political. He believed that the way of life he supported was at stake, and he willingly participated in extreme efforts to eradicate its foes. Eichmann also provides a striking contrast with Jack Bauer. In one sense, the two could hardly be more different. Whereas Eichmann blindly obeyed orders, Bauer follows only the dictates of his own conception of the good. For instance, when Bauer is ordered in Season Five to allow terrorists to release a deadly virus into a mall so that they will not be tipped off that they are under surveillance and their future, more deadly attacks may more easily be thwarted, he simply refuses to comply, having instantly devised a different, riskier plan with some chance to save even more lives. Each season provides many similar cases, and indeed, it is far easier to find examples throughout *24* of Jack openly disobeying orders than of him obeying, and it is for this reason that we call him "the Anti-Eichmann."

Yet on closer inspection it is not clear that Bauer is truly more thoughtful, in Arendt's sense, than Eichmann. On the contrary, Jack rarely shows any doubt or any patience with true discussion. He is as blindly, illiberally subservient to his own principles as Eichmann was to his commanders. Whether he is kidnapping innocent people in their homes, taking hostages at a gas station, running a secret sting operation from within CTU, killing his boss, or simply eliminating the long-established American narrative code whereby he who tortures another on film or television thereby clarifies his role as a "bad guy," Jack never exhibits the sort of self-questioning or engagement in real conversation that might count as moral debate. Jack Bauer does not discuss plans in order to determine proper goals; he speaks with others to convince them of the rightness of his vision and to coordinate their actions with his.

No Compromise

One aim guides *24*: saving innocent American lives. Much of the drama of the show stems from characters finding themselves torn between this principle and their duty to protect their loved ones— Jack's wife and daughter in Season One, Michelle Dessler in Season Three, Edgar Stiles' mother in Season Four, and so on. Ultimately, though, the series clearly contends that duty requires these public servants to be willing to sacrifice themselves and those dear to them for the sake of protecting as many of their fellow citizens as possible.

It is striking the extent to which the show does not challenge this principle with an appeal to liberal conceptions of the rule of law and the value of free debate. There are exceptions, which tend to involve the presidents Palmer. The latter portion of Season Two centers around David Palmer's efforts to prevent his cabinet from declaring him unfit for duty in order to undertake what turns out to be unjustified military action against an unnamed Middle Eastern country, while Wayne Palmer refuses to respond to the nuclear explosion on American soil in Season Six by suspending habeas corpus and affiliated rights as some of his advisors insist, on the grounds that doing so would be both unconstitutional and ineffective. Beyond these counter-examples, however, *24* almost always defines its "good guys" by their willingness to go along with Jack's uncompromising commitment to the principle of saving innocent American lives at all costs. All others, including those federal agents and police officers who sincerely believe that they are acting for the good of their country and in the name of justice, function as opponents.

This dynamic manifests itself most clearly in the shifting rotation of Jack's confederates that occurs over the course of different seasons and even within a season. Although some characters, such as Audrey Raines and Chloe O'Brian, side with Jack almost without exception, and consequently tend to argue from a Baueresque perspective in each season's inevitable CTU debates, others such as Tony Almeida, Michelle Dessler, and Defense Secretary Heller alternately serve Jack as friends and as rivals over the course of the show. Strikingly, from the point of view of *24*, these agonists are consistently on the side of the angels insofar as they agree with Jack, and count just as consistently as dramatically intriguing obstacles when they disagree. Consequently, these good guys don't care about authority or the rules, a point that a string of CTU directors are painfully slow to learn, no matter how many times Chloe disregards and disobeys their orders in order to provide technical support for Bauer's latest solo campaign.

Bauer's dedication to his principles over his compatriots animates the show. In the first episode of the first season Jack assaults his supervisor George Mason simply because he is convinced that Mason is withholding information that might allow CTU to solve the plot to assassinate Senator Palmer. When questioned about this decision Jack delivers a plea against compromise:

> You can look the other way once and it's no big deal . . . except it makes it easier for you to compromise the next time, and pretty soon that's all you're doing is compromising, because that's how you think things are done.

The irony is that Jack does not see how his analysis applies to his own behavior and to those who work with him. For someone who has watched multiple seasons of *24* it is almost quaint to recall how in the first season other characters question Jack's willingness to disregard the need for search warrants and other legal protocols. Later in the series his closest allies won't need to ask whether overriding such concerns is justified. Jack's regular practice of ignoring the law will have made his eliding it further all but involuntary. The reason he does not recognize this as a compromise is that Jack can't conceive of the law as something inherently worth preserving. All that matters is defining America's foes and dealing with them appropriately and immediately. Understood as a heroic narrative, *24* presents an unending battle between liberal and Schmittian principles, with the hero's winning side clearly siding with Schmitt.

In the most extreme situations Bauer finds his duty so clear that he is willing to threaten or harm American innocents himself in the name of saving other American innocents. What's more, he disclaims all responsibility for doing so. For example, in Season Five Jack finds himself trapped in the baggage compartment of a plane. When the pilot tries to deplete the air in the compartment to knock Jack out, Jack disables the plane's controls. The pilot asks, "What the hell do you think you're doing? You're going to kill everybody on this plane," to which Jack responds, "That's up to you." When the pilot still refuses to give in to Jack's demands, Jack answers, "Then you'll be responsible for everything that happens."

Also in Season Five Jack confronts his old compatriot Christopher Henderson at his home. Henderson admits to knowing more about the plot to release nerve gas on the local populace than he will reveal, and taunts Jack to torture him to try to get him to talk. Instead, Jack shoots Henderson's wife Miriam in the leg. Jack then notes that he has shot Miriam above the kneecap, but "if you make me shoot her again, she'll be in a wheelchair for the rest of her life. Don't you make me do this." When Henderson still refuses to talk, Jack is aghast, saying, "You don't care about anybody." Needless to say, this is a radically self-serving interpretation on Jack's part. While his reading of Christopher Henderson's lack of concern for others appears accurate, Jack fails to acknowledge his own willingness to harm someone he knows is innocent in order to serve what he believes is a higher purpose. Furthermore, Bauer apparently decides at this point not to shoot Miriam again solely because he judges that doing so would not induce Henderson to come clean.

Clearly, Jack is as enthralled with his sense of duty as Eichmann was. He is repeatedly willing to sacrifice himself, and frequently others, in order to protect that which he holds most dear, feeling that his choice in such cases is so clear as to be no real choice at all. The only noticeable tension in Bauer's calculations arises in those situations where he must choose between saving large numbers of American innocents and defending his closest friends and loved ones, particular his wife Teri, his daughter Kim, and his girlfriend Audrey Raines. Even when confronted with impossible choices between serving his country and caring for his family, Jack's struggles appear almost entirely internal. He looks out for others, and, when forced to, may negotiate with them, but he does not truly consider their view of the good as a legitimate rival to his own.

Indeed, Jack Bauer seems all but incapable of thinking from the perspective of others or valuing their aims in some rough equation with his own. That is not to say that he is selfish in the standard sense of the term. His goals rarely concern his personal well being, and in fact he repeatedly offers himself as a potential sacrifice for others. Jack's brand of paternalistic altruism, his manner of taking care of others even against their will, does not, however, count as thought in Arendt's sense. Thinking from the perspective of others entails being open to their values, being willing at least in principle to compromise not just about the means by which an end will be pursued, but about the ends themselves. A retrospective of all the scenes from *24* in which Jack Bauer has backed down in an argument would be very brief indeed! More indicative of Jack's approach to debate is the scene from Season Five in which Secretary Heller "explains" his disagreement with Jack's plan by striking him in the trachea. Heller, a Baueresque figure, knows that superior force might stop Jack, or at least slow him, but the force of another's reasoning never will.

Jack Alone

Where does all this leave Jack? Alone. Like so many other masculine heroes of American fiction, Bauer seems destined never to enjoy fully the idyllic joy of the feminized homeland that he protects. The archetype of this character was John Wayne's Ethan Edwards in John Ford's 1956 Western *The Searchers*. Wayne plays a Civil War veteran who spends years tracking the Comanche raiders who have kidnapped his niece. At the successful conclusion of his long struggle to restore his clan, the movie closes with a shot of the family's cabin door closing on Edwards, still outside and forever shut out of the peaceful space his efforts have preserved. Season after season Bauer finds himself similarly cut off from the women he loves. Teri's murder at the end of Season One illustrates this dynamic most clearly, but it is apparent in every season, from his unexplained breakup with Kate Warner between Seasons Two and Three, through his gradual estrangement from his daughter Kim, to his capture by Chinese agents at the end of Season Five just as he and Audrey Raines have begun to recapture the wordless bliss the show implies they could share if Jack were not literally and figuratively pulled away from her by his duty. *24* is open, then, about the personal costs to Jack Bauer and his friends and family of his unending efforts to protect his country explicitly from terrorism and implicitly from liberalism. The price paid for his efforts by the American political tradition is, we believe, equally great.

Jack's No Hobbit

24's temporal compression is essential for the kind of quick-paced entertainment that the show offers its viewers. Its narrative barrage of momentous decisions made on a second-by-second basis invites viewers to feel that the rule of law and due process have no legitimate place in the real world. According to Schmitt, every political and legal decision is ultimately founded upon unrestrained discretion. Liberalism's insistence on the rule of law merely disguises this decisionism, the flat assertion of will in the name of the self-preservation of a way of life that constitutes the real nature of political existence. Schmitt's Homeric moral code of the primordial distinction between those who are with us and those who are against us fits comfortably with Bauer, who after identifying friends and foes acts decisively to protect the former and vanquish the latter.

In subtle and unsubtle ways alike *24* suggests that our era is one of fundamental crisis that requires the abandonment of both liberal jurisprudence and liberal humanism's naïve optimism about human nature. The show urges that core liberal features such as consensus building, accommodating diverse opinions, and protecting against arbitrary power are unworkable in the post-9/11 world. America's terrorist enemies, so the logic goes, have identified their foes and are committed to their destruction. As Pogo didn't say, "We have met the enemy, and he is them." Jack Bauer is similarly clear-eyed about what is necessary to protect America from these terrorist assaults, and his status as the show's hero and moral center encourages us to see liberal values and institutions as anachronistic. This story is compelling, yet we question its lesson. Our closing comparison with a very different tale of Manichean struggle indicates the problem.

At a crucial point in Tolkien's *The Lord of the Rings* the hobbit Frodo offers the one ring of power to the good and wise elven queen Galadriel. Having long dreamed of this opportunity, she revels for a moment in the thought of smiting the enemies of the free peoples of Middle Earth, before rejecting this invitation to unfettered power. Tolkien's division of his fictional world into good and evil camps is, if anything, starker than that in *24*, yet his narrative offers a reversal of *24*'s moral division within its own "good guys." In Middle Earth the mark of the greatest heroes is their refusal of absolute power; at CTU the real heroes are those who recognize no limits to their efforts. No matter how anti-authoritarian Jack Bauer, our Anti-Eichmann, may be, his seizing of *24*'s closest equivalent to the ring of power, his disregard for all checks on the imposition of his own will, threatens the dissolution of the very way of life he fights to preserve. When all the barriers to the will of the most powerful are dissolved, what beyond their good will prevents them from dominating the rest of us? It is this fundamental fact of power that drives liberalism's legal and cultural efforts to restrain even good people from making decisions for others. Bauer's removal of these restraints is his most dangerous act.

Palmer's Pickle:
Why Couldn't He
Stomach It?

Georgia Testa

A nuclear bomb has been primed to explode in the Los Angeles area and the expectation is that it will kill one million people. The only person, apart from the terrorists, who knows the bomb's location, is Nina. However, the plane on which she and Jack are traveling is shot down. Before the CTU rescue team can close in on them, Nina manages to grab Jack's gun and threatens to kill him. She requests to speak with President Palmer by phone and then tells him that she will reveal the bomb's location only if Palmer gives her immunity for what she is about to do—kill Jack. To that end, she wants the CTU soldiers to stand down.

Jack tells Palmer to give Nina what she wants: he offers up his life. After some hesitation, Palmer agrees to Nina's terrible bargain but offers her immunity only if the bomb is located, so ensuring that she tells them the truth. But he is disturbed by his decision. He chokes back tears and has to be reassured by his aide, Mike, that he has done the right thing.

But has he? And why did he hesitate? He clearly didn't find the decision easy. That may be because he knew what he should do but given that it would involve Jack's death, he found it hard to do. Or it may be that he was trying to work out what he should do. One thing, however, is certain: he wasn't running through moral theories to try to identify what would be the right thing! But we will. We'll explore the kinds of considerations that could be influencing his decision and locate them within moral theories that could explain their significance. These theories can help us to assess whether Palmer's decision was, after all, the right one.

I imagine that some of you will think that simply because Jack offered up his life—told Palmer to give Nina what she wants—that Palmer's decision is the right one. Jack has consented to be killed and that settles the matter. But this, as we shall see in more detail later, is not as obvious as it first appears.

Consequentialism

According to consequentialism, the consequences of an action determine whether it is right. The action that can reasonably be expected to produce the most good in the world is the right action. Let's identify the good with the value of life.[1] How does this affect Palmer's decision? Palmer's choice is to save the lives of roughly one million people or save the life of one person—Jack. If each life matters in itself and matters equally, then a decision to save the many will result in more good than a decision to save Jack.

On this account, therefore, Palmer's decision would be the right one. In fact, it's a no-brainer, especially as Nina's cooperation is highly probable. We can trust that Nina wants to live and be free and, therefore, that she will keep her bargain. So we do not need to factor in the complication of uncertainty, which can affect the consequentialist calculation of which action is best.[2] So why did Palmer pause?

Problems with Consequentialism I: Strict Impartialism

Let's assume Palmer hesitated because he knew what he should do but found it hard to do so. Why might that be? Because he cares

1 We could equally focus on well being. It is safe to assume that each of the people likely to be killed by the bomb will have some positive measure of well being in their lives, from which it will follow that the loss of their lives will reduce the overall sum of well being in the world by a much greater amount than will the loss of Jack's life. So it would be right to take that action which will save the lives of the many. However, focusing on the value of life seems more readily to capture Palmer's dilemma.
2 Probabilities complicate matters. The good that would be realized by successful action needs to be adjusted by the probability that the action will be successful. So once we factor in probabilities it may be the case that we should try to save the few because there is a high chance of saving them but a low chance of saving the many. That way we stand a good chance of saving some.

about Jack. Jack isn't just anyone, Jack saved his life and they have a relationship. That matters. But the consequentialist calculation is impartial: no one's good or life is more important than anyone else's. So we are not allowed to weigh the losses to or of those we care about as more important. However, commitments to others, bonds of love and affection, are central to the value we find in life. It is constitutive of such relationships that we are *not* impartial in all things. So consequentialism is wrong when it requires us to violate these commitments and be impartial.

I can imagine many of you saying, "Look, there are one *million* lives at stake and so Palmer should save them and not Jack. Impartiality *is* required." But what if Palmer's choice was between saving *Keith*, his son, and saving the million? I doubt you would be quite so sure about whether Palmer should be impartial in that situation. We could explain the disparity in the following way. Although Palmer does care for Jack, their relationship is not close enough to justify being partial, and so saving Jack rather than the million is ruled out. But the relationship between Palmer and his son is of an entirely different order of commitment. So we should take account of the closeness and nature of personal relationships when considering whether they justify partial behavior and not simply the amount of good that we could do by being impartial.[3]

It would be extremely difficult to make this precise. We'd need some ranking of closeness and some ranking of the amounts of overall good that could outweigh personal relationships of different degrees of closeness. Our intuitions here are muddy. We may only be able to come up with rough and ready assessments, such that the closeness of the Jack-Palmer relationship is less than that of the Keith-Palmer relationship, and the first but not the second can be outweighed by the good of saving one million. Finer ranking details may have to be established on a case-by-case basis. But does even this rough and ready analysis provide a plausible explanation of the disparity in our reactions to the choice between Jack and the million, and Keith and the million? Let's look at the Keith scenario more closely.

In line with the ranking suggestion, there may be doubt that the good of saving one million lives is great enough to justify sacrificing

3 Some relationships impose duties of care simply as a matter of the nature of the relationship rather than the emotional closeness of it, such as the parent-child relationship.

Keith because of the nature of the relationship between father and son. Maybe more lives would have to be at stake. But the underlying assumption is that there *will* be some number of lives—some magnitude of good—that could justify sacrificing Keith. However, others may think that Keith should be saved because no amount of good could justify his sacrifice. The nature of the parent-child relationship means that consideration of the larger good does not apply here. So there are some relationships or some partial commitments that should never give way to consequentialist considerations. This takes some relationships out of the ranking I suggested above and so leaves less room for consequentialist considerations, although it may leave enough to explain why Jack should be sacrificed despite his relationship with Palmer.

Problems with Consequentialism II: The End Justifies the Means

For consequentialism, the end justifies the means: whatever action will bring about the greatest overall good is the right action to perform. So, if the only means to save one million people is to give Nina immunity for Jack's murder, that is what Palmer should do. But don't we have a basic moral right not to be killed, a right to life? Doesn't Jack have a right not to be killed even if his death would save the lives of others?

Non-consequentialists hold that we each matter in ourselves and so the fact that some action would harm us can provide sufficient reason not to take that action, even if the action would benefit a great many others. On this view, individual well being takes priority over collective well being. Rights reflect this view because they act as constraints on action; they restrict what we may do to others, even in pursuit of a greater good.[4] A right to life, understood as a right not to be killed,

---

4   For a more detailed explanation of this type of non-consequentialism, which places limits on what we may do for the overall good, see Frances Kamm, "Nonconsequentialism," in *The Blackwell Guide to Ethical Theory*, ed. Hugh LaFollette (Oxford: Blackwell, 2000). There is a stronger form of non-consequentialism which denies that consequentialist considerations *ever* matter. See Robert Nozick, *Anarchy, State, and Utopia* (New York: Basic Books, 1974) and John Taurek, "Should the Numbers Count?" *Philosophy and Public Affairs* 6 (1977): 293–316.

is basic to this account. Giving Nina permission to kill Jack would fail to respect his right to life. If it is wrong to kill a person because that would be a violation of his right to life, then it would be wrong to give someone permission to kill him.

Of course, respecting Jack's right would mean that one million other rights to life would be violated. So if we take rights seriously, shouldn't we permit the violation of Jack's right in order to prevent a great many other identical rights violations? We shouldn't. We take rights seriously as constraints on action if we constrain our actions in the way they require. The right to life rules out killing. So we respect a person's right to life by accepting that killing him is ruled out but also that giving permission for him to be killed is ruled out.[5]

But this presents a problem. It looks as though it would be wrong to permit Jack to be killed—violate his right to life—and so save one million. But I suspect that many of you will think that even though it would be a tragedy if Jack died—since he matters in himself—that Palmer should save the one million. He would be wrong to save Jack. How do we square this with non-consequentialism?

The Doctrine of Double Effect

The Doctrine of Double Effect (DDE) is meant to deal with our intuitions that sometimes bringing about the good *is* what matters. According to the DDE we are permitted to act in ways that bring about great good even when that causes serious harms to others that would normally be prohibited—harms such as death. The DDE makes a distinction between harming as a means to bringing about great good, and harming as an unavoidable side-effect of bringing about great good. We may not do the former but we may do the latter. However, certain conditions must hold:

1 The action must not be wrong in itself.
2 The bad effects of the action—or harms—are not intended but merely foreseen.

5 See Frances Kamm, "Nonconsequentialism, the Person as End-in-Itself, and the Significance of Status," *Philosophy and Public Affairs* 21 (1992): 354–389. Page references to Kamm are to this article.

3 The proportionality condition: the good effect must be sufficiently great to outweigh the bad effects. It must be worth bringing about and be sufficiently greater than the bad effect.[6]

So will the DDE license Palmer's decision? His decision would satisfy the proportionality condition. But, in order to save the one million, Palmer must get the information about the bomb from Nina. And in order to get the information from Nina, he must give her permission to kill Jack. So letting Nina kill Jack is the means to getting the information which, in turn, is the means to saving the million. Jack's death is, therefore, a means to the good. It is not an unavoidable side-effect of giving Nina a permission to kill him. If, for example, after Palmer gave his permission, Jack was beamed up by a space ship such that Nina could not kill him, she would not then give Palmer the information he wants. Jack's death would only be an unavoidable side-effect—not necessary to achieve the good end—if Nina would give up her information once she had her permission and even if she could not kill Jack. Given that is not the case, the DDE will not license Palmer's decision.

A further complication is that the action Palmer is contemplating—giving Nina permission to kill Jack—would appear to be wrong in itself, as I have explained.

Consent

As we know, Jack tells Palmer to give Nina what she wants; he gives Palmer permission to allow Nina to kill him. Could this overcome our two problems: that giving Nina permission to kill Jack is wrong in itself, and that killing Jack uses him as a means? We need to explore whether something that would normally be morally wrong can be made morally permissible by consent.

6 The proportionality condition also plays a role in assessing the morality of war. For details, see the chapter by Jennifer Hart Weed in this book. For a brief discussion of the various interpretations of the DDE, see Alison McIntyre, "Doctrine of Double Effect," *The Stanford Encyclopedia of Philosophy (Summer 2006 Edition)*, ed. Edward N. Zalta, available online at www.plato.stanford.edu/archives/sum2006/entries/double-effect/. For detailed treatment, see *The Doctrine of Double Effect*, ed. P. A. Woodward (Notre Dame: University of Notre Dame Press, 2001).

Voluntary euthanasia provides an example in which killing is made permissible through consent. It could be said that the person waives their right to life. But what matters there is that they waive their right for their own sake, in order to end their own suffering, and so we kill them for their own sake. By contrast, Jack is to be killed for the sake of others. So the role of consent is not straightforward.

As a further example, take the infamous case of Armen Meiwes who killed a person with that person's consent. Meiwes was originally convicted of manslaughter and not murder because of the consent. So while consent made a moral difference it did not make the killing morally permissible: it only made the killing a lesser wrong. However, the case was subsequently retried and this time Meiwes was convicted of murder—the consent made no difference.

Nevertheless, the Meiwes case is illuminating. The victim consented to die in order to gratify Meiwes', and possibly his own, sexual fantasies. So he chose in whole or in part to die for the sake of another. However, it seems reasonable to hold that to find sexual gratification in killing, or being killed, is a perversion of the value of sex and so that it must be wrong to kill for this reason but also to *consent* to be killed for this reason. So there was no recognizably good end for which Meiwes' victim consented to be killed. Hence there were no grounds for taking consent to be a legitimate permission to do what is normally wrong—take life. There was also doubt that the victim was of sound mind, meaning that his consent could not play an excusing role even if, in principle, consent could make a moral difference.

But these objectionable features are not present in Jack's case. While Nina's motive is perverse, what matters for this case are the motives of Jack and Palmer, for Jack gives Palmer, and not Nina, his permission to do something that would normally be wrong. First, Jack consents to die for something recognizably good—the lives of others. Second, Palmer also wants to do good—save many lives. Third, there is no reason to believe that Jack is not of sound mind. So the reasons why consent could not make a moral difference in the Meiwes case (the illegitimate motives, the lack of a good end served by the killing, and the doubts about the validity of the victim's consent) are absent from Jack's case. This suggests that we have good reasons to hold that Jack's consent makes a moral difference: it means that Palmer's action of giving Nina permission to kill Jack is not wrong in itself.

However, what of our second problem, that the DDE prohibits harming or killing as *a means* to the good? Palmer might still be wrong to bring about Jack's death for *this* reason. But Jack consents that Palmer let Nina kill him because he knows it is the only way to save one million lives. He consents to being killed as a means to the good. Does this make it permissible for Palmer to use him this way? Not according to those who hold that the DDE applies equally to actions and decisions where we use *ourselves* as a means in a way that causes our harm or death as well as to actions or decisions where we use *others* as a means, causing them great harm or death. The thought is that when we use ourselves in this way we fail to respect ourselves as persons. So Jack's consent is irrelevant. He cannot rightfully consent to be used in this way. But is this plausible?

Our countries (or Western-style democracies) are built on the principle that persons have a right to decide for themselves what they will do with their lives, and so what values they will adopt or ends they will pursue.[7] But if we respect this right, we should allow it to extend to a person's judgments about what causes are worth suffering or dying for, simply because this is part of what is involved in making personal choices about what ends to pursue and how to pursue them. Of course, we may be wrong about which things are good or worth the personal sacrifice, or even whether our sacrifice will bring about the good we intend. In such cases, our suffering or death is unjustified. It may be, therefore, that we have no right to harm ourselves in such cases or that others would be permitted to prevent us causing our own deaths or suffering. But unless we are in error about the good, the view I am presenting is that harming yourself or laying down your life for the good is permissible.[8]

It is wrong to treat *another* as a means if we involve them in *our* plans, treat them as useful for ends *we* have decided are good without taking any account of whether *they* share our ends or judgment about

7 So foundational is this principle that both liberals and libertarians, who have very different views of what a just state should be like, take as essential that people be free to make these kinds of choices for themselves. See John Rawls, *A Theory of Justice* (Oxford: Oxford University Press, 1972) and Nozick (1974).
8 Some philosophers maintain that self-sacrifice may even be obligatory in some cases. See Richard Davis's chapter for argument and examples.

what is good.[9] In such cases, whether *they* think that the good we want to bring about is worth their sacrifice is treated as irrelevant. This is wrong because it fails to respect them as persons each of whom has a right to decide *for themselves* what they will do with their lives, what values they will adopt or ends they will pursue and, in accordance with their own judgments, what causes are worth making personal sacrifices for. If we impose such a choice on them, we treat them *merely* as a means. But if we treat them as a means only when *they too* judge that the end is worth their sacrifice, and so choose to be a means to the good, then we respect them as persons. In these cases, while we treat them as a means we also treat them as a person. That is, we do not treat them *merely* as a means. Only the latter is wrong because it fails to acknowledge that the choice of whether to suffer harm or death as a means to some good is rightfully theirs and only theirs to make. We may use another as a means only if they choose to be so used.

Jack makes that choice. He says to Palmer, "Let her have what she wants" or "Use me as a means." And we now have an explanation of why it would not be wrong for him to make that choice. But it is essential to that explanation that *Jack* believes that saving the million is a cause or good worth dying for, that it is in accordance with *his* values. It wouldn't be the right kind of choice—made for the right reason—if he made it because he thought it was expected of him, or that it would make things easier for Palmer.[10] He must be able to answer "yes" to the question, "Is that what you *really* want? Do you believe that this is a cause worth dying for?" Could he answer "yes"? It is plausible that given that Jack has devoted his working life to the security of his country and that he has often risked his life to save others, that he thinks it a cause worth dying for. That is, he chooses to lay down his life because, for *him*, the lives of those others are worth it.[11]

9   The interpretation sketched here follows that of Warren S. Quinn, "Actions, Intentions and Consequences: The Doctrine of Double Effect," *Philosophy and Public Affairs* 18:4 (1989): 334–351.

10   Just as consent to be killed in voluntary euthanasia does not justify the killing of a person if the consent is given because the person thinks it is expected of them or will make things easier for others.

11   We can imagine that even if a gun was not pointing at him he would decide to sacrifice his life. If he thought that he had to defuse a nuclear bomb by detaching the detonator from the main nuclear device, but that the detonator would explode, killing him, he would do this to prevent the deaths of one million others.

Did Palmer Do the Right Thing?

According to the DDE we may not harm someone as a means to bringing about good; we may only harm them as a side-effect. But I have argued that it is wrong only to harm another as a *mere* means to the good and so without their consent or permission—without their willing involvement. If the DDE is revised to incorporate this, it will license Palmer's decision to permit Nina to kill Jack with impunity and thereby get the information about the bomb that would save a million lives, for the simple reason that Jack consents to or gives Palmer permission to use him in this way and his consent meets the conditions specified for valid consent.[12]

But we are not yet home and dry, for the revision I have suggested conflicts with the DDE requirement that we not *intend* the harmful effects of our actions. Effects that our action aims to produce are effects that are intended. When we act to bring about a good end, we perform the action with the intention of producing the good end. Any steps we take as a means to that good end are taken in order to bring about that end and so are intended.[13] And even if we perform only one action—as Palmer does—in the knowledge or expectation that this will produce a chain of events that will bring about a good end, we take that action for the reason that it will have these effects and so bring about the good end. That means we intend the effects that lead to the good outcome. Therefore, Palmer intends Jack's death, for he takes the action of giving Nina immunity because it will have the expected effect of Jack's death, the further effect of which will be Nina's disclosure of information about the bomb which will have the final effect of saving one million lives. Clearly, Palmer sincerely regrets the means he has to take to save one million other people because it involves the death of a person and a person he cares about at that. But his regret does not alter the fact that Jack's death is a means to the good and, therefore, intended.

Does this mean we should abandon the revision of the DDE I have outlined? That depends on how persuasive you find my argument for

---

12   In subsequent references to consent I will assume that the conditions for valid consent hold and that the cause or end for which a person consents to be sacrificed is good.

13   See Phillipa Foot, *Virtues and Vices* (New York: Oxford University Press, 2002), p. 20.

the revision. It depends on whether you are persuaded by the claim that it is morally wrong to use people as a means only when we do so without their consent. Accepting the revised DDE will require you to reject the claim that we should never intend harm. But why think that we should *never* intend harm? I have tried to provide an argument for an exception to this rule.[14] And there is at least one other exception. If it is permitted to kill in self-defense, then we have an example of when it is permitted to intend harm to another. In many cases of self-defense, the death of the attacker is aimed at because their death is the only means of saving ourselves. So why not accept a rule that *generally* we should not intend harm? After all, very few (if any) of the moral principles we recognize are absolute and so exceptionless.[15]

Finally, then, did Palmer do the right thing according to the revised DDE? In a sense, he did not. In some cases moral reasoning will reveal that only one action is morally permitted and so that there is *a* right thing to do. Or, you are *required* to do that thing, for doing anything else would be wrong. In other cases, however, moral reasoning may identify a number of actions as morally permissible. So there is not one action that is *the* right thing to do. This is the case with the DDE. The unrevised DDE says you *may* harm others as a side-effect of bringing about great good but would not do wrong if you chose not to take that action which harmed others. The revised version says you *may* harm another as a means to bringing about great good, and so with their consent, but that you would not do wrong if you decided not to treat them in this way. In short, therefore, Palmer would be morally permitted but not required to treat Jack as a means. In that sense, therefore, Mike was incorrect. Palmer did not do the right thing if by that we mean *the* right thing, for the revised DDE does not *require* him to sacrifice Jack. But he did not do wrong either. He did *a* right thing.

Alternatively, if you are more persuaded by the consequentialist justification for sacrificing Jack, then it would be correct to say that

---

14   Indeed, we can understand Quinn's version of the DDE, on which my account is based, as claiming that it is not intending harm that we should avoid but rather using people in harmful ways without their consent. This makes it quite a radical revision of the DDE. For further explanation, see Kamm (1992).

15   When it comes to euthanasia, people disagree about whether death is a harm and so whether harm is intended.

Palmer did *the* right thing, for consequentialism *requires* that we take that action that we expect will produce the greatest sum of good. But on either account I have provided, I hope it is clear why Palmer found his decision hard to stomach.

But did he have to stomach it? Did Jack die? Of course not, as we all know. Jack tricks Nina into stepping into the line of fire of a CTU sniper. They were told by Palmer not to close in on Nina but to stay in position. The sniper shoots and wounds Nina, who drops her gun. Defenseless, she is captured, and Jack lives to fight the day—and many others![16]

---

16 I would like to thank Rob Lawlor for helpful discussion of this chapter.

12:00 PM–3:00 PM

CTU
HEADQUARTERS___

The Ethics of Torture in 24: Shockingly Banal

Dónal P. O'Mathúna

Season Six of 24 opens with a shocking display of the results of torture. Our hero, Jack Bauer, has survived two years in a Chinese prison. The usually proud, defiant Jack shuffles slowly off a plane, shackled and bedraggled. A glimpse of his scarred back and hand reveals that he's been through something terrible. Later in the season, Audrey Raines also returns from Chinese custody. Torture has left her cowering, bruised, and battered—a broken woman.

Torture shocks us, which is one reason it's usually hard to justify. "Almost anyone looking at the physical act of torture would be immediately appalled and repulsed by the torturers."[1] Those who witness torture on 24—even other counter-terrorism agents—usually express horror. Such reaction is typical and expected, which makes it disturbing when, in Season Two, President David Palmer fails to flinch as the screen on his desk shows Roger Stanton, Director of the National Security Agency, being tortured. Stanton screams as he is electrocuted barefoot in a bucket of water. The agent informs him the pain will only get worse, much worse. How could anyone inflict such pain on a fellow human being?

Ethics is concerned with how we treat one another. One approach called *deontology* says we should never act in ways that treat people as merely means towards our ends or goals. Torture certainly seems to do that: reducing people to mere means to get the information we want.

Back at the airport, the Chinese are trading Jack to the Americans,

---

1 Elaine Scarry, *The Body in Pain: The Making and Unmaking of the World* (Oxford: Oxford University Press, 1985), p. 35. Page references to Scarry are to this work.

who will in turn trade him to today's terrorists. Bill Buchanan, Jack's boss and friend, now Director of CTU, is told by the Chinese that for two years Jack has remained silent. Whatever torture they inflicted, it simply hasn't worked. It's done no good at all.

Utilitarianism, another approach to ethics, focuses on results. Something is ethically justified if it leads to good outcomes for lots of people: the greatest good for the greatest number in the long run. One utilitarian argument is that torture can be justified if it saves large numbers of people, or avoids much harm. So does torture work? Does it save large numbers of people?

Jack is to be handed over to the terrorist Abu Fayed who will give CTU vital information on Hamri Al-Assad's location. Assad has waged a 20-year war of terrorism on the US, and is believed to be behind a recent spate of suicide bombings on US soil. Fayed wants Jack so he can avenge his brother whom he says Jack tortured and killed in Beirut. Torture has long-term implications, leaving Fayed with a deep-seated hatred and desire for revenge.

A third approach to ethics, *virtue ethics*, looks at the impact of actions on people's characters, their virtues. War and violence change people, yet torture seems particularly destructive of individual character, and not only for the one tortured. Jack's torture begins with Fayed's aborted attempt to cut off Jack's fingers. What *kind* of person does such a thing? Well, Jack for one. Later we see Jack slice off the Russian consul's finger with a cigar cutter to find out where the suitcase bombs are located. In Season Two he refuses to give Marie Warner pain killers for her bullet wound. Instead, he pushes the bullet into her bone to force her to reveal where the nuke is hidden.

Yet Jack is the hero. He not only combats terrorism, he effectively navigates the moral morass around him. His moral compass is nearly always right—or at least so we like to think. If Jack sometimes resorts to torture, maybe there are good reasons for it.

Cultural Context of Torture

According to the United Nations' *Convention Against Torture and Other Cruel, Inhuman or Degrading Treatment or Punishment*, "No exceptional circumstances whatsoever, whether a state of war or a threat of war, internal political instability or any other public emergency, may be invoked as a justification of torture."[2] Signed by over 130 nations, this convention builds upon the three hundred year old ban on cruel and unusual punishments in the English Declaration of Rights and the two hundred year old ban in the US Constitution.[3] Only deviant totalitarian governments or terrorists carry out torture. Even if *they* use it, *we* shouldn't.

Military tradition supports the prohibition of torture. The nineteenth-century *Devising a Military Code of Conduct* states, "the modern law of war permits no longer the use of any violence against prisoners in order to extort the desired information or to punish them for having given false information."[4] This ethical position has deep roots. The Roman Cicero, the fifth-century Augustine, the fourteenth-century age of chivalry, and the *Military Code* see war as justified only if necessary to attain peace. The *Military Code* bans torture and cruelty because "military necessity does not include any act of hostility which makes the return to peace unnecessarily difficult" (TEW, 579). This is precisely the sort of hostility afflicting CTU agent Curtis Manning, who cannot overcome his hatred for Assad for having tortured and beheaded his comrades during the Gulf War. Tragically, Manning's hatred and desire for revenge forces Jack to shoot him, thus preserving Assad's life.

The world of 24 suggests that views about torture may have changed. Allegations arise regularly that the US and its allies permit the use of torture in the war on terror. Photographs of hooded detainees, naked prisoners cowering in the face of snarling dogs, and men standing with electrical wires dangling from their bodies, speak loudly of the reality of torture. Mike Novick, President Palmer's Chief of Staff, claims death during torture is akin to accepting civilian casualties with bombings: "A few people may have to die to save millions."

Torture in 24 both reflects the way the world has become, but also makes it easier to accept torture in practice. A 2006 BBC News

---

2   Office of the High Commissioner for Human Rights, "Convention against Torture and Other Cruel, Inhuman or Degrading Treatment or Punishment," December 10, 1984, available online at www.unhchr.ch/html/menu3/b/h_cat39.htm.
3   Michael Wilks, "A Stain on Medical Ethics," *The Lancet* 366 (August 2005): 429–431.
4   *The Ethics of War: Classic and Contemporary Readings*, ed. Gregory M. Reichberg, Henrik Syse, and Endre Begby (Oxford: Blackwell, 2006), p. 571. This work will be referred to herein as TEW.

survey found that almost one-third of 27,000 people surveyed in 25 countries agreed that "Terrorists pose such an extreme threat that governments should now be allowed to use some degree of torture if it may gain information that saves innocent lives."[5] In the US, 36 percent held this view, as did 43 percent in Israel, 42 percent in Iraq, 24 percent in Great Britain, and 14 percent in Italy. Countries facing political violence have a greater tendency to approve torture to prevent terrorist attacks. However, an overall majority in the world (59 percent) still favors an absolute ban, viewing torture as an inherently immoral activity that weakens respect for human rights.

Defining Torture

Torture is difficult to define precisely. Sometimes those being appropriately interrogated will claim they were tortured. And often those who truly torture will claim they were merely conducting a "coercive interrogation." Whether the distinctions are legitimate or euphemistic word-smithing has important consequences for detainees. In Season Five Christopher Henderson is clearly being tortured when he is strapped to a hospital bed and injected with hyoscine pentathol, an alleged truth serum. Henderson is a disgraced agent suspected of being in league with terrorists. Typical of torture, Henderson is tied down, unable to fight back or defend himself. In this regard, one cannot help but think, too, of Roger Stanton, Marie Warner, and a host of others. Intense pain brings people close to losing consciousness and to the brink of death.

But of course 24 also presents us with situations in which pain is inflicted—say, during a fight or a shoot-out—but we wouldn't typically classify these as instances of torture. In such cases each person in the fight can at least defend themselves. Pain can also be inflicted for another's good as in some medical procedures. Torture inflicts pain for reasons that have nothing to do with the good of the one tortured.

Torture must also be distinguished from coercion. Jack initially pleads with Henderson to disclose his information. He tries various methods to coerce the information from him. Earlier in Season Five,

5   "One-third support 'Some Torture'," *BBC News*, October 19, 2006, available online at www.news.bbc.co.uk/2/hi/in_depth/6063386.stm.

terrorists "shot" hostages on live TV in an attempt to coerce the government to meet their demands. These acts are repulsive, but they do not constitute torture. Under coercion, someone still makes a rational decision to do what is demanded. Under torture, the pain obliterates rationality. The person will do or say anything for the pain to stop. Coercion seeks to get the person to go along with the appeal; torture seeks to break the person.

Torture starts when persuasion, bribery, or coercion fails (or is not even attempted). Torture targets autonomy itself, and tries to overwhelm the tortured person's rational control over his own decisions. It does so "by literally terrorizing them into submission. Hence there is a close affinity between terrorism and torture. Indeed, arguably torture is a terrorist tactic."[6] The torturer uses drugs, deprivation of normal sense perception, severe pain, confusion, or anything else to gain control over the person's whole being. The goal is not just information, but to "break the person." "The self-conscious aim of torture is to turn its victim into someone who is isolated, overwhelmed, terrorized, and humiliated. Torture aims to strip away from its victim all the qualities of human dignity that liberalism prizes."[7] David Sussman argues that "torture is uniquely 'barbaric' and 'inhuman': the most profound violation possible of the dignity of a human being."[8] The victim's body is made an object to be manipulated and controlled by the torturer and used against the person's will.

Part of the twisted nature of torture is how even the victim's emotions are turned against himself.[9] In Season Six, Morris O'Brian is tortured into arming the terrorists' nuclear devices. Jack expresses disbelief that Morris "gave in" and betrayed the cause. Morris is driven away, deeply ashamed, yet he was the one deeply violated. Torture is not just a physical beating; it is a violent raping of a person's soul. Morris is then overwhelmed with guilt, especially when reminded of what he did. Studies show that those tortured are plagued

---

6 Seumas Miller, "Torture," in *The Stanford Encyclopedia of Philosophy (Summer 2006 Edition)*, ed. Edward N. Zalta, available online at www.plato.stanford.edu/entries/torture.

7 David Luban, "Liberalism and the Unpleasant Question of Torture," *Virginia Law Review* 91 (2005): 1430. Page references to Luban are to this work.

8 David Sussman, "What's Wrong with Torture?" *Philosophy and Public Affairs* 33 (2005): 2.

9 The origin of the word "torture" comes from the idea of twisted, as in "tortuous"; torture was whatever left the body twisting uncontrollably.

for years with self-destructiveness, failure to reintegrate into their families, and an inability to take control of their lives.[10] Recovery is not easy when a torturer has used "the prisoner's aliveness to crush the things that he lives for" (Scarry, 38). Some survivors of torture have such psychological damage that they fail to ever return to normal, rational decision-making.

Thus torture usually involves some combination of the following: intentional infliction of extreme physical or psychological suffering; restriction of the person into a defenseless position; substantial curtailment of the exercise of a person's autonomy; manipulation of the person's sense of time and place; and an attack on the person's will, with a goal of breaking the person. Although we may have difficulty defining torture, it is clearly recognizable when encountered. Torture is very different from a physical beating or a manipulative deception. Torture goes deeper than the pain, which may tear the skin; torture seeks to tear the soul.

The reasons for torture vary, each raising different considerations.[11] Torture can be done for personal satisfaction, where the torturer is a sadist or psychopath. Torture can be used to terrorize people into submission, as some dictators have done. On *24*, the focus is on *interrogational torture*, where detainees are tortured to get information. Backward-looking interrogational torture tries to extract confessions from detainees about past activities. On *24*, we primarily see forward-looking interrogational torture, used to get information from detainees about a future event. People who argue that forward-looking interrogational torture is ethically justified will usually claim that the other uses of torture remain unethical.

Arguments for Torture

The torture scenes on *24* are an extended commentary on the main argument used to ethically justify torture: Henry Shue's classic "ticking

---

10   Robert Oravecz, Lilla Hárdi, and László Lajtai, "Social Transition, Exclusion, Shame and Humiliation," *Torture* 14 (2004): 4–15.
11   Vittorio Bufacchi and Jean Maria Arrigo, "Torture, Terrorism and the State: A Refutation of the Ticking-Bomb Argument," *Journal of Applied Philosophy* 23 (2006): 360. Page references to Bufacchi and Arrigo are to this article.

bomb argument."[12] The innovative style of 24, with its frenetic pace and action in "real" time, contributes to the continuous reminder that the clock is ticking. Time is always running out, and this has constant implications for what must be done. In Season Five, Homeland Security sends Karen Hayes and Miles Papazian into CTU to resolve their problems. Miles argues that Karen should authorize the torture of Audrey Raines to gather information about the terrorists' nerve gas attack. Miles uses core aspects of the ticking bomb argument: "We don't have the luxury of time. Intel indicates that an attack is imminent—within an hour. Tens maybe hundreds of thousands of Americans are at risk. And we just got information that Audrey Raines knows about it."

The ticking bomb argument is basically a utilitarian argument. The good consequences of discovering the sought-after information outweigh the bad consequences of torture. Finding and diffusing the bomb prevents many deaths and injuries; the harm of inflicting pain on the bomber, of denying his dignity, of violating his rights, is a small price to pay in comparison. Nonetheless, Bill Buchanan defends Audrey, arguing that she deserves different treatment. Karen replies: "If she is guilty, she doesn't deserve anything." Implicit in the ticking bomb argument is the claim that people can lose their right not to be tortured when the consequences of not extracting their information are high enough.

Torture, however, is one of several strategies normally not accepted in Western liberal democracies. The war on terror has helped promote a new, very utilitarian political philosophy. In Season Five, we saw martial law introduced. Behind the scenes in Season Six, the rights of those with Middle Eastern or Muslim connections are curtailed. The seriousness of the terrorist threat justifies what wouldn't normally be tolerated. Chief of Staff Tom Lennox takes a very utilitarian approach to ethics, telling Karen Hayes, now National Security Advisor: "Security has its price. Just get used to it, Karen."

24 graphically and dramatically portrays the urgent need for torture and its apparent legitimacy. Modern law enforcement agencies are placed in difficult situations. Traditionally, such agencies dealt

12   Henry Shue, "Torture," *Philosophy and Public Affairs* 7 (1978): 124–143. Page references to Shue (1978) are to this work.

with crime after the fact and sought evidence for conviction. Rules dictate the searching and seizing of property and how confessions are obtained—if convictions are to result. But the mandate at CTU, and in the war against terror, changes this. Now the goal is to prevent terrorist attacks, and extracting information from captured suspects can do much good. In Season Two, the terrorist leader Syed Ali is tortured into disclosing the location of the nuclear bomb. Under torture, Roger Stanton names the same location. *24* gives life to the ticking bomb argument.

Even when a bomb goes off, the argument gains support. We didn't see the horror, pain, and devastation of the nuclear blast in Season Six. The mushroom cloud over a modern city conveyed enough of the effect. If torture could have prevented the bomb, would that not be justification enough? Fritz Allhoff, a utilitarian who accepts this view, believes it is so obvious and rational that it does not need defending. "If anyone wants to disagree with the permissibility of torture in this [ticking bomb] case, I simply do not know what to do other than throw my hands up in exasperation." Any argument to the contrary he finds "hopelessly implausible."[13] Yet such arguments do exist, and several are dramatized throughout *24*.

Arguments Against Torture

The main argument against torture is that it treats human beings in undignified ways. Torture is not just painful; it is humiliating, degrading, and terrorizing. The person is treated as an object. When introducing his ticking bomb case, Shue admitted, "No other practice except slavery is so universally and unanimously condemned in law and human convention" (1978: 124).

Most people are shocked when they see, read, or think about what one person does to another during torture. Consider the people on *24* who writhe in pain as torture drugs flow through their veins. In Season Two, Jack screams into the bloody face of terrorist Syed Ali, and then reaches down and appears to break his fingers. In Season Six, Jack cuts off the Russian consul's finger to find out where the

---

13   Fritz Allhoff, "A Defense of Torture: Separation of Cases, Ticking Time-bombs, and Moral Justification," *International Journal of Applied Philosophy* 19 (2005): 257–258.

remaining suitcase nukes are located. These scenes elicit an emotional response which is itself part of the argument against torture. "If we treat someone in a way we generally find shocking, we do not treat her as a person—or, at least, we do not if we treat her that way against her will and without benefit to her."[14] Shock alone is not a sufficient argument, but it alerts us that something may be very wrong. Detainees are kept naked, cold, wet, hungry, or sleep deprived; some are forced to stand for days, their cells soaked with random noise, bright lights or darkness; others are placed in sexually degrading or other humiliating positions; their religious icons desecrated. Such practices are defended as necessary interrogation techniques, "torture lite"; means to important ends.[15]

24 does not portray this side of torture, though it is in the background, as when we glimpse Jack's scarred hand throughout Season Six. The ticking bomb argument that permeates 24 shows torture as a rational choice, a necessary evil when time is of the essence and the stakes are immense. Torture on 24 is sane and somewhat sanitized, mirroring the image in the ticking bomb argument. "Torture to gather intelligence and save lives seems almost heroic. For the first time we can think of kindly torturers rather than tyrants" (Luban, 1436).

Apart from Jack, Agent Burke is CTU's main torturer. A good-looking young man, his character is never developed, though he appears season after season. Maybe we don't want to know what sort of person he is and would rather think of him as the stereotypical "kindly torturer." But what does he do while waiting for the call to come in and torture someone? Maybe he's at home with his family, the call comes, and he kisses his child goodbye saying, "Sorry honey, Daddy's gotta go to the office." Maybe he must return quickly from a training course in Guantanamo. Or maybe he's at CTU, reading up on the latest research on "truth serums" or practicing new techniques on lab animals.

The ticking bomb argument suggests that torturers materialize when the need arises. 24 shows this is not the case. It was Christopher Henderson who taught Jack his methods. Agent Burke has training and equipment to support his work. If torture is accepted, society

---

14   Michael Davis, "The Moral Justification of Torture and other Cruel, Inhuman, or Degrading Treatment," *International Journal of Applied Philosophy* 19 (2005): 168.
15   Mark Bowden, "The Dark Art of Interrogation," *Atlantic Monthly* 292 (3): 51–76.

will need "a professional cadre of trained torturers" supported by biomedical research and legal developments (Luban, 1445). Such training is hardly so neat and clean as *24* portrays it.

Investigations at Abu Ghraib note that the torturers must have received "systematic training" in torture techniques developed else-where.[16] This training turns ordinary young men and women into torturers who dehumanize their victims. Torture not only devastates the one tortured, it ruins torturers' lives. Studies of torturers show they have a variety of psychological and social problems, often resorting to drug and alcohol abuse.[17] The father of a Greek military torturer said at his trial, "I had a good boy, everybody said so. Can you tell me who turned my son into a torturer and destroyed him and my family psychologically?" (Haritos-Fatouros). Torturers' relation-ships suffer also, with even their military comrades viewing them with contempt, as "defiled" (Arrigo, 554). *24* is thus unrealistic in portraying Burke, and Jack especially, as unaffected by torture. In the real world, torture changes torturers, often dehumanizing them. Their destruction must be included in any utilitarian calculation.

Central to the utilitarian argument is the assumption that torture works. As President David Palmer watches Roger Stanton resist tor-ture, he confidently notes that "everyone breaks eventually." But Jack withstood two years of Chinese torture; and Henderson didn't break at CTU. In Season Six, when Jack tortures his own brother, Graem, with drugs and a plastic bag over his head, he gives up some infor-mation, but not the crucial pieces. Later, as General Habib also appears to succumb to torture, he slips in a way to warn his comrade, Fayed. Sometimes torture works, but most times it doesn't (Arrigo, 549–550). Of those tortured legally in France from the sixteenth century through the eighteenth century, between 67 and 95 percent did not confess. The Nazis used all sorts of torture on the resist-ance movement, yet got little information. An estimated 5 percent of

16   Mika Haritos-Fatouros, "Psychological and Sociopolitical Factors Contributing to the Creation of the Iraqi Torturers: A Human Rights Issue," *International Bulletin of Political Psychology Online* 16 (2), February 2005, available online at www.security. pr.erau.edu/browse.php. Subsequent citations are given in the text under the author's name.
17   Jean Maria Arrigo, "A Utilitarian Argument Against Torture Interrogation of Terrorists," *Science and Engineering Ethics* 10 (2004): 553. Page references to Arrigo are to this article.

the American prisoners-of-war tortured by the North Vietnamese gave the anti-American statements demanded of them. Steve Biko withstood years of torture in South Africa.[18] Even people who believe some torture is ethical admit it only works "sometimes"[19] and that "there are many instances of torture that are totally inefficacious by any measure."[20] Others say the idea that torture works is "one of those false beliefs of 'folk psychology'" (Arrigo, 563).

The ticking bomb argument is based on having the actual bomber in custody. But once torture is accepted, it spreads to other suspects. In Season Four, Paul Raines is tortured because his name is on the lease of a building used by terrorists. That makes him "a prime suspect" and eligible for torture. Jack douses him in water and sticks live electric wires in his chest to get some information—but certainly not a bomb's location. In Season Five, Audrey Raines is tortured, yet she was innocent, framed by the terrorists. According to past history, "a torture interrogation program . . . can anticipate that at least half to three-quarters of terrorist suspects may be arrested mistakenly" (Arrigo, 557). In reality, authorities can never be sure they have the right person. And when torture is accepted for the rare extreme incident, its application spreads. Recent history in the war on terror shows that torture has been accepted as part of "a more general fishing expedition for any intelligence that might be used to help 'unwind' the terrorist organization" (Luban, 1443). That is certainly the picture we get from 24, where torture is employed with increased frequency and less justification.

Overall, the ticking bomb argument is viewed by some as a "dangerous delusion" and an "intellectual fraud" (Luban, 1452). Its details are so far removed from reality that it lulls people into thinking it is realistic and compelling. In reality, the committed terrorist is unlikely to break, especially knowing he must endure torture for a short time before the bomb goes off. Some terrorists are unafraid of death. Syed Ali is defiant in the face of Jack's threats, saying he woke

18 Steve Biko and Millard W. Arnold, *The Testimony of Steve Biko* (London: M. T. Smith, 1984).
19 Uwe Steinhoff, "Torture—The Case for Dirty Harry and against Alan Dershowitz," *Journal of Applied Philosophy* 23 (2006): 342.
20 Sanford Levinson, "The Debate on Torture: War Against Virtual States," *Dissent* (Summer 2003): 82. See the chapter by R. Douglas Geivett for further discussion of whether torture is an effective means of collecting information.

up knowing he would die that day. Jack says he'll make him die in more pain than he ever imagined. Syed replies that will only bring him more pleasure in paradise.

In proposing the ticking bomb argument, Shue compares torture to cancer: "There *is* considerable evidence of all torture's metastatic tendency" (2003, 143). He has since reversed his position, concluding that his own argument is artificial and unrealistic. "Justifications for torture thrive in fantasy," he wrote in 2003.[21] Shue now thinks it would be more reasonable to believe that a dedicated terrorist being tortured on the morning of 9/11 would lie about his plans rather than tell the truth. But apart from those arguments, Shue states "the ultimate reason not to inflict agony upon other human beings is that it is degrading to all involved: all become less human" (2003, 91).

Torture's impact spreads beyond those directly involved. Allowing torture turns the whole liberal, democratic system of justice, law, and order upside down. "In its basic outline, torture is the inversion of the trial, a reversal of cause and effect. While the one studies evidence that may lead to punishment, the other uses punishment to generate the evidence" (Scarry, 41). Torture goes against the presumption of innocence and the right to a fair trial. It goes against human dignity as inherent and applicable to all humans—even criminals and terrorists. It undermines the belief that everyone has basic rights, including the right not to be treated in cruel, inhuman, or degrading ways. The utilitarian approach holds that human dignity is something earned, conferred by others, and therefore something that can be taken away. According to this view, the dignity of some people may be violated for the good of society.

This idea becomes part of a running debate in Season Six over proposals to curtail basic freedoms. President Wayne Palmer and Karen Hayes reject this notion, arguing that the gradual erosion of individual rights and human dignity will further undermine the fundamentals upon which a just society is built. Torture plays a key role in this erosion of core values. "Any State that sets up torture interrogation units will lose its moral legitimacy, and therefore undermine the political obligation of its citizens" (Bufacchi and Arrigo, 366).

---

21 Henry Shue, "Response to Sanford Levinson," *Dissent* (Summer 2003): 91. Page references to Shue (2003) are to this article.

It's Not That Simple

Again and again, 24 dramatically portrays why it is tempting to view torture as sometimes ethically acceptable. Torturing the person with his finger on the button can seem like the right thing to do to prevent destruction. But things aren't usually that simple. Torture did not get Fayed to give up the nuclear bombs. He was tricked into believing he was being rescued. Torture almost gave the plan away when General Habib warned Fayed about the plan. Old-fashioned police-work, good luck, and a Hollywood shoot-out saved the day, not torture.

At the same time, 24 shows many of the problems with torture. Even if the ticking bomb case is accepted, the practice of torture spreads quickly. Others, many of them innocent, get caught in the web of torture interrogation. When the prisoners talk, they might be telling the truth, or they might not. People will often say anything for the pain to stop. The benefits are not as clear-cut, and the costs extend far beyond the one tortured. The torturer's life is often ruined, and the program corrupts the military, police, political, medical, and legal systems it involves. Ultimately, all of society is impacted. Peace after terrorism may be difficult to imagine, but torture will make it even more difficult. Places like Algeria, South Africa, Chile, Greece, Israel, and Northern Ireland demonstrate the difficulties of social repair after torture is institutionalized (Bufacchi, 367).

Rather than violating someone's dignity in (often vain) attempts to obtain information by torture, another approach is to appeal to people's dignity. By refusing to deny others their dignity, a better way is proposed. That may have its price. The current justice system risks letting some guilty people go free rather than wrongly convict the innocent. So too, a society that refuses to torture *may* let some people sit in prison while bombs go off. However, it is not certain that even torture will get them to reveal where the bombs are located. Using torture risks the bomb's devastation on top of our own moral defilement and social degeneration.

The banality of torture in 24 should shock us into realizing how easily and quickly torture becomes acceptable. 24 dramatizes the need for torture, but also shows its problems. However, torture in 24 remains compatible with comfortable TV entertainment. The images from Abu Ghraib and testimonies from people actually tortured are harrowing and grotesque. We should never forget this, nor be seduced by simplistic images that misrepresent the real world. Torture in *24* and the ticking bomb case are artificial and sanitized. Nevertheless, *24* provides an important way to explore the ethics of torture. We must do so openly and very, very carefully. Denying the fundamental rights and dignity of any person is a dangerous and degrading proposition.[22]

22   Much appreciation is expressed to Pat Brereton, John Keane, and the editors for their valuable input on earlier drafts of this chapter.

Loyalty and the "War of All Against All" in *24*

Eric M. Rovie

It's almost impossible to take anything at face value when you're dealing with turncoats, traitors, terrorists, moles, and counter-moles. In a world where everyone (except Jack, of course!) is willing to double-cross you, there's little room for trust and even less for loyalty. Jack has been betrayed by his lover, his fellow agents, his former mentor, his brother, his father, and even the President of the United States, his employer! Almost every major character on the show has been betrayed, falsely accused, imprisoned, tortured, or even killed by someone who they once thought was a friend. All of this leads us to ask a philosophical question about the world of *24*: What can we learn about trust and loyalty from Jack Bauer and his cohorts? We find a rather pessimistic view of the world on the show, so let's take some cues from the pessimistic philosopher Thomas Hobbes (1588–1679) with an eye towards answering the question "Can Jack ever trust *anyone*?"

What is Loyalty? What is Trust?

Let's start by considering the nature of loyalty. When one is loyal to someone or something, one maintains a disposition to remain faithful and committed to that person or thing despite challenges that may arise along the way. More importantly, when one is loyal, one should, presumably, defend or stand behind someone or something that has been accused of doing wrong. A loyal spouse, for instance, should assume (absent compelling evidence to the contrary) that her husband is not cheating on her despite the fact that rumors have been circulating to the contrary. We should be careful not to lose our grasp on reality though. If a wife catches her husband in the act of cheating, it wouldn't be disloyal to deny what she saw with her own eyes. She might be willing to forgive her husband, but that's another matter. Of course, sometimes the "cheating" isn't exactly what it appears to be. When Kim Bauer discovers some seemingly inappropriate conversations and goings-on between her boyfriend, Chase Edmunds, and fellow CTU analyst Chloe O'Brian, she seems to clearly be in the right in questioning Chase's fidelity. While she is shocked to discover that Chase has a daughter, Angela, and that Chloe has been helping her friend Chase with the child, she is happy to learn that there is nothing romantic linking the two of them. Loyalty would not require Kim to simply assume, despite the apparent evidence that Chase and Chloe were having an affair, that Chase would never cheat on her. At some point, suspicions must be raised. So we want to avoid the kind of unthinking loyalty, often described as blind loyalty, in favor of a presumption of faith and commitment even when that faith is tested.

Notice that loyalty can apply at lots of levels and to lots of entities. One can be loyal to individuals, groups of persons, abstract entities, ideologies, political systems, political leaders, clubs, sports teams, animals, and even inanimate objects. In practice, my loyalty to the St. Louis Cardinals is drastically different from the loyalty I have to my daughter Jillian, but the general concept is the same. I will stand behind both, regardless of the troubles they may cause me, unless some very strong and compelling reason forces me to withdraw my support. There is a fine line between loyalty and fanaticism. If my love of the Cardinals leads me to neglect my duties as philosopher, teacher, parent, or good citizen, I might have crossed some sort of line. If, for example, I take it upon myself to bludgeon a Cubs fan with a baseball bat because I love the Cards so much, I'm probably not loyal. Instead, I'm a fanatic, anti-social lawbreaker.

Loyalty is generally considered a virtue, although it may be a virtue that can be overridden by other considerations.[1] To be fair, we should

---

1 No less of an authority than Donald Trump has claimed it to be a virtue. In fact, Trump claims loyalty is the *highest* virtue (www.donaldtrump.trumpuniversity.com/default.asp?item=109435) and, since he's the President of Trump University, I'm guessing we should believe him. Other, less authoritative, figures who have endorsed loyalty as virtue (but not necessarily the highest virtue) include Socrates, Aristotle, Marcus Aurelius, and the authors of many Old Testament texts.

consider what we might contrast loyalty with, if not something as insidious as blind loyalty or fanaticism. Consider, for instance, that loyalty might undercut impartiality, which, in many cases, is a useful virtue (or state of mind) for the promotion of justice and fairness. A judge's presumed loyalty to his own friends or family members, for example, would preclude him from presiding over cases involving them. It would be difficult for a sitting judge to remain impartial enough to provide a fair trial if his son was involved in the case, and that allows us to impose restrictions on the cases certain judges can preside over. A judge whose son was the defendant would be asked to recuse himself from the case, or be forced to do so. But, if loyalty conflicts with impartiality, aren't we stuck in a muddle? The answer may be "yes" and "no": we might, ideally, need to have these two virtues in our arsenal of character traits, and we might be forced to choose between them at certain moments.[2] So, at the end of the day, we need to at least consider the nature of loyalty, why we should have it, and why it might be a dangerous thing. Shortly, we'll consider how it affects the world of Jack Bauer, but first, a word on trust.

It should be pretty obvious that trust is connected with loyalty. At the very least, it would be hard to be loyal to someone or something you didn't trust. Trust itself, however, isn't easy to define or describe. Some consider trust to be placing faith in strangers.[3] To trust someone in this way is, roughly, to believe that person will act in a manner consistent with your expectations, although it seems obvious that this doesn't just apply to strangers. Trust is, to a large degree, predictive: to trust is to assume that you have good reason to believe something will come to be.[4] It is to believe that you have some reason to expect

2 Aristotle might tell us to use *phronesis*, or practical wisdom, to decide whether we should be loyal or impartial in any situation.
3 Eric Uslaner, *The Moral Foundations of Trust* (New York: Cambridge University Press, 2002).
4 There are, of course, huge problems with the nature of prediction. We should be clear to distinguish between statements of prediction and claims of knowledge: to say that we *know* our friend is loyal is probably to overstate the case. We should say it is likely, given what we know about him, that he will remain loyal. But we can't *know* that he will remain loyal unless we've got a window to future events. The philosopher David Hume, among others, has much to say about this kind of logical argument (*inductive* logic). See David Hume, *An Enquiry Concerning Human Understanding*, ed. Tom Beauchamp (Oxford: Oxford University Press, 1999), particularly Section IV.

that someone's (or something's) future actions, commitments, or activities will be as you expect them to be. To trust that something will be the case need not be a good thing. If I say that I trust that the caged dog will bite when freed, I'm not encouraging bad dog behavior, but simply stating what I think will likely be the case. Jack Bauer, for instance, may trust that nothing Nina Myers says or does can be believed because of her past history of double-dealing.

When we use trust in a more positive sense (when we say "I trust you with the keys to my place") we are saying not only that I have predicted what you will do, but also that it is something that I will accept you doing, or that I want you to do. In the weakest sense, trust is saying that I predict that you will not do something that I don't want you to do. It is to say that I believe you will not rob me blind when I hand you the keys to my house and drive away for the weekend. When Wayne Palmer helps Jack (a suspect in the murder of Wayne's brother, President David Palmer) uncover information about David's murder and then helps Jack secure evidence on the conspiracy from a bank vault, Wayne seems to be operating at a high degree of trust. Even though Jack and Wayne don't really seem to know each other all that well, Wayne takes Jack's promises to solve David's murder in this positive sense of trust.

I am not implying, of course, that trust and loyalty aren't in some way related to each other. In fact, it might be the case (although I won't explicitly endorse that view here) that trust is the base upon which loyalty can be built. Understood in this way, it would be argued that one can't really have loyalty without some degree of trust. I can't be loyal to a friend unless I have some reason to believe he's fulfilling his responsibilities in our relationship by not talking about me behind my back, not stealing from me, and not being a cannibalistic serial killer. It should also be clear that one can have trust without being loyal. I can make a deal to pay someone to repaint my house and trust that the painter (a stranger to me) will, in fact, paint my house after he receives payment.[5] I have no sense of loyalty to this unknown painter, but I can have trust (much of it

---

5 One reason this trust might exist, as Hobbes will note, is because we have a network of legal and political protections that allow consumers to make deals like this. In Hobbes' state of nature, which we'll discuss shortly, this trust would seem unlikely to exist.

based in the legal recourse I would have if he failed to do the work) that he will perform the job as requested. So let's consider loyalty to be a larger, more inclusive, state of mind than trust for the purposes of the discussion here.

Watch Your Back, Jack

Is there loyalty in the world of *24*? Can anyone be trusted? Probably not! While there are at least a few characters who seem to be relatively trustworthy (consider that only four people: President David Palmer, Chloe O'Brian, Tony Almeida, and Michelle Dessler, could be trusted with the knowledge that Jack was still alive following his faked death at the end of Season Four), one of the reasons *24* is such riveting television is that you're never really sure if the main characters are trustworthy. While it would be hard to imagine Jack being disloyal to the country (and maybe Chloe being disloyal to Jack), everyone else is fair game for a double-cross. And we certainly have to consider that the primary focus of Jack's loyalty is to the country and not to any particular person. After all, he shot and killed his acting supervisor, Ryan Chappelle, in the third season to prevent a biological attack on Los Angeles. Clearly, Jack considered his duty to be to the citizens of Los Angeles (and to President David Palmer, who approved the execution) and not to the person who was his superior at CTU. Outside of his close relationships with David Palmer, Chloe O'Brian, and his daughter Kim, the main object of Jack's loyalty seems to be to his country and his job, protecting the United States from terrorism.

So we're left with a question: What can philosophy tell us about the nature of loyalty and trust in the topsy-turvy world of *24*? Can we glean any wisdom from philosophers that would help Jack Bauer? To look for an answer, let's turn to the first great English philosopher, Thomas Hobbes.

Hobbes, Trust, and *24*

Much of political philosophy today rests on the shoulders of Thomas Hobbes and, in particular, on his most famous work, *Leviathan*, first published in 1651.[6] It would short-change Hobbes to say he was exclusively a political philosopher. His contributions range over all of the philosophical subfields, but he is certainly best known for the social contract theory found in *Leviathan*.[7] According to Hobbes, human beings are better off coming together in groups, giving up the absolute freedoms of isolated lives without society (his famous term for this pre-social world is the state of nature), and handing over enforcement of the well being of society to a powerful and fearful sovereign.[8] According to Hobbes, we "contract away" our freedoms for the sake of security because a world where we are free of all rules is also a world where we face constant danger, struggle, and strife. Hence, Hobbes' theory of political society is a "social contract theory." As he famously puts it, life before society is absolutely free but also "solitary, poor, nasty, brutish and short" (89). To protect ourselves we give up many of our freedoms, and, in return, we receive protection from harm, through the efforts of the sovereign. There is much more that could be said about Hobbes' arguments for political society, and about the moral considerations that attach to his political theory, but we'll leave them mostly untouched. Instead, let's consider the nature of Hobbes' view of the nature of trust and loyalty, in light of his political theory, and connect it back to 24.

Did Hobbes think that, after the social contract, the sovereign and his subjects would trust each other? The answer, once again, seems to

6   There are many editions of Hobbes' classic available, but the version from the *Cambridge Texts in the History of Political Thought* is loaded with helpful features, including insightful essays, a careful index, and a concordance with other popular editions. Thomas Hobbes, *Leviathan*, Revised Student Edition, ed. Richard Tuck (New York: Cambridge University Press, 1991). Hereafter page references to this edition of *Leviathan* will be included parenthetically in the text. There is also a very nice version of parts of the text, edited by Jonathan F. Bennett and available online at www.earlymoderntexts.com. Bennett's version features the text modified and "translated" into contemporary English. Given the awkward language, grammar, and punctuation of Hobbes' work, Bennett's version is a nice starting place. My citations to the text here will be to the Tuck edition.
7   For an insightful overview on Hobbes' life, contributions to all areas of philosophy, and influence on contemporary philosophy, see A. P. Martinich, *Hobbes* (New York: Routledge, 2005).
8   This sovereign would need to be as frightful and terrifying as the sea monster (leviathan) described in the Hebrew Bible, a being without fear and without limited power. See *The Book of Job*, Chapter 41.

be "yes" and "no." On the one hand, it would be silly to give someone absolute power over your life if you didn't trust them with it. Why give up freedom to someone who might brutalize you at the first opportunity? But, on the other hand, Hobbes does leave the door open for the possibility, however slight it may be, that there may be recourse available to the subjects who are mistreated by their sovereign. As he says, "The Obligation of Subjects to the Soveraign, is understood to last as long, and no longer, than the power lasteth, by which he is able to protect them" (153). And when Hobbes points out the "mutual relation between Protection and Obedience" he seems to be recognizing that citizens who do not receive their end of the transaction (freedom for security) may lose the inclination to obey the sovereign (491). More seriously, Hobbes says the negligent government of princes is naturally punished with rebellion and with slaughter, putting some burden on the sovereign to govern well (254).

We could be very skeptical about Hobbes' argument and the general concept of trusting in our government. As viewers of *24* we might be downright cynical about the amount of loyalty we should place in our government, considering that high-ranking governmental officials (all the way up to the president!) have their hands in very dirty places. Don't we have to assume that at least one figure in any president's cabinet is somehow involved in an evil plot against the country? We might be right to be cynical, but there's a more telling point to be found backing up Hobbes' argument for political society, and it has to do with the reasons why people ought to keep their promises.

In chapters 14 and 15 of Leviathan, Hobbes lays out some of the laws of nature that apply to all men[9] for their own benefit and preservation. The important law of nature for our purposes is the third law of nature: "that men perform their Covenants made, without which, Covenants are in vain, and but Empty words" (100). We can replace Covenant in Hobbes with the more common words promise or agreement. The breaking of an agreement constitutes an unjust action, a moral wrong.[10] But what reason, beyond Hobbes' belief, do we have

---

9   Hobbes was not worried about gender equity in his discussion of laws of nature. For our purposes, when Hobbes refers to *men* we can assume he means rational human beings. While he might have deliberately left women out of that category, we don't.

10   Thomas Hobbes, *On the Citizen (De Cive)*, ed. Richard Tuck and Michael Silverthorne (New York: Cambridge University Press, 1998), p. 44.

to believe this is a law of nature? Is there any real reason to keep one's promises? There are at least two very good reasons to do so, according to Hobbes:

1 *Non Self-Contradiction.* One should not contradict what one had maintained in the beginning. Promising to walk someone's dog, and then deciding not to walk the dog after all, is to be intellectually inconsistent, and Hobbes thinks all humans strive to avoid that kind of inconsistency (93). What sense is it to say something and then not hold true to those words you say? Even worse would be to promise to do something knowing that you intended not to keep that promise! Hobbes calls such a false promise-maker the "Foole," but we might just as easily think of that person as someone who lies to attain advantages in society.
2 *Fear.* Breaking a promise brings consequences. If I promise to walk Sparky for you, and I fail to, it will lead you, at the very least, to be mad at me. At worst, you might stop being my friend. Hobbes says that "right and force" is often sufficient to compel parties to perform their covenants made (96). There will be some cases where there are no formal legal remedies for those who have suffered broken promises, of course, as in our dog-walking case. But Hobbes points out that someone who is known as a promise-breaker "cannot be received into any Society" and faces being an outcast and social pariah for his wrongdoings (102).

So keeping our promises seems to be bound up in both internal obligations of intellectual coherency and external concerns about the results of the broken promise. We seem to have strong reasons to keep the covenants we make, according to Hobbes' moral and political theory. So can we apply this lesson to *24*?

The State of Nature is Alive and Well in Los Angeles

Consider, once again, the general relationship between promises and trust, and between trust and loyalty. It would be difficult to trust someone who was known not to keep their promises. So we could assume that one important element of the "predictive" element of trust is that we know that the person we are trusting will "keep their covenants made," as Hobbes would say. A history of promise-breaking would certainly lead to a potential denial of trust, and a trusting relationship usually implies that you believe the person you trust will keep whatever promises they make in almost ideal situations.[11]

If keeping promises is part of being trustworthy, then we can move on to loyalty. We loosely defined loyalty as a disposition to remain faithful and committed to a person or thing despite potential challenges that might arise along the way. Loyalty seems to require trust, as we have seen, although one may easily trust without any preexisting loyalty. What does this three-way relationship between trust, loyalty, and promise-keeping have to offer Jack Bauer and the agents of CTU? Consider three possible examples:

1 *Chase Edmunds.* Imagine you are a new agent, assigned to work with Jack. You know Jack's history with CTU, but you also know that Jack has gone "dark" and worked on projects without the authorization of the director. While performing some field work, you overhear Jack making some questionable phone calls and seeming to be preoccupied with something other than the current case. Do you have reason to trust Jack? Do you have reason to think that Jack would keep his promises to you? Do you consider Jack to be loyal to CTU if he is not following orders directly?

2 *Jack Bauer.* Imagine you are Jack Bauer, and you are told by a terrorist mastermind that there are biological weapons positioned in strategic locations throughout Los Angeles. The terrorist offers you a simple choice: kill your supervisor or the bombs will be set off, killing thousands. Assuming you have evidence that this is not a bluff, do you have reason to believe that the terrorist will keep his promise not to set the bombs off if you kill your boss? Would your own loyalty or trustworthiness be questioned if you actually did kill your superior?

11 Note that changes in the situation don't change the fact that you *made* the promise. They may just mitigate the degree to which you're held responsible for breaking that promise. If I promise to walk Sparky for you, but on my way to your house, I'm hit by a truck and hospitalized, I've still broken my word, but I'll probably be easily forgiven. If, on the other hand, I decide to stop and have a few beers on the way over, and end up passed out in an alley, I'm probably not likely to be forgiven. A promise is still a promise, but some circumstances may justify forgiveness while others do not.

3 *Stephen Saunders.* Imagine you are Stephen Saunders, the terrorist who orders Jack to kill his boss in the previous example. If
Jack does what you ask, what reason do you have to keep your
end of the bargain? Isn't the fact that you are the one holding all
of the cards the relevant factor here, or is there something that
would prevent you from going back on your word even if it
would be better for you if you did set the bombs off?

These cases are obviously based on events from the Season Three of
24. Case one roughly follows the dilemma of Chase Edmunds early in
that season, when Chase thinks Jack's loyalty is compromised because
of his drug use and his relationship to the Salazar drug family. Of
course, Jack has not turned on the country . . . he's just in "deep cover"!
The second and third cases occur later in that day, when terrorist
Stephen Saunders forces Jack to kill Ryan Chappelle to cut short
CTU's pursuit of Saunders. We should consider what Hobbes might
say about these cases or, more appropriately, what Hobbes might
say to these individuals. But before we hear what Hobbes has to say,
let's think about the nature of trust and loyalty again for a moment.
Recall that we offered, earlier, a rough definition of loyalty as a disposition to remain faithful to someone or something despite obstacles
and challenges to that disposition. And we proposed that the positive
sense of trust is to have a predictive belief that someone will do what
we expect them to do, and that the thing they will do is what we want
them to do, or at least not something we don't want them to do. Let's
apply these considerations of trust and loyalty to the three cases,
keeping in mind the Hobbesian foundations for their application.
   We could start by asking what reasons, if any, Chase would have
for trusting Jack. What reason would Jack have for believing that
Saunders would keep his promise? And what reason would Saunders
have for not setting the bombs off after all? Is there any chance that
loyalty, and not just trust, would come into play here? Can Chase
trust his new partner, given that he knows little about him and is
faced with the apparent evidence that Jack is working against CTU?
Can Jack trust someone who is a terrorist to ever keep a promise
made? Does Jack's loyalty to Ryan Chappelle override his loyalty to
the country or to CTU? Can Saunders, given the fact that he isn't
playing by the normal set of rules, expect that his enemies will play
by the rules and keep their promises? Recall that Hobbes has set out

two main reasons to keep promises, but I'll actually divide the second reason into two distinct types:

1 *Non Self-Contradiction.* It would be intellectually dishonest for someone to say they were going to do something (protect the country or not set off the bombs) when they intended to do the opposite. While this kind of reasoning might be at play here, it's not clear that the folks who populate the world of terrorism and counter-terrorism are really Hobbesians in the sense of worrying about the law of non self-contradiction. I think we can toss this one out as a possible reason for promise-keeping.

2 *Fear of Social Consequences.* If I break a promise, I may become a social outcast. Friends and family members will cease to trust me, and I'll find myself without all of the benefits that living in a civil society allows. The problem here, if this fear of social consequences is supposed to motivate Jack to stay loyal to CTU or Saunders to refrain from bombing Los Angeles, is that being a social pariah is probably not a major concern for someone who is about to turn traitor against his government. And, while I don't know much about the world of international terrorists, I would hazard a guess that they don't worry too much about how the rest of society feels about them outside of their circle of supporters. So, I think we can also dismiss the fear of social consequences as a motivating factor in promise-keeping in these cases.

3 *Fear of the Leviathan.* For Hobbes, the other main source of fear is not simply that we'll become socially excluded from our world, but also that we may face serious and deadly reprisals from the agent empowered to protect society from itself, namely the sovereign. In this sense, we act at least in part (many believe in large part) out of the fear of punishment from the sovereign. Imprisonment or even death might be the result of failing to hold up our end of the social contract, whatever that may be. This would seem to be the most effective reason for believing that promises should be kept in the world of *24*.

Given these three Hobbesian reasons that motivate us to stand by the contracts, promises, and commitments we make, is there any reason to be loyal or to believe that others will stand by their promises in the world of *24*?

The War of All Against All

Unfortunately, the answer is "no." Ultimately, none of the three reasons Hobbes offers to explain loyalty and trust can hold up in the world of brutal uncertainty that is the world of *24*. Consider the three cases presented before: Chase Edmunds, Jack Bauer, and Stephen Saunders. It would seem that each of these cases would fail to be supported by Hobbes' reasons for promise-keeping or loyalty. Chase, for instance, might feel conflicted about doubting his loyalty to his own partner (and the father of his girlfriend!), but ultimately could excuse the breach of loyalty for the sake of a broader loyalty, to his country or to CTU. Jack might face serious social and legal consequences for killing Chappelle, even under duress (note that Jack only does so under the direct authorization of President Palmer), but ultimately is willing to shrug off those concerns for the greater good of the country and the safety of the people of Los Angeles. And how seriously do we think that a terrorist like Saunders will take the Hobbesian law of non self-contradiction, much less the fear of social or political punishment? Not only is his stated goal to "make American clean again," but he has revenge on his mind for his imprisonment and torture following a botched operation in Serbia. To be a terrorist, one must be willing to operate outside of the standard world of social consequences and political order! Saunders is not afraid of the sovereign (President Palmer) or his agents (the police, the CIA, CTU), and sets out to show just how unafraid he is by successfully blackmailing the most powerful man in the world.

Consider one last possibility for the source of loyalty: to the Leviathan, as representative of the ultimate source of loyalty, the country itself. But even this case fails, because, as Hobbes points out, the Leviathan can be ousted if his misdeeds are great. This was clearly the situation in Season Five, when President Charles Logan was revealed to be, in part, involved in the murder of President Palmer, among others, in an attempt to bring Jack out of hiding. If we can't be loyal to our partners, our friends, our president, our family, or even our country, is there any loyalty at all in *24*? The simple answer is "no." The world of *24* is such a nightmarish world of presidential treason, espionage, double-crossing, and shady dealing that all of the characters in it should be very afraid of trusting anyone else, ever. We, as audience of the show, know we can trust Jack Bauer (he is, after all, the hero of the show), but beyond that, not much can be known with any degree of confidence, and that kind of confidence is essential for trust. As much as we want to trust Chloe, or the president, or any other character we've grown attached to, we are always left with lingering doubt. The only thing that would protect the people in the world of *24* from collapsing into Hobbes' state of nature is some reason to keep one's word, and those reasons don't seem to be present there. There is little concern with self-contradiction, and not much reason to fear social or legal/political punishments. I think Hobbes would look at the various seasons of *24* as the embodiment of his "war of all against all." At the very least, being involved in the life of Jack Bauer seems like an existence that is pretty dangerous! Given the body count on the show, it would seem living in Los Angeles would not be a safe bet. It is the state of nature come vividly to life! It's a chaotic world where nerve gas is used on shoppers in malls, where the deadly Cordilla virus is unleashed on unsuspecting hotel guests, where terrorists cause nuclear meltdowns that kill innocent civilians, and where nuclear warheads, stolen from the government, are launched at the city. Talk about "solitary, poor, nasty, brutish, and short"!

It seems pretty obvious that philosophy can teach us something about trust and loyalty, and it seems clear that we can glean some interesting philosophical consequences from the world of *24*. Whether these consequences have much bearing on the "real world" will depend on how similar our world is to Jack Bauer's world. Hopefully, they're not that similar. But watch your back . . . your best friend might not be who you think she is.[12]

---

12   Thanks to the editors of this book, particularly Ron Weed, for comments on the first draft of this chapter. I also thank Grant Christopher for his comments, and to many of the students in my courses on the morality of war for commenting on a much earlier version of this argument.

Who Dares Sins: Jack Bauer and Moral Luck

Rob Lawlor

24 is popular largely because Jack breaks the rules and gets results against all odds. Of course, other things being equal, Jack ought not to break the rules. But other things are not equal. Jack breaks the rules for particular reasons, and people should not follow rules blindly. Still, if Jack breaks the rules he needs to justify his decision. It's one thing to ignore your superiors, and to break the rules, when you can be certain that your actions will be successful. But breaking rules in order to implement a plan that is risky is another matter.

Of course, Jack does succeed. There may be hiccups along the way, but eventually Jack always comes out as the hero. Still, we need to ask: Is the fact that Jack succeeded enough to justify his actions?

Moral Luck and the Outcome of Actions

Commonsense morality suggests that whether a person acted rightly or wrongly should not depend on luck. However, the philosopher Bernard Williams has argued that luck does play a role.[1]

Consider the bombing of Japan in 1945.[2] Bernard Williams would claim that the bombing could not be justified at the time of the decision. If it could be justified at all, it could *only* be justified by the

---

1 Bernard Williams, "Moral Luck" in his *Moral Luck* (Cambridge: Cambridge University Press, 1981). See also Thomas Nagel, "Moral Luck" in his *Mortal Questions* (Cambridge: Cambridge University Press, 1979).
2 See Piers Benn, *Ethics* (London: UCL Press, 1998), pp. 103–104.

outcome—the surrender of the Japanese. If the outcome was different, our judgment of the bombing would be different. But the outcome could not be guaranteed; an element of luck was involved.

Likewise, Jack takes great risks to achieve particular outcomes. Because he succeeds and saves millions of innocent people from another terrorist attack, Jack is a hero. If he failed, our judgment would probably be different.

For the purposes of this chapter, let's assume that Jack's actions *would* be justified *if* the outcome he is hoping for could be guaranteed. Now let's ask: Can Jack's actions be justified given that the right outcome *can't* be guaranteed? Does the rightness or wrongness of Jack's actions depend on the outcome? Does the rightness or wrongness of Jack's actions depend on luck?

To address these questions, consider a particular example from Season Six. Jack receives a call from Cheng Zhi, who tells Jack that if he wants to see Audrey Raines alive again, he must steal a component from the suitcase nukes that Jack has just secured from terrorists. Jack must deliver the component to Cheng. But this would give the Chinese access to Russian defense technology. Jack knows that if he delivers the component the Russians will know the leak came from the United States. This would almost certainly lead to a third world war. But Jack has a plan. He thinks he can get Audrey back without letting Zhi get away with the component.

If he succeeds, he will have saved Audrey's life without leading to another world war, and Jack will, once again, be the hero. But if he fails, the consequences would be devastating and Jack would be judged to have done a great wrong. Should our judgment depend so much on the outcome of Jack's actions?

Many people seem to have conflicting intuitions about this. If we think that we need to see what the outcome is before we can judge Jack's actions to be right or wrong, then it looks like we have to accept the conclusion that the rightness or wrongness of a person's actions can depend on luck. However careful Jack is in constructing his plan, he cannot guarantee its success with 100 percent certainty, and so it must depend—at least to some extent—on luck.

Alternatively, we may deny that Jack's actions can be made just or unjust as a result of luck. We should thus be able to reach a conclusion about the rightness or wrongness of his action *before* we see what the outcome is.

Typically, this is presented as a dilemma. Both options have attractive and unattractive features. On the first account, it seems right that the actual outcome should have some effect on our judgment. If Jack is successful, he will be a hero. But it also seems an unattractive implication that the morality of our actions depends, at least in part, on luck. On the second account, we can avoid this conclusion, but we have to give up the plausible belief that the outcome should make a difference.

Typically, it is thought that we have to choose between these two unattractive options, but I will argue that there is a third and more plausible alternative, namely that the success is merely *evidence* that the action was right (but the action was right *before* we had this evidence).[3] Therefore, the fact that we cannot *know* if an act is right or not before we act does not necessarily entail that the outcome *made* the act right. We can appeal to the outcome of our actions without claiming that this is, in anyway, an appeal to moral luck: it is *evidence*.

To demonstrate the difference between an appeal to moral luck, where the outcome *makes* an act right or wrong, and this alternative account, which appeals to evidence, consider two different scenarios which both involve an element of luck.

Scenario 1: The Roll of a Die

Imagine that Jack arrives at CTU and finds a parcel waiting for him. In it, he finds a note and a standard six sided die. The note tells him to expect a call, and tells him that he must receive the call in his office, alone, and with the die.

Jack goes to his office and waits for the call. His phone rings and he answers. The voice on the phone tells Jack to roll the die.

"Who is this?" Jack demands to know.
"That is not important. Just roll the die."
"Why?"
"I will explain after, but for now just roll the die on your desk."
Jack rolls the die. "Now what?"
"Just roll it a few times, to prove it's not loaded."

3   The position I defend here is argued for in more detail in my "Luck, Evidence and War," *Journal of Applied Philosophy* 23 (2006): 247–257.

Jack rolls the die a few more times. Finally, he loses his patience.
   "Now are you going to tell me what this is about?"
   "You rolled a 3," the stranger says.

Jack looks around his office, trying to spot the hidden camera. He is unsuccessful.

Finally, having established that he can see Jack, and also that the die is not loaded, the man on the phone explains that he has a nuclear bomb, which he is ready to detonate in Los Angeles. He doesn't have any demands, and he is not fighting for a cause. He's just playing a game.

"You have two choices. Either you can say '6' or you can say 'other'."

Beyond the obvious probabilistic calculation, Jack has no idea what number he will roll. The aim of the game is to guess correctly whether he will roll a 6, or some other number. Jack is not required to specify further than that. He does not have to pick a different number. The choice is 6 or any number other than 6.

If Jack predicts correctly, the terrorist will tell Jack where the bomb is, and he will not detonate it. If Jack fails, he will detonate it immediately.

There are no tricks. There is no reason to say "6," suspecting that the terrorist has fixed it so that Jack will roll a 6. If he rolls a 6, it will be by chance alone. The terrorist is waiting. All he has to do is give his answer, "6" or "other," and then roll the die. If he refuses to roll the die, or if he delays in any way, the terrorist will detonate the bomb immediately, and, for good measure, will detonate a second bomb in Los Angeles as well.

Jack says, "other." Weighing the probabilities, this is the obvious choice. But now consider the two possibilities that may follow. First, Jack rolls a number other than a 6. Everyone is happy that Jack made the right choice.

Alternatively, Jack rolls the die and, as a matter of bad luck, he rolls a 6.[4] New York is destroyed. But clearly this was just a matter of

---

4   And, again, let's *stipulate*, that this was only a matter of luck, and we should not conclude that Jack should have known it was fixed. We know for certain that it was purely a matter of luck, and Jack knew the odds.

bad luck. Surely we cannot blame Jack for saying "other." He did the right thing, but was unlucky. And the actual outcome should not make us reconsider our judgment that Jack's choice could be justified.

Now suppose that Jack says "6" before rolling the die. And remember that we have stipulated that we are 100 percent sure that it is not a trick. Jack knows the odds. In this case, it seems clear that we do not have to wait for the outcome in order to make a moral judgment. Given that the odds are clearly against Jack, surely we have to conclude that Jack cannot justify his choice, no matter what the outcome is, and this judgment should not be altered by luck.

Scenario 2: The FA Cup Final

Now imagine a second scenario. The gambling terrorist demands that Jack predict the outcome of a soccer match.[5] Manchester United are to play West Ham in the FA Cup final. If the game is not decided in normal time, it will go to extra time, and then to penalties. So the game will be decided one way or another, so there are only two options: Manchester United will win or West Ham will win. The consensus is that Manchester United are the overwhelming favorites, and the bookies are giving odds of 6 to 1 for West Ham to win.

Is this example any different from the first? You might think that, if Jack predicts that West Ham will win, this is comparable to saying "6," before he rolls the die. They are the clear underdogs. But there is a difference. To illustrate this, we must remember that Jack is exceptionally brilliant at everything. Regardless of the issue, we have reason to think that Jack's judgment is better than anyone else's. This includes soccer. Let's assume his knowledge of English football teams and his awareness of strategy are both impeccable.

Everyone else predicts that Manchester United will win, but Jack believes they are mistaken. This is the significant difference between this scenario and the first. If Jack says "6" in the first scenario, he is

5   Given that the terrorist is unlikely to be American, but—following the precedent of 24 to date—is more likely to be from China, Russia, or some unspecified Middle Eastern country, the terrorist is more likely to be interested in soccer than in baseball or American football.

simply being capricious, irrational or superstitious. But this needn't be true in this case.

Let's assume Jack has been following English football very closely, and he thinks that Manchester United will be complacent, and he also thinks that Manchester United will struggle against the new formation that West Ham have recently started to play with. He doesn't merely think that West Ham *could* win (no one denies that), he really believes that everyone else is mistaken and that West Ham ought to be seen as the favorites. The odds, he thinks, are in their favor.

Now Jack has a dilemma. Does he trust his own judgment, or does he go with the opinion of others? Well, this is Jack Bauer we're talking about, so we all know what he would do. He's going to bet on West Ham.

Whatever we think of his choice in this case, it is clear that it's quite different from choosing 6 in the first scenario. Even if we think that Jack's decision is the wrong one, it is not capricious, irrational, or superstitious.

If Jack does end up rolling a 6 in the first case, this doesn't give us *any* reason to think that we misjudged the probabilities, or to think that Jack was justified after all. It just shows that Jack was lucky. But the second case is different. If West Ham do win, it's plausible to think that we should question our original assessment of the probabilities, and to think that the result does actually vindicate Jack's choice. He wasn't just lucky, he really did get it right.

This is important because, if we believed in moral luck and we believed that the outcome of an action could make that act right, then we shouldn't treat these two cases differently. On this account we couldn't say that Jack did the wrong thing if he said "6." We would have to wait for him to roll the die and see what he rolled. On this account, if he did in fact roll a 6, this would make his action right after all. But this seems implausible.

We should conclude that, if the outcome is important to our moral judgment in *some* cases, it is for some reason other than just luck. The second scenario demonstrates that one reason the outcome can be important is because the outcome can provide evidence, retrospectively, for the rightness or wrongness of particular decisions.

However, because it is the evidence that is important, and not the outcome itself, it is possible for Jack to predict that West Ham would win, and for West Ham to beat Manchester United and win the FA

Cup, without this providing any evidence that Jack was justified in his choice. Jack could say "West Ham," and West Ham could win without this vindicating Jack's decision at all.

To know whether Jack's decision was justified, we would need to know whether or not there was any evidence to suggest that Jack's judgment was good. To know this, it is not enough to know who won. We would also need to know how they won.

Imagine that Manchester United did not look the slightest bit complacent and did not appear to struggle with West Ham's new formation. However, uncharacteristically, Manchester United did struggle to score. It looks like it will be a 0–0 draw and go to extra time. Finally, in the last minute, the West Ham goalkeeper kicks the ball deep into the opposition half. As a result of a freakish combination of events, this leads to a goal. First, there is a strong gust of wind, second the Manchester United goalkeeper is (uncharacteristically) out of position, and finally the ball lands on a loose piece of turf and bounces unpredictably. As a result, the ball bounces over the keeper and into the net: a freak event that no one would have predicted.

If this is how West Ham won, this outcome does nothing to vindicate Jack's judgment. As such, despite the good outcome, we should say that he acted arrogantly and recklessly (and ultimately wrongly) when he decided to bet the safety of New York on West Ham rather than on Manchester United.

Saving Audrey Raines

Now let's return to Season Six of *24*. Jack insists that he can have the best of both worlds. He can save Audrey while also avoiding a third world war. He has a plan and he guarantees that the component will not fall into the hands of the Chinese. Things don't go according to plan, but Jack does eventually get the outcome he wanted. Audrey is saved, the component is destroyed and the Russians are satisfied. Jack is the hero once again. Or is he?

As we've seen, it's not enough to consider the outcome. We need to examine the events to see whether or not they provide evidence to justify Jack's actions. Remember, in order to justify his actions to the president, Jack insisted that he could *guarantee* that the component would be destroyed, and that it would not fall into the hands of the

Chinese. For the sake of argument, let's stipulate that Jack's actions would only be justified if it were true that he could guarantee the destruction of the component. (Also Jack himself seems to accept this claim as well, when trying to persuade the president to let him save Audrey.)

So now, let's consider the evidence. On the face of it, the evidence seems conclusive. Jack was not able to destroy the component, and the Chinese did take possession of the component. Ultimately, the fact that Jack was able to destroy the component later is irrelevant (especially when one considers the circumstances, as we will shortly). His failure provides strong evidence to suggest that the success of his mission was not guaranteed and his actions were not justified.

Some may insist that Jack would have destroyed the component if CTU hadn't interfered. Jack was about to detonate the explosives when Doyle opened fire, ultimately leading to Jack being shot. So it was Doyle's fault.

But this response won't help. It may be true that Doyle should be blamed for opening fire, but this is consistent with the fact that these events demonstrate that Jack could *not* guarantee the destruction of the component. If you say something is guaranteed, that means that *nothing* can go wrong, whether the problem comes from yourself, the enemy, or other members of CTU. If you can't guarantee that other members of CTU won't ruin it for you, you cannot guarantee it. Perhaps Jack could guarantee it if he had the cooperation or at least non-interference of CTU but – even if this is true – this is irrelevant because, by the time Jack got to the hotel, he knew that he did not have the cooperation of CTU.

Second, even if we take Doyle out of the picture, these events demonstrate what *could* have happened. If Doyle could ruin Jack's plan by opening fire prematurely, one of the Chinese soldiers could ruin it in the same way. It also demonstrates the extent to which Jack was vulnerable. The Chinese could have simply shot him before he even got into the hotel, and before he even set up the explosives. The outcome that Jack was aiming for was far from guaranteed.

Alternatively, you might argue that Jack didn't guarantee that the component would be destroyed immediately, only that it would be destroyed. And Jack did manage to destroy it in the end. And, furthermore, it wasn't a result of luck: it was a result of Jack being Jack—the best and most determined agent on the planet.

Remember that in order to evaluate the claim that Jack's actions could be justified, we need to look beyond the outcome, and examine the actual events that led to it. If we can show that Jack's success did rely (even partially) on luck, then it is not true that the destruction of the component was guaranteed, and therefore his actions could not be justified. Why? Because only a 100 percent guarantee would be acceptable under these circumstances.

Consider the events leading up to the eventual destruction of the component. There are numerous examples of luck: in the hotel, even if Doyle hadn't messed up, one of the Chinese soldiers could have shot Jack; Jack could have been shot in the head and killed, rather than in the chest; when Jack was in custody, Cheng Zhi could have asked someone other than Phillip Bauer to repair the circuit board; Cheng Zhi could have taken it back to China before getting it repaired (in which case, this wouldn't have led to Jack being released, and finally being able to track down Cheng Zhi); Phillip Bauer could have decided that he didn't need to take Josh with him (in which case, Jack never would have known his father was involved *and* he would not have been released); having infiltrated CTU, the Chinese could have been more ruthless and shot and killed Jack and everyone else while they were all unarmed; the Chinese soldiers could have had more men, with better training, such that even Jack wasn't able to fight his way out.

In short, there is a long list of factors that were beyond Jack's control, where Jack depended on luck, and the list goes on. Clearly, Jack could not 100 percent guarantee the success of his plan, and the actual outcome does not vindicate his decision to try to save Audrey.

Jack did succeed, but his success was too dependent on factors beyond his control. Clearly, he could not *guarantee* the destruction of the component and therefore his actions were not justified.

In this chapter, I have concentrated on a single example from Season Six. However, I think my arguments will condemn Jack elsewhere too. He frequently takes risks, and does so against the judgment of his superiors, and in all cases there will be factors beyond Jack's control, where his success relies partly on luck. Maybe each of these examples would have to be explored individually but, provisionally at least, I suggest that Jack is not a hero. He's a liability. He just happens to have been exceptionally lucky.

3:00 PM–6:00 PM

MOLES, DOUBLE-AGENTS, AND TERRORISTS___

3:00 PM–4:00 PM

Living in a World of Suspicion: The Epistemology of Mistrust

Scott Calef

It is a mark of prudence never to trust wholly in those things which have once deceived us.
René Descartes, Meditation One

I'm sorry. I don't know what else to do. I'm running out of time.
Jack Bauer, Season Two, approximately 12:04 AM

The life of a CTU field agent is perilous indeed, and Jack's is more dangerous than most. He's kidnapped by the Chinese, exposed to Sentox nerve gas, and forced to explode a natural gas facility on site—all in a day's work. He's been tortured, shot to fake his death, and blasted out of the sky by a surface to air missile. Frequently forced to turn rogue and go it alone, move into hostile situations without backup, or work undercover with no protection other than his wits and risky ruses like heroin addiction, he always comes out on top in the end. Jack Bauer is the paradigm case of a maximally self-sufficient and independent operative—to the dismay and consternation of his directors at CTU and Division.

And yet, the fact is, even Jack can't do it alone. He needs people he can trust, and people who trust him. Where would Jack be without Chloe, Tony, Curtis or Buchanan? On the other hand, the information he has and pursues is often so sensitive and vital to national security that he must guard its secrecy with his very life. Extreme care must be taken to divulge data only when absolutely certain of the recipient's reliability. And he can be wrong. For example, when Jack gives Secretary Heller evidence implicating President Logan, Heller betrays Jack (with near disastrous results). Bauer must trust, and he must suspect, and sometimes direct both attitudes towards the same person at the same time.[1] Everything depends upon getting the balance right— a fact which terrifies his outwardly stoic superiors.

The tension created by the conflicting needs to trust and suspect is largely what makes *24* so dramatic. President Palmer, Jack Bauer, George Mason, Karen Hayes, and numerous others in the series confront vital issues of national security with much less than 24 hours to gather relevant data and act decisively. In matters concerning war, peace, terror, and the lives of millions, one hopes to base decisions on well-confirmed facts, not speculation, on trustworthy sources, not duplicitous traitors, on sound intelligence, not feelings or hunches borne of intense emotion. And yet, again and again, Jack and others must act on their instincts and trust (or ask others to trust) that proof will emerge in time. Lacking proof, direct orders from superiors are contravened and protocol breached. Thin resources are diverted to pursue possibilities and leads in ways that cannot be rationally justified given the primary mission. Who is doing what or communicating with whom must often be kept secret as agents and politicians operate with multiple, sometimes conflicting, agendas simultaneously. Conspiracies are everywhere and anyone could be a mole. Who then can be trusted? Or, more generally, when is trust permissible, and when is it morally incumbent upon us to suspect our co-workers, spouses, friends, children, or leaders?

Evidentialism and Suspicion

Trust and suspicion concern belief. When I trust someone, I believe them, and when I suspect them, I don't.[2] The question, then, is when

---

1 For example, it's clear Jack doesn't—and shouldn't—trust Christopher Henderson. And yet because he needs him, Jack gives him autonomy and a gun as they invade a Russian sub armed with multiple-warhead missiles. They complete their mission, and then Henderson tries to take Jack out.

2 Even when I'm trusting someone to do something rather than to tell me the truth, still, I believe that they'll do it.

am I rationally or morally justified in believing someone or something, and when am I not? Philosophers, predictably, have differing opinions about this.

"Evidentialists" like David Hume (1711–1776) say we should proportion our belief to the strength of the evidence. This suggests three things. First, overwhelming evidence justifies solid conviction. For example, if President Palmer is shot in the throat by a sniper rifle while writing his memoirs, we're justified in thinking someone wants him dead. After all, there's no reason to suppose it was an accident. He wasn't duck hunting with Dick Cheney. People don't often inadvertently shoot people in the throat while cleaning their assault weapons, and when they do, it's rarely a former president who's in the way. We can be sure Palmer was targeted by someone who meant him harm.

If evidence for a theory is altogether lacking, on the other hand, we should reject it. If someone believed the wild speculation that Nina Myers came back from the grave to kill Palmer, or that Jack's daughter Kim killed the president because she thought, after watching *Taxi Driver*, it'd impress her boyfriend, we can dismiss those accounts without further ado.

Things get interesting when the evidence is ambiguous, inconclusive, or susceptible to multiple interpretations. Then evidentialists advise us either to withhold judgment until more definitive data come to light or to believe tentatively and provisionally. Suppose we think the Season Five attacks on Palmer, Dessler, and Almeida are motivated by their knowledge that Bauer is alive. This is plausible; it would be a very odd coincidence if three of the four people known to have this information were killed or injured within minutes of each other for some unrelated reason. But if Chloe O'Brian, who also knows Jack's situation, goes about her daily business unmolested, we might conclude that the hits were unconnected, or connected by something other than Bauer, or that O'Brian herself is the shooter, or that the shooter has some special reason for sparing her, or that the shooter died before completing the mission, or that the shooter somehow didn't know Chloe was in the loop. While we still might entertain the hypothesis that Jack is connected in some way, we need to know more to be sure and should be open to revising our assessment. If Chloe is subsequently targeted, our original hypothesis receives additional confirmation. If she never is, then the original hypothesis would be, to that extent, undermined.

Scott Calef

Other evidentialists, like William Clifford (1845–1879), are more strict and hold, not that the strength of our belief should be proportionate to the weight of the evidence, but that we shouldn't believe at all without "sufficient" evidence. Clifford famously wrote: "it is wrong always, everywhere, and for everyone, to believe anything on insufficient evidence."[3] If we do so, we fail not just intellectually, but morally. Clifford provides a parable involving a ship owner whose aging vessel is of doubtful seaworthiness. If the owner believes the ship sound because of wishful thinking rather than the kind of evidence that only a thorough inspection could provide, and allows it to set sail full of innocent and unsuspecting passengers, he sins. Clifford claims the man is guilty even if, happily, the boat makes port safely. Although the owner's careless and unfounded optimism wasn't contradicted by events, he didn't avoid wrongdoing, only detection. By believing without sufficient evidence, he weakened our habit of inquiring into things. This, for Clifford, is a "sin against humanity" because it's our demand for evidence and the rational investigation of claims that enables civilization to rise above savagery. If religious fanatics and zealots in shows like *24* seem to us barbaric, maybe that's because their lives are completely controlled by violent and improbable ideologies that they cling to without a shred of proof. Syed Ali, for example, would willingly die what he imagines to be a martyr's death for his faith—and take the rest of us with him.

For the philosopher, *24* offers parables of its own. Jack, questioning Marie Warner at Norton airfield, finally wrests from her vital information that a nuclear device will be detonated at Arco Towers. If Jack plays a hunch that Marie is lying and that the device is still at the airport, without any proper warrant for that conviction, he too sins against humanity. If he's wrong, we're all the worse for it. Or consider Jack's conviction, on the basis of a 20-second interview with Syed Ali, that Ali is telling the truth about the Cyprus audio being a forgery. The physical evidence in favor of the recording's authenticity is uncontroverted, yet Jack believes in its fabrication anyway. Though in both instances he's right, he's gambling with the lives of millions.

3   Quoted by William James in his essay "The Will To Believe," in *Essays in Pragmatism*, ed. Alburey Castell (New York: Hafner Publishing, 1948) p. 93.

132

He may be congratulated as a hero, but like Clifford's nonchalant and well-insured ship owner he was lucky, not good, and guilty, though undiscovered.

This assessment, though, might seem too harsh under the circumstances. For Clifford, when we lack sufficient evidence we have a duty to suspend judgment and wait for additional information. But that's a luxury the President of the United States and CTU agents can't always afford. When Jack is working under crushing time constraints extreme urgency forces him and others to make decisions now, not later. Does this mean that Jack acts irrationally or immorally when he makes snap judgments based on incomplete intel? When, if ever, can we legitimately trust, believe, and act without critical data?

Of course, everything depends on the circumstances. In general, though, I'm inclined to think that when a decision must be made quickly, one can't be criticized for making it without all the facts. And do we ever have all the relevant facts? How do we know? No matter how confident Jack and others may be, a shocking plot twist is always just a few clock ticks away. To say, "Wait for the facts" amounts to saying we should wait until the truth is known before we commit. But then, what's truth? Clifford's view suggests truths are propositions that correspond to the facts, and that we mustn't accept something as a matter of fact without good reason. American philosopher William James (1842–1910), on the other hand, was a pragmatist. James defined truth as what works in the way of our believing. That is, something is to be considered true if it produces a minimum of conflict with our other beliefs.[4] For pragmatists, truth isn't a matter of believing something which corresponds

---

4   James writes: "A new opinion counts as 'true' just in proportion as it gratifies the individual's desire to assimilate the novel in his experience to his beliefs in stock. It must both lean on old truth and grasp new fact; and its success . . . in doing this, is a matter for the individual's appreciation. The reasons why we call things true is the reason why they *are* true, for 'to be true' *means* only to perform this marriage-function [of giving human satisfaction in marrying previous parts of experience with newer parts]" ("What Pragmatism Means" in *Essays in Pragmatism*, p. 150). In this respect, the pragmatic theory of truth resembles the Coherence Theory of Truth, according to which "what is said (usually called a judgment, belief, or proposition) is true or false [insofar as] it coheres or fails to cohere with a system of other things which are said" (Alan R. White, *Truth* [Garden City, NY: Anchor Books, 1970], p. 110).

to an independently existing state of affairs.⁵ It's a matter of having intellectual commitments which cohere together and are mutually consistent. James writes that "ideas . . . become true just in so far as they help us to get into satisfactory relation with other parts of our experience."⁶ "True" beliefs thus are beliefs that work by minimizing cognitive dissonance.⁷ They enable us to avoid doubt and confusion by not clashing with our other commitments and experience. This suggests that as long as Jack isn't ignoring evidence at his disposal,

---

5   The notion that truth is a correspondence between propositions and states of affairs is called the Correspondence Theory of Truth. Although this theory has many adherents and a certain commonsense appeal, it's also problematic. For example, "correspondence" is somewhat vague. How exactly do true utterances "correspond" to the world? Are the elements of a true sentence related to one another in the same way that objects in the world are? It's unclear what this means and, on at least one interpretation, it's dead wrong. In the sentence, "Jack is on the chopper," the word "Jack" is to the left of the word "chopper," but in the real world Bauer isn't to the left of the chopper, he's *in* the chopper. So the elements of the sentence are not related in the same way as the objects they describe. The correspondence or "fit" between the sentence and the world isn't like the fit of a comfortable pair of shoes or like the correspondence between the lines on a topical map and the steepness of the terrain represented. How then *are* we to understand this correspondence? Second, the correspondence theory doesn't work very well for negative sentences. If I say "No one is working behind President Logan's back" or "The lone gunman doesn't exist," what corresponds to what? What do these sentences refer to, and what exactly am I talking about? The universe as a whole? I certainly don't *seem* to be thinking about the universe as a whole, so why choose that interpretation rather than another? If, at 8:00 PM on Season Five, I say "Edgar Stiles is dead," I'm speaking the truth. But then, there is no Edgar, so what does the name in the sentence signify? The person who *used* to be Edgar? But the sentence is in the present tense and the person referred to is, as it were, past tense. How is this a correspondence?
6   "What Pragmatism Means," p. 147.
7   James notes that "The process [by which an individual settles into new opinions] is always the same. The individual has a stock of old opinions already, but he meets a new experience that puts them to a strain. Somebody contradicts them; or in a reflective moment he discovers that they contradict each other; or he hears of facts with which they are incompatible; or desires arise in him which they cease to satisfy. The result is an inward trouble to which his mind till then had been a stranger, and from which he seeks to escape by modifying his previous mass of opinions. He saves as much of it as he can, for in this matter of belief we are all extreme conservatives. So he tries to change first this opinion, and then that (for they resist change very variously), until at last some new idea comes up which he can graft upon the ancient stock with a minimum of disturbance of the latter, some idea that mediates between the stock and the new experience and runs them into one another most felicitously and expediently. This new idea is then adopted as the true one. It preserves the older stock of truths with a minimum of modification." ("What Pragmatism Means," p. 148.)

he can choose the hypothesis which best comports with his past experience and expertise. Certainly, Jack and others often face doubt and must scramble as quickly as possible to find more pieces of the puzzle. But in the meantime, he needn't withhold judgment altogether. He needn't succumb to paralysis. He can embrace the theory that works best (even if no theories are watertight).[8]

Living, Momentous, and Forced Decisions

James and Clifford agree that we shouldn't believe contrary to the evidence. That would be irresponsible. But James insists that when an issue is intellectually undecideable (or perhaps, as 24 illustrates, undecideable in the scant time available to us to make a choice) we're free to follow "the passions." The passions are all those factors, other than the evidence, which might incline us to a particular choice or conviction—things like desire, hope, fear, and love. More specifically, for James, we're permitted to choose between competing hypotheses when the option is intellectually undecideable and "living, momentous and forced."

A "live" option is one where each of the opposing positions seems viable or credible or has something to commend it. It's necessary for the option to be live if we're to go beyond the evidence because, if one of the choices isn't feasible, the decision has already been made.[9] Suppose Almeida and Dessler wonder whether Mason, exposed to plutonium and beginning to show symptoms, should be relieved of duty. He's still doing a good job—indeed, a better job than ever—but he's also distracted and his faculties will soon begin to fail. Both relieving him of command and allowing him to continue are acceptable, at least for the time being.[10] The choice between them is live. Or

8 Thus, James also famously defines truth in terms of its utility, or usefulness: "You can say . . . either that 'it is useful because it is true' or that 'it is true because it is useful.' Both of these phrases mean exactly the same thing" ("Pragmatism's Conception of Truth," in *Essays in Pragmatism*, p. 162). Also, " 'The true', to put it very briefly, is only the expedient in the way of our thinking" (p. 170).

9 For simplicity, I'll assume we're only considering two alternatives.

10 This can be considered a choice between the hypotheses "Mason should be relieved" and "Mason should be allowed to continue . . . for now." Similar adjustments can be made for the other examples to follow.

consider the position of President Palmer during Season Two when his ex-wife Sherry suddenly appears at the OC and begins trying to insinuate herself back into his confidence. He can recognize the value of her contributions, but also has every reason to distrust her motives. Letting her stay on with a provisional security clearance, or sending her away, are both real possibilities. The choice between them, according to James, is a living one. On the other hand, most of us would probably not consider allowing President Logan to remain in office after his collaboration with terrorists has come to light a live option. To do so, for most of us, would be unthinkable. There's no up side.

"Momentous" decisions, for James, occur when we may not have another chance to decide, the choice can't be easily reversed or undone, and something of considerable importance hangs in the balance. The choice has to be momentous if we're to go beyond the evidence because if we can always decide later or change our minds, there's no pressure to act prematurely on insufficient data. We can safely pro-crastinate. *24* is replete with examples of momentous choices. During Season Three, Ramon Salazar hands Jack a firearm and orders him to shoot Chase Edmunds. If he doesn't do it, Jack's cover is blown and they'll probably both be killed. Jack can't postpone making a choice or Salazar will probably do it himself. Whether he submits or resists, he can't easily undo the choice. Once he points the gun at Chase and pulls the trigger, there's no turning back. Nor will it be possible to change his mind later if he initially refuses. Finally, something of considerable importance hangs in the balance, since only if Jack protects his cover can he hope to prevent Salazar from turning a deadly virus over to the highest bidder—Nina Myers, as it turns out. The "option" between shooting and not shooting is momentous. (It may also be "forced," as we'll see below.)

"Forced" decisions arise when the consequences of not choosing are the same as making one of the choices. For example, during Season Five, Sentox nerve gas was released in CTU after terrorists infiltrated the building using Lynn McGill's stolen key card. Most of the surviving personnel were in the situation room, but corrosive elements in the gas were causing the protective seals around the door to rapidly deteriorate. Chloe's attempts to disable the ventilation system were futile due to a remote program that could only be shut down manually, and McGill was one of only two people who could possibly reach the location and intervene before succumbing to the gas. When McGill is asked to sacrifice his life to save the others, the decision is forced. If he can't make up his mind about whether or not to cooperate, that's tantamount to refusing since in both cases everyone will die. Jack's decision about whether or not to murder Ryan Chappelle is also forced. If Jack dithers, wrings his hands and can't decide whether to act that's functionally equivalent to choosing not to make the kill. And in that case, Stephen Saunders exposes the general population to a lethal virus.

So what has all of this to do with trust and suspicion? For Clifford, we should never believe anyone or anything without sufficient evidence. In an effort to arrive at certainty, Descartes (1596–1650) rejected as false anything that was in the slightest degree doubtful. These policies protect us from making mistakes. But the certainty of avoiding error doesn't come risk free because, while we won't believe a lie if we follow Clifford's advice, neither will we believe the truth when our source is (unbeknownst to us) reliable. When we withhold judgment, we don't believe one way or the other even when more good would have resulted from trusting the person. Thus, the certainty of avoiding error may result in the loss of a vital good.[11] We also cut ourselves off from possessing whatever truth we would have believed if we had guessed correctly. By refusing to believe and so resolutely act, Jack may avoid inadvertently mistaking error for truth. He may also fail to prevent a nuclear detonation. In other words, where something like preventing a terrorist strike is at issue, Clifford's stance amounts to risking a loss of truth and a vital good for the certainty of avoiding error. James' stance amounts to a willingness to risk error for a chance at acquiring truth and a vital

---

11 James' essay addresses belief in God in particular. Assume that whether God exists or not is intellectually undecideable. Clifford would say, then, that we must remain agnostic. James points out, though, that if the benefits of faith are only available to those who believe, by withholding assent we deprive ourselves of the good that faith might deliver. So Clifford prioritizes the certainty of avoiding error over the possibility of obtaining a vital good. For James, rationality doesn't *compel* us to prioritize as Clifford does.

good.[12] For James, in a world where we will certainly err occasionally in spite of our greatest precautions, we needn't be so afraid of mistakes that avoiding them becomes our highest duty. It's not that Clifford's position lacks merit; rather, the point is that we may freely adopt James' without violating any intellectual duties or standards of excellence when the matter is intellectually undecideable, living, momentous, and forced.

The Cyprus Audio

Let's try to apply these principles to a concrete example. Consider Season Two's controversy over the Cyprus audio. The vice president, Mike Novick, the joint chiefs, and Ryan Chappelle all regard its authenticity as absolutely verified through sophisticated analyses by teams of independent experts. Based on all of the information at their disposal, including their acquaintance with Bauer's maverick tendency to put his hunches ahead of the facts, protocol, and chain of command, they uniformly support a war of retaliation without delay. Clifford would probably agree that, for them, regarding the Cyprus recording as genuine is justified. If the unanimous verdict of many experts from multiple agencies doesn't constitute "sufficient evidence," it's hard to say what would.

Palmer, on the other hand, isn't so sure, and argues against an immediate strike on the grounds that Bauer thinks the audio a forgery. Prescott, Novick, and the majority of the president's cabinet easily discount the unconfirmed suspicions of a single agent, however. They consider the president's reliance on Bauer a sign of instability, if not outright disability. Unfortunately for the president, the proof Jack needs seems a mirage, constantly receding as he approaches nearer. First, Syed Ali, who denies being in Cyprus at the time, is assassinated; then, a chip believed to contain a copy of the source recording for the audio file is heavily damaged. It's inauthenticity is implied (but not proven) by the killing spree and torture Kingsley's men undertake in a vain attempt to recover and suppress it. Finally, Jack finds Hewitt, who claims to be able to replicate the specs on the forged

---

12 The "vital good" can be the prevention of a great evil, like a terrorist strike or assassination of a political figure.

recording, but Hewitt dies before he can demonstrate the process and technique by which it was created. Jack has reason to believe the recording a falsification, but not proof.[13] Palmer's skepticism about the audio, in turn, is derived from Jack. He trusts Jack, because he knows the kind of man Jack is. Because the president knows Bauer and has the utmost confidence in his integrity, honesty, frankness, powers of observation, sober-mindedness, and unique ability to render an on-the-ground assessment, he regards the audio's status as unknown. The president refuses to start a war until every shred of doubt has been eliminated, and that means giving Jack up until the bombers drop their payloads to disprove the audio. The recording's trustworthiness is perhaps not intellectually undecideable, but is, for the president, undecided. To engage in war without following up every lead would be a dangerously precipitous action that risks destroying US credibility forever. This Palmer cannot do.

Who's right? It's hard to say without clarifying what constitutes "sufficient" proof or evidence and when the authenticity of something like a recording can be regarded as definitively established. These notions are bound to be somewhat slippery. And as long as

---

13   The most commonly discussed modes of reasoning are induction and deduction. Induction involves reasoning from a sample to a whole group or population. For example, "Every episode in Season One of *24* was exciting, so all episodes of *24* must be exciting." This reasoning is at best probable, since there's always the (unlikely!) possibility that some episode will prove a letdown. Deductive reasoning involves drawing inferences which are supposed to be not merely probable but necessary. For example, "Everybody who works at CTU is stressed out. Jack works at CTU. Therefore, Jack is stressed out." In addition to these, American philosopher and logician Charles Sanders Peirce (1839–1914) identified a third type of reasoning he called "abduction." Abduction involves inference to the best explanation. We notice some facts which we want to understand. We reason that if a particular hypothesis were true, the facts would be nicely explained or accounted for. Indeed, they would be better accounted for than they would be by any other competing hypothesis we can think of. Thus, we conclude, the hypothesis is probable (or at least, possible). Abduction is therefore a logic of hypothesis formation, or of making educated guesses. This is what Jack—and indeed, almost any crime scene investigator—does all the time. If there are facts that can't be accounted for on the hypothesis that the Cyprus audio is authentic, Jack is justified in believing an alternative hypothesis, such as that it is a forgery designed to drive up the value of Caspian Sea oil reserves. Nothing that I say in what follows should be thought to suggest that Jack is believing against the evidence. Rather, he is reasoning abductively, forming hypotheses based on the facts at his disposal in an attempt to make the best possible sense of them.

they are, it's hard to say that suspicion or skepticism is out of place. The difference between President Palmer and Vice President Prescott is that the former regards the audio's authenticity as open to question and the latter as conclusively verified. As viewers, we can see the reasonableness of both positions (largely because, like Palmer, we've had opportunity to acquire confidence in Jack's abilities and integrity). But what if additional proof can't be obtained before the bombers are in position? To postpone attack anyway risks tens of thousands of additional American lives, since the three countries implicated would acquire the opportunity to ready their defenses. Would it be wrong to call off the attack, as Novick and Prescott assume? Or is Lynne Kresge right when she protests that, though she disagrees with the call, it's the president's decision to make?

In the absence of timely definitive proof—and from Palmer's position, the evidence isn't conclusive enough—and where the option is between the competing hypotheses that the recording is genuine or that it is false, or the hypotheses that he should attack without hesitation or delay attack indefinitely, Palmer can let his "passions" decide. He can allow his reluctance to risk the lives of innocent citizens in foreign countries, and not the evidence, to determine his decision. Kresge is right. As the president, it's his decision to make. For the decision to attack or not attack is living, momentous, and forced. It's living because both options are open. Though Palmer is choosing delay under the circumstances, that's not because going to war is unthinkable. He wouldn't hesitate to strike back if he were convinced of the intelligence supporting the mission. The choice is momentous because, obviously, a great deal is at stake and a decision, once reached, may be irrevocable. And the decision is forced. Refusing to make a decision about whether or not to attack has the same consequences as choosing not to do so.

Clifford seems to suggest that the consequences of our action are less important than the reasons for our actions. If I don't have adequate reasons, I shouldn't act even if the consequences would be beneficial. James, on the other hand, while not neglecting the rational factors, allows consideration of consequences when the information is inconclusive. The problem with James' approach is that it seems to justify the Prescott faction no less than Palmer and his supporters. This is because, if the veracity of the Cyprus audio is undecideable, Prescott can allow his passions to decide, and on that basis order an attack. For that option is, for him as for Palmer, living, momentous, and forced. But is that what we want to say? Do we want to embrace a theory which would justify military action based on faulty, fabricated, or incomplete intel? When it comes to something as extreme as entering a war against three Middle Eastern countries, can we allow anything less than absolute assurance in the justice of our cause to propel us to strike?

Unfortunately for those who like simple answers, *24* doesn't give us any. That's partly why it's such an intelligent and compelling drama. I imagine that most viewers of the show find it easier to go along with President Palmer. That may be because, as viewers, we have access to information that neither he nor the vice president have—we have access to Bauer in the field. Therefore, we know the president's support for Jack is well placed. But if we put ourselves in the actual positions of President Palmer and Vice President Prescott —if we couldn't look through the windows of our televisions at what Jack is hearing, seeing, and doing—things could go either way. The evidence might caution us against a headlong rush to war. And, we might feel that Prescott is, if not right, at least reasonable. The "evidence" does favor the view that the Cyprus audio is genuine.

And in a way, that complicates Clifford's view. Believing people isn't just like believing statements. If circumstantial evidence suggests a man's wife is unfaithful, the right thing to do might be to trust her anyway and assume there's a harmless explanation for her unusual behavior. You can't really love without trust, and love isn't rational. Perhaps we shouldn't believe propositions without sufficient evidence; perhaps Clifford's right that to do so is intellectually criminal. But when it comes to people, reason isn't all that counts. James' "passions" matter too. If Palmer doesn't believe Bauer, he not only risks losing the truth. He risks the loss of vital goods as well—the respect and friendship of an honorable man, as well as human lives.

The Cruel Cunning of Reason: The Modern/ Postmodern Conflict in 24

Terrence Kelly

It is tempting to view 24 as an allegory for a "clash of civilizations." However, the conspiracy-within-the-conspiracy structure of 24 reveals a much richer kind of conflict. As Jack Bauer struggles to defuse terrorist threats, his adversaries have included not only Islamic fundamentalists, but also Russian separatists, business cartels, fellow anti-terrorist agents, and no less than the President of the United States. The conflict in 24 is not simply East/West, or Fundamentalist/Secular, or Muslim/Christian. Instead, 24 represents something deeper, a conflict between two modes of practical rationality and the forms of social organization they give rise to: modernism and postmodernism.

Modernism can be characterized by bureaucratic and expert-oriented social systems in conjunction with a form of reasoning that emphasizes efficiency and rules. *Postmodernism* can be characterized as fragmented and open-ended social organization in conjunction with a form of reason that emphasizes plurality, indeterminacy, and contingency. Both modernism and postmodernism have self-destructive tendencies, or as Jacques Derrida (1930–2004) calls them, "auto-immunities."[1] These auto-immunities are exacerbated by the conflict between agents operating from these divergent perspectives.

1 Jacques Derrida and Giovanna Borradori, "Auto-Immunity: Real and Symbolic Suicides: A Dialogue with Jacques Derrida" in *Philosophy in a Time of Terror: Dialogues with Jürgen Habermas and Jacques Derrida*, ed. Giovanna Borradori (Chicago: University of Chicago Press, 2003). Page references to Derrida and Borradori are to this work.

The dramatic tension in *24* is fueled by the anxiety created by a new world disorder in which the modernist confines of the Cold War have been replaced by a threat that has gone postmodern. Jack Bauer personifies the auto-immunity of an increasingly frustrated modern hero who sacrifices his own humanity to fight an enemy that is fragmented, decentered, and, hence, never fully present. Jack's Sisyphean fate is a cautionary tale for those imagining a "war" on terrorism.

Modernity and Auto-Immunity

The actions of Jack Bauer and CTU are classic examples of modern rationality and social organization. Max Weber (1864–1920) argued that "modernity" is characterized by a turn to secular, bureaucratic, market-based, and technical social systems. As modern states grow in size and complexity, Weber argued that *efficient* organization and administration becomes the foundational social/political principle. Thus, in the name of efficiency, the modern state becomes increasingly bureaucratic in structure. It becomes differentiated, specialized, rule-bound, hierarchical, and insulated from destabilizing feedback. This compartmentalization allows modern administrative systems in the public sector to become more "automated" and better able to manage complex state functions and the increasing risks of a technologically driven society. State leaders need not be experts in (or even aware of) each area of risk addressed by the state. Administrative systems, stocked with experts, continually regulate risk and the implementation of public policy.

However, the turn to instrumental rationality and bureaucratic systems comes at a high price. Weber observed that a bureaucratic and efficiency oriented state tends to treat citizens as objects to be processed by administrative systems. Thus modern society slowly builds its own "iron cage" in which the freedom and the distinct personality of human beings are leveled in the name of efficient systemization. Modern life—for all its tremendous complexity—is purchased with human freedom.

Weber's "iron cage" thesis was dramatically defended by Max Horkheimer (1865–1973) and Theodor Adorno (1903–1969) in

Dialectic of Enlightenment.[2] Having fled Nazi Germany to, of all places, Southern California, Horkheimer and Adorno argued that democratic and authoritarian societies both suffer from the fact that the modern "enlightened" project, with its emphasis on science and efficiency, destroys the very values it aims to realize: human autonomy and democracy. In "enlightened" societies, culture, for instance, has become an industry manufacturing knowledge and preferences for economic and/or political gain—all, of course, in the name of consumer freedom and choice. At the same time, although increasingly efficient, social organization suffers from an impoverished practical reasoning and culture that no longer contemplates moral values.

Horkheimer and Adorno dramatize the self-destructive tendencies of enlightenment reasoning in the myth of Odysseus. While Odysseus is able to use his cunning to survive extreme dangers, he does so at terrible personal cost. Horkheimer and Adorno summarize Odysseus' condition: "the title of hero is only gained at the price of the abasement and mortification of the instinct for complete, universal and undivided happiness" (57). It is little wonder that in the "Myth of Er," Plato imagines Odysseus choosing his next life as that of a "private man who minds his own business"—a nobody.[3]

Jack Bauer, Modern Odysseus

Without doubt, Jack Bauer is a modern hero, perhaps *the* modern hero, of post-9/11 America. One can hardly overstate the cunning Jack uses to survive the most hopeless situations. In Season Six, while chained to a chair and being tortured, Jack is able to escape by faking his death and then biting (yes biting!) into the jugular vein of the guard who bends over him to check his pulse. However, for all his cunning, the sobering fact remains that Jack is ultimately a bureaucrat carrying out organizational goals in the most efficient manner possible, but at the cost of the complete abasement of his personal happiness.

2 Max Horkheimer and Theodor Adorno, *Dialectic of Enlightenment* (New York: Continuum Publishing, 1997). Page references to Horkheimer and Adorno are to this work.
3 Plato, *The Republic*, trans. Allan Bloom (New York: Basic Books, 1968), Book X, 620c.

It's startling to think of Jack as a bureaucrat. His action in the field is so fluid and requires so much ingenuity that at first glance he seems more like a Sartrean existential hero, that is, a radically free individual unconstrained by rules and conventions and living by a code entirely of his own creation. However, for all the appearance of freedom, Jack serves as an agent of a bureaucratic, vertically structured organization. Jack's ubiquitous cell phone places him in virtual contact/control with his superiors (whether the head of CTU or the president himself),[4] and while Jack occasionally defies the orders of his superiors, the fact is that he knowingly and loyally serves them. Their decisions, however frustrating, are typically obeyed.

For example, in Season Six the president has offered a terrorist, Hamri Al-Assad, immunity for his crimes provided that he continues to assist CTU in an anti-terrorist operation. Curtis, at times Jack's right hand man at CTU, is flabbergasted. Al-Assad has committed numerous atrocities against Americans (including members of Curtis's special forces unit several years ago). He simply cannot accept this arrangement. Jack's response is bureaucratic: "It's not our call." The president has made his decision, and as good members of the vertically structured, bureaucratic system, Jack insists that Curtis honor that decision. When Curtis cannot, and attempts to kill Al-Assad, Jack shoots and kills Curtis. As Jack stumbles down the street and collapses onto a lawn weeping and vomiting, we see not a Sartrean existential hero expressing his radical freedom, but a tool of an administrative system nauseated by the abasement of its own humanity in order to "get the job done."

Killing his friend Curtis is but one of the many abasements Jack suffers in the name of "the job." His wife is killed by fellow CTU agent Nina Myers, Jack's ex-lover turned terrorist mole; he is estranged from his daughter, becomes addicted to heroin, is "traded" off to be killed by a terrorist in exchange for information, and must fake his own death to avoid prosecution by malevolent members of his own administrative system. It's little wonder that Season Five begins with Jack, having faked his death at the end of Season Four, living the quiet life of "Frank Flynn," a day laborer in Mojave, CA. We do not know if Jack is happy in this life, but as with Odysseus in

---

4 See the chapter by Read Mercer Schuchardt for an analysis of the pervasive influence of the cell phone in 24 and everyday life.

the "Myth of Er," he has chosen the life of a "nobody." Too often Jack's cunning saves "Agent Bauer" at the price of Jack's own humanity.

The destruction of Jack's flourishing as a human being is not only evidenced by his terrible suffering and the loss of family and friends, it is also witnessed in Jack's deformation as a moral being. In Season Two, Jack is ordered to infiltrate a gang that is possibly connected to a terrorist plot. Jack's plan: murder a witness in protective federal custody who was to testify against gang members, and then bring his severed head to a meeting with the gang as a token of trust. Efficient? No doubt. But Jack's moral sensibility has clearly been replaced by a cruel cunning in which anything done to this (undoubtedly evil) witness is acceptable provided that it efficiently furthers the aims of the mission. Jack's increased use of torture, sometimes with surprisingly little provocation, is also symptomatic of the deterioration of what Kant would call his "moral personality."[5] Of course, in a heavily criticized element of *24*, all turns out well because the people Jack tortures are (usually) evildoers with critical information that is truthfully and quickly shared. But Jack's instrumentality in this matter is at times jarring.

Jack's auto-immunity, his self-destructive tendency, is reflected in the administrative system as a whole. Executives in the system are willing to trade on human lives (usually Jack's) with surprising ease. Romantic relationships continually strain the work of CTU, occasionally leading to betrayal and murder (for example, Nina Myers' romantic entanglement with Jack and Tony Almeida), and at any rate, almost always turn out badly. Like Jack, other members of the system increasingly adopt a questionable instrumental perspective in their approach to torture. In Season Four, CTU agents torture various suspects (for example, Sarah Gavin) who turn out to be innocent but, following the instrumental logic to its bitter end, the CTU agents endorse their decision because it helped exonerate the suspects. Even Defense Secretary Heller endorses the torture of his own son, despite his son's innocence.[6]

---

5 For Kant, we express our "moral personality" when we determine our own will via the use of moral reasoning as opposed to the "pathological self" that allows itself to be determined by external forces such as appetites. See Immanuel Kant, *The Critique of Practical Reason*, trans. Lewis White Beck (Upper Saddle River, NJ: Prentice-Hall, 1993).
6 Adam Green, "Normalizing Torture, One Rollicking Hour at a Time," *New York Times*, May 22, 2005.

Finally, the policies adopted by CTU and the US government exhibit an auto-immune, self-destructive response to the terrorist threat. The broader authorization of torture, the establishment of detention camps and sweeping quasi-legal searches, and the exchange of lives in the coarsest utilitarian terms erode the very values that are being "defended." The United States in 24 becomes decidedly less free and democratic. Even the president is not immune from the destructive demands of instrumentality. In Season Two, after a nuclear bomb has been detonated on American soil (thanks to Jack, in the desert and not in LA as planned), an audio recording surfaces identifying a number of countries behind the plot. President Palmer is urged by his cabinet to respond with vigorous military retaliation. When Palmer refuses because he suspects the authenticity of the recordings, he is removed from power because he is "incapacitated"; his moral qualms are simply not compatible with the instrumental logic of the system. Even the president is a tool.

So at the personal level (Jack), intersubjective level (members of CTU), and system level (US government), 24 dramatically highlights the auto-immune responses of the modern form of practical rationality. Jack's humanity, the relationships between the various members of CTU, and the policies of the US government all become instrumentalized to the point of tragedy. Like Odysseus, Jack and America survive, but in a self-destructive fashion.

The Specter of Terrorism

In James Bond films, SPECTER is an organization that is every bit as modern and bureaucratic as MI-6, complete with a Number One as the chief executive officer. The terrorism that Jack Bauer faces could not be more different. The threat he faces is typically decentered, pluralistic, and faceless. It is not represented by an organization, it does not reside in a geographic place, and its agents are motivated by radically different values and styles of reasoning. There is no "Number One" or "Dr. Evil" who, like a puppeteer, guides the unfolding plot that threatens America. There are certainly key individuals behind the threat, but their links are not vertical. For example, in Season Two, Jack is trying to find a nuclear bomb that Muslim extremists are planning to detonate in Los Angeles. The extremists, in turn, are being supported by a consortium of European and American business-men. The plan, as it turns out, is to (1) detonate a nuclear bomb in LA, (2) fabricate evidence that several Middle Eastern states were behind the attack, (3) allow this evidence to be "discovered" by CTU which (4) will lead to a massive military retaliation by the US, thereby (5) sending oil prices soaring, and (6) realizing tremendous profits for the business consortium.

The agents in this plot are extremely pluralistic in their motives, reasoning, location, and relations to one another. The Muslim extremists couldn't care less about oil prices; they want to strike at America on religious, and perhaps geopolitical, grounds. The consortium has no religious stake in the attacks and reasons from a modernist view seeking to maximize their economic resources. As a result, while they enable one another, no one is really *in charge* here. The consortium enables the terrorists, but once they have the bomb, the terrorists are relatively self-contained, with their own logic and motivations. Likewise, the terrorists are, quite frankly, pawns in a "larger" game. But it is unclear that they care. While their motivations are being utilized by the consortium, the terrorists themselves do not *serve* the consortium in any intentional way.

Many agents within the terrorist conspiracy are not, in and of themselves, postmodern in their reasoning.[7] The Islamic terrorists can be reasonably read as pre-Moderns striking out at the demythologizing effect of Modern Western societies. On the other hand, the business consortium is motivated by very modern considerations of market manipulation and efficient planning. What makes the terrorist threat postmodern is that such diverse motivations, values, and forms of reasoning are improbably aligned into a *constellation* of action. In Season Two, this constellation is both pre-Modern and Modern, both religious and secular, both Western and non-Western.

---

7 This is an important point to stress. Obviously, there is no necessary connection between terrorism and postmodernism. Many terrorist groups are not postmodern in structure and reasoning. Furthermore, there are many movements that arguably *are* postmodern in reasoning and structure (e.g., the peace movement in the US) that would categorically reject terrorist actions. The unique challenge that Jack faces is that significant forms of contemporary terrorism *do* happen to be postmodern in structure and reasoning.

As a result, the constellation that Jack confronts never fully presents itself; there is always another element to the plot that acts from a distance, from behind the curtain, from far away in time and space. This makes the terrorist threat, to borrow Derrida's metaphor, a "specter." It is nothing like the SPECTER in the world of James Bond. Rather, it is a specter in the sense of being something that appears but never fully; that acts, but never entirely in person; that haunts as much as it attacks. As Derrida puts it, the specter is "an apparition which . . . will not present anyone in person, but will strike a series of blows to be deciphered."[8]

The great challenge of fighting such a threat is that there is no opportunity for a "decapitation" strike. There isn't a Dr. No to find and kill, no predictable logic to follow, no "secret island" to locate. Jack is forced, thread by thread, to follow a tangled maze of terrorist threats, and this tangling helps insulate the terrorists from direct assault. As they are deployed in decentered networks or cells, they elude the head-on confrontations at which modern organizations excel.

Of course, such a logic carries its own auto-immunities, its own self-destructive tendencies. The favored terrorist tactic of suicide bombings leaves no person behind for accountability, but it also literally destroys the attacker. For many terrorists, their own humanity is also effaced by the cause. Furthermore, as one could imagine, constellations of such disparate styles of reasoning produce rather unstable social arrangements. For instance, in Season Six, Abu Fayed has lost the nuclear scientist he needs to arm several nuclear devices. He contacts Darren McCarthy to secure another scientist for this task. McCarthy, as opposed to Fayed, is not an Islamic fundamentalist and so his loyalty to the cause is hardly suicidal. As such Fayed engages in an almost humorous use of threats and monetary offers to cajole McCarthy into action. Because they are decentralized and pluralistic, agents within the terrorist constellation cannot count on loyalty, institutional accountability, or shared "thick" ethical concepts to coordinate action. Rather, they must work through a plurality of language games, often at the price of their own interests or authenticity.

---

8 Jacques Derrida, *Specters of Marx* (New York: Routledge, 1994), p. 99. Cited herein as *Specters of Marx*. In this context, Derrida is discussing Marx's use of the terms "specter" and "haunts" to describe Communism's confrontation with Europe.

Teetering On the Edge of the End of History:
24 and Contemporary Terrorism

In the giddy years after the fall of Communism, Francis Fukuyama declared that we had reached "the end of history."[9] This expression has its source in Hegel's (1770–1831) confidence that, in modernity, social life had reached its rational zenith. While there would obviously continue to be historical and social developments, the fundamental structure of society would, barring catastrophe, not change from its optimum, modern (democratic/market) form.[10]

24 presents us with the potential catastrophe that pushes modern societies beyond the end of history. The anxiety about this catastrophe resonates with viewers because the current geopolitical situation bears numerous similarities to Jack Bauer's. While it is unlikely that the conspiracies are as rich and (soap) opera-esque as in *24*, in contemporary terrorism modern societies face a threat that is also decentered, non-institutional, pluralistic, and never fully present. And it is also dangerous. With the proliferation of nuclear, biological, and chemical weapons, contemporary terrorism raises the possibilities of mass destruction and significant social destabilization. Terrorism haunts modern societies as much as—or more than—it attacks them. As Derrida remarks about such specters, "no one talks of anything else. But what else can you do, since it is not there, this ghost, like any ghost worthy of its name" (*Specters of Marx*, 100).

Terrorist organizations are described as "networks," but this already over-unifies them. Terrorists and the various states, organizations, and individuals who support them often have various, and not entirely consistent, religious, geopolitical, and economic goals. Bin Laden, who is never present, occasionally makes "appearances" which haunt or terrify some and inspire others. Terror "cells" form spontaneously even in Western states such as Britain and the United States, and while it is comforting to think about "training camps" where junior extremists go for finishing school, the reality of modern

9   Francis Fukuyama, *The End of History and the Last Man* (New York: Free Press, 1992).
10   G. W. F. Hegel, *The Philosophy of Right*, trans. H. B. Nisbet (New York: Cambridge University Press, 1991).

terrorism is so decentered that, were catastrophe not so close at hand, these images would be laughable. As Derrida glosses it:

> The worst, most effective "terrorism" even if it seems external and "international" is the one that installs or recalls an interior threat, *at home* and recalls that the enemy is also always lodged on the inside of the system it violates and terrorizes. (Derrida and Borradori, 188)

The fear of the threat that is already "inside" has, as in Jack's America, produced various self-destructive, auto-immune responses in order to locate and expel the foreign body. Those responses are familiar to viewers of *24*: authorization of torture, restriction of individual liberties, disproportionate military reactions, a decline of democratic deliberation, a vague and constant paranoia color coded in "threat levels," and the equalization of dissent with treason. And as in *24*, one cannot help but wonder if these auto-immune responses are the goal of the terrorist attacks. Consider Jürgen Habermas's reflection on living in New York a few months after 9/11:

> The repeated and utterly non-specific announcements of possible new terror attacks and the senseless calls to "be alert" further stirred a vague feeling of angst along with an uncertain readiness—precisely the intention of the terrorists.[11]

In Marxist revolutionary theory, armed resistance and terrorist attacks are never meant to confront the government head-on. Rather, they are intended to spur the government into disproportionate responses that highlight the state's illegitimacy—to "heighten the contradictions" as the Maoists would say. In its auto-immune response, the government is no longer able to distinguish between the healthy and dangerous elements of society because the threat is always already perceived to be interior. As a result, legitimate elements of society (for example, civil liberties) and the international community (for example, international law) are inadvertently undermined. The result

11 Jürgen Habermas and Giovanna Borradori, "Fundamentalism and Terror: A Dialogue with Jürgen Habermas" in *Philosophy in a Time of Terror: Dialogues with Jürgen Habermas and Jacques Derrida*, ed. Giovanna Borradori (Chicago: University of Chicago Press, 2003), p. 26.

is that the United States suffers a staggering loss of legitimacy in the hearts and minds of citizens worldwide.

I'm Gonna Break My Rusty Cage . . . and Run

If there are similarities between *24* and the current situation faced by modern societies, what is to be learned from *24*? Are modern societies doomed only to reinforce the bars of the iron cage, to trade freedom and democracy for efficiency and security? Can the threat of a terrorism that has gone postmodern be confronted without auto-immunity?

To understand the potential for a constructive response to contemporary terrorism, it is worth reconsidering the account of modernity offered by Weber, Horkheimer, and Adorno. The iron cage thesis they support relies on a highly deterministic account of the philosophy of history, according to which the tendencies of modern rationality come to organize both social structures and the interior life of individuals in strictly instrumental terms.[12] In other words, society comes to be organized in terms of efficiency and means-ends reasoning, and this in turn shapes the outlook of individual members of society in the same way. Thus the macro mirrors the micro elements of society. In such a philosophy of history, individuals have become "cultural dupes" who are no longer aware of the iron cage that their society has become, that they unwittingly build and reinforce. In other words, individuals fail to see the broader destructive implications of modern rationality—whether in their own practical outlook, or as operationalized in social institutions. This "behind the back" philosophy of history is quite common in theories influenced by the Marxist approach to the problem of ideology.

However, such strong social determinism is neither philosophical nor empirically tenable. Ethnography and ethnomethodology have made clear the ways in which everyday actions require significant creativity and self-reflexivity—of which instrumental calculation is merely one of many considerations in everyday interaction.[13] Philosophers such as Jürgen Habermas have noted that Horkheimer

12 See Axel Honneth, *The Critique of Power* (Cambridge, MA: MIT Press, 1993).
13 Harold Garfinkel, *Studies in Ethnomethodology* (Englewood Cliffs, NJ: Prentice-Hall, 1969).

and Adorno, while correct in their assessment of the instrumental dimension of enlightenment rationality, overly globalize this insight into an implausible account of practical rationality and social development. Modern rationality, argues Habermas, has other dimensions that can contain the "colonizing" effect that instrumental rationality can have on social life. After all, the arguments offered in *Dialectic of Enlightenment* itself are surely not mere cogs in the culture industry, but rather represent a use of reason that aims at generating a principled agreement among rational individuals to further the aims of human liberation and flourishing. This dimension of practical rationality, which Habermas calls "communicative rationality," is used when we deliberate with others in order to arrive at a rational consensus on norms that are acceptable to all.[14] It is in this form of reason that we exhibit our "moral personality" and preserve our humanity against the potentially corrosive effects of instrumental reasoning.

Indeed, even in the crisis of the perpetual now of *24*, we see glimmers of such reasoning. For example, in Season Two, President Palmer refuses to authorize retaliatory strikes because he believes, based on Jack Bauer's word, that the evidence demonstrating the involvement of other nations in a domestic nuclear attack has been fabricated. Palmer trusts Jack *and* acts upon the moral principle that aggressive military action is unjustified in the face of such doubts. Palmer knows from the discursive products of international law as well as his own moral compass that, in principle, military aggression cannot be justified by evidence that is suspect. Palmer's moral personality shines through as he holds his principled stance even as he is removed from office by his own cabinet. Likewise, one can reread Jack's killing of Curtis in Season Six as motivated by Jack's *promise* to protect Al-Assad. Regardless of the terrible consequences, Jack follows through on the moral imperative of that promise. The entire incident may well be best understood in the context of *both* instrumental (bureaucratic) and communicative (in this case moral) imperatives.

---

14 See Jürgen Habermas, *The Theory of Communicative Action: Volume One*, trans. Thomas McCarthy (Boston: Beacon Press, 1984) for his critique of the iron cage thesis and *Dialectic of Enlightenment*. See also Jürgen Habermas, *The Pragmatics of Communication*, trans. Maeve Cooke (Cambridge, MA: MIT Press, 1998) for his account of communicative rationality.

Despite these occasional flashes, communicative reasoning overall does not do very well in *24*. After all, by the time they call Jack Bauer, "it is already too late." The immediate nature of the threats that Jack faces requires administrative responses and, as such, efficiency easily outpaces deliberation, with all the auto-immune disorders that follow.

In the real world the situation is not so bleak. While some aspects of the management of terrorist threats will necessarily be administrative and crisis-driven, there are significant opportunities to develop principled and communicative responses as well. The development of broad international coalitions against terrorism, the strengthening of international law and institutions of justice, the expansion of human rights, the remediation of poverty and global market inequities, and the promotion of democracy can all be developed from communicative and deliberative responses to terrorism. Such responses offer the potential for long-term effectiveness against terrorism without the self-destructive tendencies dramatized in *24*.

Such principled responses are not possible, however, to the degree that the management of terrorism is imagined as a "war." As a war, the management of the risk of terrorism becomes, as in *24*, a crisis of the perpetual now. In the milieu of this crisis mentality, the openness required by communicative rationality is closed off and replaced by instrumental/administrative logic. To the degree that dissent is equated with treason, morality is equated with being "soft on terrorism," and unilateral action replaces international consensus building, the fragile requirements of principled deliberation are destroyed. In the absence of such deliberation, the cruel cunning of instrumental reasoning becomes the dominant mode of risk management. In this mode, those of good faith, like Jack Bauer, forfeit their own humanity and moral personality in service to the system, while others use the crisis to cynically advance anti-Enlightenment interests. Either way the result is the same: in the name of freedom, justice, and democracy the United States (and the world) becomes less free, less just, and less democratic.

The Knowledge Game Can Be Torture

R. Douglas Geivett

Senator: Mr. Smart, how many arrests did Control make last year?

Maxwell Smart: I don't know.

Senator: Who's the number one man in your organization?

Maxwell Smart: I don't know.

Senator: How many cases were assigned to Control last year?

Maxwell Smart: I don't know.

Senator: What would you do if you were fired, Mr. Smart?

Maxwell Smart: They can't fire me. I know too much.[1]

Jack Bauer knows his stuff. And it's a good thing, too. If he didn't, he wouldn't last one hour, much less 24. Counter-terrorism expert, field agent with the grit to survive unthinkable torture, a man whose reflexes have saved dozens of lives (including his own dozens of times), a sharpshooter when handling a Glock, the improvisational wunderkind of CTU, jet pilot, helicopter pilot, and everything-else-kind-of-pilot, decryption whiz, explosives specialist, seat-of-the-pants chemical engineer, a regular guy generally at ease telling the President

---

1 This snippet of dialogue is from the popular television series *Get Smart*, a phenomenon of the 1960s. Maxwell Smart, a.k.a. Agent 86, is a spy working for a secret government entity called Control, its nemesis a criminal element that goes by the name Kaos (pronounced like "chaos"). The name Smart is deliberately ironic. Max is a bumbler, who can be counted on for solving all of his cases . . . but always by accident. See www.imdb.com/title/tt0058805/quotes.

of the United States what he should do in nerve-jangling situations, and—by his own lights, of course—a team player. That's our Jack. And when there's serious trouble lurking about, even the most ambivalent CTU director wants agent Bauer on the case.

What explains the—sometimes enthusiastic, often grudging—deference toward Jack Bauer? In a word, *expertise*. CTU, the president, the country, depend on Jack Bauer for his inimitable expertise as a counter-terrorist agent. At the core of his expertise is a fund of knowledge that enables him to act with responsible authority in matters of national interest. Jack knows enough to be practically indispensable as a field agent in the arena of counter-terrorism. Here are a few of the most important *kinds* of knowledge Jack has:

- Knowledge of the way clever and determined terrorists think and behave.
- Knowledge of the politics of American engagement with an elusive enemy.
- Knowledge of the interpersonal dynamics that may compromise a high-stakes mission.
- Knowledge of the psychology of human motivation.
- Knowledge of protocols of various kinds (for example, the use of weapons, the testing of evidence, the navigation of unfamiliar territory, etc.).

Jack Bauer is a commanding figure and a go-to guy because of what he knows and what he can accomplish on the basis of what he knows. If we observe closely and in the right way, we may learn a few things from Jack about the knowledge game. This chapter explores a few of the connections between *24* and epistemology. But first we must ask, what is epistemology?

When I'm asked what I do for a living, I like to say, "I'm an epistemologist." It sounds so . . . medically sophisticated. Of course, epistemology has nothing to do with medicine. It has, rather, to do with belief, and the status of belief. Beliefs vary in status; that is, they are not all "created equal." Some beliefs are better than others. Epistemologists explore the ways in which one belief may be better than another.

In epistemology truth is our aim, and evidence is our game. But there are many different kinds of evidence. And there are pitfalls in the pathway to truth. Trouble arises when we demand evidence of one kind for determining the truth-value of a proposition that simply cannot be determined on the basis of that kind of evidence.[2]

In the sections that follow, we'll consider two themes, the nature of expertise and the value of testimonial evidence, as these are developed in *24*.

Get Me Jack Bauer

In *24*, the importance of expertise is illustrated time and again. For example, in Season Four, Jack is working for the Department of Defense. He drops in on CTU Director Erin Driscoll to talk budget numbers. Standing in her office, he sees there's an investigation in progress. Driscoll is watching live feed from a camera hidden in some shop. Ronnie Labelle, head of Field Ops, is seen questioning the shopkeeper about a terrorist who might be connected with a bombing earlier in the morning. As he watches the proceedings, Jack's instincts engage. Speaking of the shopkeeper, he says, "He's hiding something." Driscoll seems mildly annoyed and says, "It's being handled, Jack." She doesn't see anything unusual in the shopkeeper's demeanor, and neither does Labelle. But Jack continues, expanding on his observation: "The store's open for business, but the blinds are closed. There are no other employees. This guy is way too nervous. Trust me. He's hiding something." Driscoll recognizes the possible relevance of this and asks Labelle to back off a bit. Then Jack notices something else, something the others miss. There's a subtle shift of the shopkeeper's eyes, a brief glance to his right. In Driscoll's office, they replay the feed in slow motion. With this for confirmation, Jack advises Driscoll to tell Labelle he should look for something on the shopkeeper's right. Sure enough, the terrorist is spotted. The shopkeeper has been lying to cover for him.

---

2   It is rumored that Soviet cosmonaut Yuri Gagarin said, during his orbit of the earth on the first manned spaceflight (1961), "I don't see any God up here." Some speculate that these words were falsely attributed to Gagarin (for propaganda purposes) by Nikita Khrushchev, First Secretary of the Communist Party of the Soviet Union. The very idea that God's existence might be visually tested while circling the earth for an hour-and-a-half is transparently ludicrous.

In this incident, Jack is initially given the brush-off. But soon he is vindicated. Jack scores points with Driscoll and Labelle. He'd told Driscoll, "Trust me." But the CTU director needed a reason. Without one, Jack's entreaty is an impertinence. With a few simple observations, Jack coaxes a modicum of deference out of her. Yes, come to think of it, it is odd that the blinds are closed. Then he sees the eyes shift. Now Jack can tell Driscoll how to instruct Labelle, and expect compliance from her. Why? Because he knows his stuff. With his knowledge of what to look for and the few clues at his disposal, Jack effectively takes control of the situation. Driscoll, however reluctantly, cedes authority in this instance.

Expertise gives one standing as an authority. Knowledge by itself doesn't have this effect. Jack could have kept his observations to himself. His knowledge would have remained intact. But he wouldn't have been much use. Expertise is a matter of placing one's knowledge and skills at the disposal of others, in the service of some good. This makes it a kind of virtue.

What I'm suggesting is controversial. You might think that expertise has nothing to do with a disposition to do the right thing on the basis of what one knows. But there clearly is a difference between "know-how" that can be directed toward ends that are either good or bad, and "know-how" that is naturally directed, by the character of the individual, toward the highest goals. We generally think of expertise as a quality that says something admirable about the *person*, that is, the expert. This notion of expertise as a virtue—or, if you prefer, of expertise wedded to virtue—is richer than the conventional notion because it recognizes a unity of two states: being knowledgeable and being disposed to act responsibly on the basis of what one knows.

I'm prepared to suggest something even more controversial. Knowledge is itself a good that has for its natural goal responsible action in the world appropriate to the knowledge one has and the circumstances of one's life. A knowledgeable but impassive individual does not hold his knowledge in the right way. Inherent in the concept of knowledge is a special kind of goal-directedness, where the relevant goal in any case is the realization of some good. This does not mean that knowledge that is not *enacted* on behalf of some good fails to be knowledge. But that is a corrupt form of knowledge. It isn't admirable, and it isn't expertise.

There's more to say about Jack's intellectual virtues, on the basis of this one incident. It reveals that Jack is a careful observer. In this instance, his observational skills may be so neatly honed that his awareness of relevant detail (the shifting of the eyes, for example) is more reflexive than deliberative. It may seem deliberative because Jack traces the steps of a deliberative (almost deductive) process for Erin Driscoll. But this is probably more for her benefit than it is a reflection of any process he has consciously followed himself. This is a remarkable phenomenon. It isn't only that Jack makes speedy judgments without the benefit of deliberative reasoning. He does so efficiently and usefully. Of all the things available for awareness as he watches the proceedings, Jack picks out what is salient given the aims of the investigation. And he does so spontaneously.

In this case, Jack's thinking parallels, without engaging in, a step-wise process that can be spelled out for Driscoll. It isn't always this way, as we'll see in a moment. But here it helps that Jack can rattle off the specific components of his evidential base for the judgment that the shopkeeper is prevaricating. Jack is able to persuade Driscoll by pointing to relevant evidence. He naturally and appropriately assumes that Driscoll will take this to be evidence. And Driscoll does. They are on the same wavelength. It is important to draw attention to this, since many people today claim to be immune to the blandishments of evidence. We are exquisitely evidence-sensitive. We have this sensitivity in common with one another. And we contribute to the common good when we seek to be responsible in believing the things we believe and to enable others, on the basis of good reasons, to believe these things as well. This form of altruism is compatible with our fallibility and the distinctiveness of our respective points of view.

Sometimes Jack makes spontaneous critical judgments without the need to persuade someone else. And sometimes when this happens, Jack seems (even to himself) to be going on a hunch. But a hunch is something like a guess backed by strong conviction without much in the way of evidence. A hunch may turn out to be a lucky guess, or not. But Jack has a habit of making "lucky guesses." Part of what I mean by "habit" here is that there's a pattern of "hunching" and getting things right. But I also mean that this pattern is a function of habit. That is, Jack is *habituated* to making spontaneous judgments, without the benefit of careful deliberative reasoning. I suggest that if Jack did not have a track record of "hunching" correctly, he would not have a habit of trusting, and therefore acting so successfully on, his hunches.

Is Jack's successful track record a happy accident? I don't think so. I believe it's the result of long practice in the trenches of counter-terrorism, and a growing fund of knowledge from which Jack can draw, as needed, in a host of unique settings. In numerous situations, he knows what to do or think without *thinking about* how he knows it. This, too, is a mark of expertise. And it explains the halo of authority recognized by Jack's colleagues and by political leaders right up through the chain of command to the President of the United States.

This "halo of authority" speaks of something acknowledged and respected by others. It's why, when something goes wrong in the world of counter-terrorism, the president or the CTU director is telling someone, "Get me Jack Bauer!"

Hostile Witnesses and Testimonial Evidence

It isn't always easy knowing what kind of evidence gives us the indication of truth that we seek. On the other hand, there are plenty of things we believe, without reticence, on the basis of evidence that we often do not cross-examine. Two sources of evidence that account for much of what we believe—more-or-less uncritically—are sensory perception and human testimony. Philosophers have long explored the epistemology of sensory perception. But until recently, the epistemology of testimonial evidence has been generally neglected. It happens that testimony is an important source of evidence in Jack Bauer's labors on behalf of national security. It's time we consider this dimension of *24*.

In his capacity as expert, Jack often must interrogate a hostile witness, that is to say, an "uncooperative informant." Situations of this kind are layered with epistemological complexity. Some of the more significant difficulties relate to the nature of testimonial evidence.

We begin with a common instance of testimonial grounding for belief that guides action. Suppose you're driving your car in an unfamiliar city and you stop to ask a stranger for directions. This seems like a reasonable thing to do. But would it be reasonable if you weren't prepared to believe what the stranger tells you? Why stop to ask if you aren't going to believe the stranger? And would it be reasonable to believe the stranger? After all, she is a stranger, which means you don't really know whether she's a reliable informant. This description of a commonplace is thought by some philosophers to expose epistemological difficulties in the acceptance of testimony. Whenever we rely on the testimony of others, whether they are strangers or not, we run the risk of being misinformed, whether intentionally or unintentionally. What is the status of a belief that is based on testimonial evidence?

We'll return to this general form of the problem in a moment. First let's notice some complications that are introduced when an informant refuses to inform. Jack Bauer has plenty of experience with "uncooperative informants." If the stakes are high and he thinks torture may help in the extraction of critical information, then he's demonstrably willing to rip the electric cord from a lamp, insert the two wires on one end into an electrical outlet, and test the juice on the sensitive skin of a would-be informant. (It has no doubt been argued that this is one reason why we watch *24*.) Now, what is the value of this exercise?[3]

Some have argued that torture "doesn't work," that it's not an effective means of collecting information. There are several reasons for wondering whether it works or not. One prominent claim is that, when threatened with torture or while undergoing an escalating series of torture tactics, the subject is an unreliable informant because he's liable to say whatever it is he thinks you want him to say in order to avoid the infliction of (additional) pain. This is more likely in cases of police interrogation where the subject is asked to admit guilt, and there is little evidence that would countermand such an admission. But admission of guilt under such circumstances differs from cases where information that is sought during interrogation can be cross-checked against other evidence for corroboration or disconfirmation. If information extracted during interrogation matches up with evidence collected by other means, that information will provide vital confirmation. It may even contribute detail that is not otherwise knowable.

Be that as it may, we have the advantage here of stipulating that torture is an effective information-extracting tool since that is how

---

3 We are not here considering the *ethics* of torture. We are reflecting on what might be called the *logic* of torture, for epistemological purposes.

it's portrayed in *24*. For our purposes, it doesn't matter whether this portrayal is accurate. We are interested in residual complexities, even assuming that torture is (some significant percentage of the time) successful in squeezing information out of an unwilling informant.

Jack Bauer has two kinds of experience with torture. He has been the victim of torture, and he has resorted to torture during the interrogation of individuals. From these experiences, Jack must generalize about the psychology of human motivation and then apply his knowledge of human psychology when making any decision about whether to use torture.

Sometimes Jack has good reason to believe that torture will get him the information he wants. For example, in Season Six, Jack needs information from a Russian diplomat about the location of the launch site for a series of nuclear weapons aimed at densely populated California cities. He breaks into Russian consular offices in Los Angeles, in violation of laws guaranteeing immunity for foreign dignitaries, holds the highest ranking official hostage in his own office, and threatens to clip off fingers if the official refuses to reveal launch locations. It appears for awhile that this particular renegade apparatchik will not relinquish information under any circumstances. But when Jack removes one digit from his left hand, he changes his mind and blurts out the general whereabouts of the computer-guided missiles. This can be corroborated, so Jack can trust the report. In fact, Jack believes the official. And it happens that the official's report is accurate.

It doesn't always work out that way. One of the most dramatic episodes of *24* involves Jack's interrogation of Nina Myers in Season Two. Joseph Wald has presented conclusive evidence that Nina (herself a CTU operative) is connected with a group of terrorists who have scheduled a nuclear bomb to go off that day. Nina is about to be interrogated for the purpose of learning where and when. CTU Director George Mason takes first crack at her. We're not surprised that his limp efforts are ineffectual. Nina seems to be getting the upper hand with her demand for a full presidential pardon, complete with third-party certification. Only then will she give up her contacts, background material, and critical intel. Jack receives a call from President David Palmer informing him that he has authorized a "shadow asylum" in exchange for the information they need.

At this point, Jack confronts Mason. "I want the case," he says. "I know how she thinks . . . and you know it." Mason doesn't trust

Jack to play by the rules, so he refuses. But Jack manages to blackmail Mason, whom he'd seen taking anti-nausea pills to counteract the effects of lethal radiation exposure.

While standing by for the certificate of pardon to reach CTU, Jack waves off Michelle Dessler, who's brought him Nina's file. "I know Nina," he says. Soon after, with pardon in hand, Jack heads for the interrogation cell and tells Mason, "I'll show her this. I'll start her talking. Then I'll get you everything you want, even the stuff she doesn't want us to know."

Inside the cell, Nina starts in with additional demands. But Jack will not acquiesce. Heated dialogue ensues:

Nina: Stop wasting time. I'm sitting here looking at the president's signature.
Jack: I'm here; he's not. And I'm not going to make a move until I believe you're credible.
Nina: I'll only get the pardon if I stop the bomb. Why wouldn't I do everything I can?
Jack: Because you're worse than a traitor, Nina. You don't even have a cause. You don't believe in anything. You would sell anyone and everything out to the highest bidder. *So stop wasting my time. Give me a name!*
Nina: Don't even bother, Jack. If you lay a hand on me, you'll be taken off the case . . . You're just going to have to follow my lead.
[Jack rams Nina against the wall and starts choking her.]
Jack: You are going to tell me everything I want to know, or I swear to God, I will hurt you before I kill you, and no one will stop me. Do you understand me?
[With spot-on timing, George Mason pulls Jack out of interrogation.]
Mason: Alright, you're done. Get out of here.
Jack: Why?
Mason: Why? Because you've lost it. That's why.
Jack: George, right now she thinks she's won the lottery. She's in control. You want her to tell the truth? You take that away from her.
Mason: By killing her? Yeah, that'll work.
Jack: No, by giving her someone to answer to, someone to be afraid of. She has to believe that I'd be willing to put my revenge in front of finding this bomb . . . You need to let me go back in there, show her that I have the power to do anything I want to her . . . All I need is five minutes. Just don't let anyone in that room. And raise the thermostat ten degrees.

So Jack goes back in. He even traces the outline of her head against the wall with bullet holes. Somewhat rattled, Nina still will not give up the name of her contact. She'll only say that he's in Visalia. Jack's expression suggests that he doesn't believe her. He certainly doesn't trust her. Yet he boards a plane with her . . . headed for Visalia.

What's going on here? Even if Nina is telling the truth, the only thing she has said is that her contact is in Visalia, California. She won't say any more than that. Should Jack believe her? He probably wouldn't be justified in believing her. But it doesn't matter. He doesn't have to believe her. What he can do, and it's about the only thing he can do, is go to Visalia, with Nina in handcuffs, to see what unfolds. This is the responsible thing to do even though he doesn't believe her. Notice, he doesn't believe she's lying, either. He doesn't know whether she's telling the truth or not. So he suspends judgment. He makes no belief commitment, and plays the hand he's been dealt by acting *as if* she was telling the truth. But he does this for the sake of finding out the truth.

From the cases we've examined, we've learned that testimony, even when it is offered under extreme duress, may be valuable. Testimony extracted during interrogation may be offered in such a way that it can be corroborated simply by checking reality against the statements given, as in the case of the Russian diplomat. The check cannot be performed without the testimonial evidence, since it's the testimony that reveals the means of verification. This in itself is reason to believe the testimony. Sometimes, however, the information is too vague and cannot be corroborated in this way. In that event, while it may not be reasonable to believe the statements given, it may be reasonable to act as if the statements are true, and hope to come by better information along the way, as in the case of Nina Myers.

These lessons have general application. Consider the stranger giving directions. If she offers confident and frank advice about how to reach our destination, we may be justified in believing her. After all, we have no reason not to, and she isn't reporting under duress. If her directions are specific enough, that will be additional reason to accept her testimony. Details will permit corroboration along the way. If the stranger is taciturn or seems unsure of herself, and her directions are more general, then we may not believe her statements. But we may proceed as if her directions, as vague as they are, are accurate. In due course, we may come by better information, even if it consists in ruling out the path suggested by the stranger and starting over.

A Risky Venture

Our two topics, the expertise of Jack Bauer and his dependence on the testimony of uncooperative informants, converge. Jack is himself an informant, delivering information to those who depend on him. But this information often is only as reliable as the sources he has interrogated. His expertise, then, must extend to his ability to obtain reliable information from uncooperative informants. The enterprise of responsible believing is always a risky venture. But in the high stakes arena of counter-terrorism, the knowledge game can be torture.[4]

4   I wish to thank Rich Davis for helpful discussions of epistemological themes in *24*, and for his suggestions regarding specific scenes of epistemological interest.

TECHNOLOGY, OBJECTIFICATION, AND THE CLOCK___

How the Cell Phone Changed the World and Made *24*

Read Mercer Schuchardt

For the "message" of any medium or technology is the change of scale, or pace or pattern that it introduces into human affairs.
Marshall McLuhan, *Understanding Media*

The television program known as *24* is a documentary of the cell phone's complete takeover of contemporary life. All else is commentary.

Despite satellite uplinks, computer databases, a plethora of interconnected digital technology, and the usual primetime prescription of guns, cars, babes, and bad guys, the story loses all plausibility, most of its narrative structure, and more than half of its screen time if you remove the cell phone. This does not mean that *24* is about the cell phone; it merely means that the medium of the cell phone is the hidden ground upon which the figure of the show appears. Everything about *24* derives from this primary fact of media change: the content, the compression of time, the picture-in-picture display, the character types, the character hierarchy, the location of the dramatic action, the genre of performances, the network upon which the show plays, the time slot at which it originally aired, the actors' increasing but understandable inability to separate reality from fiction, the audience's imitation of the actors, and the audience's limited leisure time within which to understand the world through television.

When you introduce a cell phone to a culture, you don't get the old culture plus a cell phone. You get a completely restructured culture, one whose relationships, time commitments, interests, beliefs, fears, hopes, and primetime television shows are themselves radically reoriented towards the communication made possible by the cell phone itself. Like many of technology's Faustian bargains, the cell phone's greatest blessing is simultaneously its greatest curse: you're always reachable. Hidden behind this assumption is the lurking imperative: you should always be available. Moreover, this applies to anyone— wife, lover, friend, boss, colleague, terrorist, president. To enhance our opening claim: *24* is the documentary of what your life would look like if all your cell phone calls were as important and special as you'd like everyone to think they are. Our guide through the show will be Marshall McLuhan and the media ecology school of thought that he created.[1] If you are just tuning into the work of Mr. McLuhan, then Season One of *24* is both an excellent primer for exegesis of the show and for an introduction to the media ecology perspective.

Manhattan's twin towers fell on September 11, 2001. Within six weeks of that event, on October 26, 2001, the USA PATRIOT Act was passed with no debate. Two weeks later, on November 6, 2001,[2] Episode 1 of Season One of *24* aired for the first time on Fox TV.[3] The opening shot of the season is the twin towers of Kuala Lumpur,

1 The Media Ecology Program at New York University's Department of Culture and Communication was founded by Neil Postman in 1971 and survived until his death in 2003. It was known as the New York School of media ecology; it owes its existence to what is now known as the Toronto School of media ecology, whose work is presently carried on by the Canadian scholars whose work or studies were influenced by McLuhan's Centre for Culture and Technology, which existed from its founding in 1963 to McLuhan's death in 1980. Both "schools" have active members in the Media Ecology Association, founded in 1998 by Lance Strate (chair of the Fordham University Communication and Media Studies program, and a former student of Neil Postman's), with a website at www.media-ecology.org.
2 In 1998, November 6 was also the release date of significance for the movie *The Siege*, whose poster's headline declared, "On November 6, Our Freedom Is History." The film deals with the loss of civil liberties after martial law is declared in response to Muslim terrorist bombings in New York City. Civil libertarians and conspiracy theorists kicked up a stink about the film prior to 9/11, and afterwards many saw it as the *Wag The Dog* film that scripted many of the 9/11 events and subsequent political fallout.
3 Fox TV is Rupert Murdoch's station, long known to be the furthest to the right on the ideological spectrum among the major networks. This mirroring of the show's "realness" in a political climate that matches it, is one of the great uncommented reasons for the show's popularity. Just as a caption reflects and confirms the reality of the photograph above it, so does *24* act as the caption for the images we see on the nightly news. Neither one may, in fact, be real, but by virtue of their mutual confirmation of each other, even far-left liberals, moderates, and independents are ga-ga over the show.

the world's then-tallest buildings. The first character we meet, Victor Rovner, introduces us to the three technologies that drive the story-line of the show. In order of appearance, they are the cell phone, the Internet-connected computer, and the geosynchronous satellite. Of these, the cell phone is the visible manifestation on earth of what has been true in the heavens since the late 1960s. McLuhan pointed out that the satellite makes a proscenium arch over the planet and, no offense to Shakespeare, turns the whole world into a literal stage. By extension, this makes every human an actor on that stage, with the implication that someone is always watching. This total surveillance society is only possible by virtue of the cell phone-to-satellite matrix, which makes everyone with a switched-on cell phone traceable to within 3 meters of his or her actual, realtime location.

To Heraclitus' ancient dictum that "war is the father of all things," McLuhan added, "War is never anything less than accelerated technological change."[4] *24* emphasizes the implicit corollary: techno-logical progress is the history of conquerors. Like the Internet—the information superhighway leased to the citizenry during times of peace—the cell phone is also a technological outgrowth of the mod-ern battlefield's need for wireless communication. Thus, most late twentieth-century communications gadgets are properly understood as stealth military technologies that have been declassified due to overexposure in the modern urban warfare zone. In practice, this has also meant that the time lag between military and civilian use of a technology has gotten shorter and shorter. And this decreased lag is precisely the drama borne out in Season One of *24*. In every episode we witness the tension between Jack Bauer's civilian life and his mili-tary life, and then see it magnified when his wife, in her search for their daughter, calls in to Nina for "favors"—almost always in the form of an extralegal use of military technology to track and trace her daughter's kidnappers. Because Jack is such a loving father, he has to continually circumvent CTU protocol in order to save his family; because his wife is an equally aggressive defender of the sanctity of the home, she too will break convention to acquire the tools and techniques necessary to serve justice. The message to the viewer is clear: you must fight to the death if you want to keep your family

4 *Understanding Media* (New York: McGraw-Hill, 1964), p. 101.

together. As such, the show embodies two of McLuhan's most prophetic insights: (1) "World War Three—A TV guerilla war with no division between civil and military fronts,"[5] and (2) "Under conditions of rapid change, the family unit is subject to special strain."[6]

After Kuala Lumpur, the first character in America we meet is CTU's own Richard Walsh, when he says "Excuse me a moment" in order to take a cell phone call. We learn that Senator Palmer's life is in danger. In the next scene, we meet the Bauer family and within two minutes Jack receives a phone call from his colleague Nina requiring him to get to CTU immediately.

And that's the set-up. For the next 24 hours, a series of cell phone calls between these four elements—(1) CTU, (2) Palmer's campaign, (3) the Bauers, and (4) the escalating layers of "bad guys"—will heighten our tension, increase our heart rates, and sell us the fear so necessary to maintaining our interest in the show and the terror-ridden world it wants us to believe we live in. Almost every scene will use the cell phone as the narrative device deployed to rapidly yank us into the next scene, and visually premature jump cuts will make sense only by accompanying voiceovers of a phone call between two discrete locations. We constantly see characters in search of each other as simultaneously being so close, yet so far away. For each scene with a cell phone in it, there is a subsequent scene with a missed call, a misunderstood word, a dying battery, a bad reception, a call waiting, a please-leave-a-message-after-the-beep, a plaintive, "Why didn't you call?"

The Splintered Life

Touted by its makers as being "ripped from today's headlines" (a phrase also associated with *Law and Order*), 24 will progress to the point where it comes to mirror the paranoid emotional state so familiar to any habitual news-watcher, and progress from there to actually

5 *Take Today: The Executive As Drop-Out* (New York: Harcourt Brace Jovanovich, 1972), p. 152.

6 *The Mechanical Bride* (New York: Vanguard, 1951), p. 156. Hereafter cited parenthetically in the text as *Mechanical Bride*.

become a proxy or substitute for the news itself. Oddly, this will be accompanied by a sense of relief and gratitude, because the show is about as accurate at monitoring the prescribed state of fear as the daily color-coded terror alerts were, which is to say they represent a sort of national mood ring, and should long ago have moved to the weather segment of the news. In our increasingly busy, multi-tasking lives, where both mom and dad have to work in order to make the mortgage, the rising cost of gas, and cover the decreasing value of the dollar, *24* will become the placebo antidote for the fact that we never spend meaningful time together anymore, except, perhaps, on the cell phone. The show will mirror our personal reality while confirming our growing fear of a fantastic but seemingly real external threat, and thereby win the domestic war on terror before a single shot is fired—simply by coercing us into an entertained acceptance of the world the news media presents to us. As a bonus, the show will offer us the illusion of a lone white male hero who defends all that we most dearly wish to be possible—a sane, intact, and meaningful family life in a sane, intact, and meaningful society. If he dies, we die, and in our allegiance to Jack Bauer we pledge our allegiance to the State that produced him, the National Emergency Entertainment State[7] from which there is no escape, no chance of opting out, and nothing to do but sit tight and hope you survive the repetition and escalation of the

---

7 By "National Emergency Entertainment State" I am not hyperbolizing, but referring to the increasing confluence of (1) *entertainment as distraction from the realities of our political economy* and (2) *fear of the unknown as coercive guarantor of participation* as being the two dominant factors in American life. Independently, they are cause for concern, but when combined, they make for odd bedfellows indeed. My favorite example of this came in the summer of 2004 when Coca-Cola produced the "You Can Win, But You Can't Hide!" campaign, in which a GPS navigation device and an RFID chip were installed in special cans of Coke sold in 12-packs. The idea was that you could drink Coke all summer, but if you won the lucky can, *you couldn't get away no matter where you were* from the corporation that would show up "Wherever you are!" to reward you with a 3,600 pound Chevy Equinox SUV delivered by helicopter—a quasi-military operation in and of itself. Whether intentional or not, the campaign combined the pleasure of summer fun with the horror of a total surveillance society in such a bizarre combination that it made the Constitutionally guaranteed freedom to "the pursuit of happiness" seem like it had become a mandatory law that was now intermittently demanded of citizens in order to sustain capitalist democracy itself. If the Coke campaign was the second of such imperial decrees, the first came when President Bush urged Americans, three days after 9/11, to go to Disney World.

formula from Season One to Season Seven, to whenever the next "War On Abstractions"[8] is declared.

It is not surprising that it makes for deadly serious entertainment. The first season had exactly zero jokes, laughs, or comic relief moments. It was as dreary as going through airport security, the one semantic environment where joke-telling is literally against the law. And as tragedy, it is constant: the constant tragedy of raising kids! The constant tragedy of the war on terror! The constant tragedy of American race relations! The constant tragedy of American politics! Of trying to win Orange County! Of petty criminals! Of Kosovar blowback! Of trying to save your marriage! Of overlapping story-lines! Of being two people at once! Of being three! As the screen splits, so too does Bauer's personality—father, husband, agent, lover, friend, employee, criminal, hero, savior! At one point, Bauer asks for cameras to cover every square inch of the adjacent hotel room, giving him two angles of every area. This is the multi-tasking porn that makes up large portions of the show itself, and that we are required to see Jack in light of: yes, he's the CTU top agent protecting the president, but right now he's got to kill the president in order to save him. We understand the necessity of schizophrenia, quadrophenia, or whatever it takes to get you through the night. And we only understand this because we have the necessary accessory to the splintered life, the cell phone.

The phone that keeps us together. Keeps our illusions tabulated. Keeps our data, our dates, our birthdays, our important memos, our urgent must-do lists. Keeps us amused with games in between all that seriousness.

---

8 In living American historical memory, these abstractions are The War on Hunger, The War on Poverty, The War on Drugs, The War on Illiteracy and The War on Terrorism. In all cases they are endless wars because the enemy is an undefeatable abstraction. Not to be crass, but the poor, hungry, drugged, illiterate, and violent will always be with us. Literacy, the one really achievable goal of a culture for the majority of its citizens, is perhaps the one goal most actively being avoided in America today. Unlike poverty or hunger (somewhat overlapping issues), literacy is at least a "solve it once, solve it for a lifetime" type of problem, whereas hunger could strike anyone up to three times a day.

Gender Blender

It is precisely its ability to capture the splintered life so well that allows *24* to offer something entirely new in the history of television: a genre and gender blender of media consumption. McLuhan said, "Horse opera like the sports page, is a man's world, free from the problems of domesticity. Soap opera is a woman's world, laden with personal problems" (*Mechanical Bride*, 157). *24* is a brilliantly original combination of these two. It is the sexual tension of Scully and Mulder, but this time with children, marital difficulties, curfews, and counselors thrown in. It is daytime television plus primetime television. It is TV for him and her, in one program, implicitly acknowledging that both men and women have no time anymore, since each is required to be at work 24/7/365. No time to relax, no time to watch TV, no time to work on relationships, in fact no time for anything except possibly a one-hour show that can take care of all of it. *24* is that one show that husbands and wives can watch together, tolerate each other through the end of, and thereby confirm both their relationship commitment as well as its problems, its malleability, and its hope of a solution. It is the serial suspense of the cliffhanger meeting the morbid magnetism and endless escalation of the soap opera drama. *24* is a cliff opera at best, a soap hanger at worst. While it is arguable that the show's femininity is of a rather masculine nature, that is merely indicative of the times we live in, itself largely a subset of the technology and media available to us.[9] But for McLuhan, writing in 1951, the picture was quite different, and in the time between then and now we see how far we've come in media consciousness. He uses the term "horse opera" instead of "cliff hanger," but with that one substitution we see quite clearly what *24* hath wrought:

> Horse opera and soap opera, then, embody two of the most important American traditions, the frontier and the home town. But the two traditions are split rather than fused. They show that radical separation between business and society, between action and feeling, office and home, between men and women, which is so characteristic of industrial man. These divisions cannot be mended until their fullest extent is perceived. (*Mechanical Bride*, 157)

9   On this topic, see my forthcoming book, *The Disappearance of Women: Technology, Pornography, and the Obsolescence of Gender* (Dallas: Spence, 2008).

And there it is: the cell phone is the primary technological mechanism by which "these divisions" have been mended, because the cell phone is the communication technology that forces us to perceive, beyond any reasonable doubt, that the border between business and society, between office and home, between men and women, has indeed entirely collapsed in on itself. And the cell phone is both a pusher and enforcer of this new perception. It's a distracting form of entertainment as well as a serious social obligation. Thanks to the cell phone, we are now always at work, even while at home. Every day we come home exhausted, we both identify with Jack Bauer—"Today is the longest day of my life"—and we feel comforted by his existence because, unlike Jack, we will at least get some sleep. Thanks to the cell phone, we are now always talking to our spouse, even while at work, while commuting, while at the gym, while coming home— "Should I pick up anything?" We are now always socializing while working, and working while socializing. For a man to have two cell phones—one for the wife, one for the mistress—is no longer a sign of being Italian. Even today's increased emphasis on sexual contact was predicted by McLuhan as the price for living in the modern city, to compensate for the incredible loneliness and anxiety that the city produces.

Events Occur In Real Time

While the show is the first to "occur in real time," the reality behind the scenes is quite different:

- Two episodes are filmed simultaneously over a period of 15 days.
- Completing an entire season, including pre- and post-production work, takes ten and a half months.
- Roughly 25 hours of footage are edited into one episode of the show.[10]

Like the law of animation, the production of this seemingly "real-time" show comes at a very high cost. Think of it as primetime maple syrup: just as you need 40 gallons of sap to make 1 gallon of liquid

---

10   See www.imdb.com/title/tt0285331/trivia.

gold, so too does one full 24-hour day require nearly a year of intense coordinated effort. The resulting concentration of production effort into a golden hour of programming actually results in a show that is, in fact, only 42 minutes long. The commercial breaks take 3 minutes each. And yet the effect on the viewer is equally exhausting— watching these 42 minutes feels like a full day's work. When the commercial break does come, we see the minute counter while hearing the offscreen audio tickdown, echoing the human heartbeat pumping at full volume. The rhythmia comes back when the show resumes. The only time the audience can breathe is during the commercials. This implies a subtle corollary within the action of the show itself— during commercial breaks, no crisis gets to its breaking point—the characters themselves can take these few minutes, sponsored by corporate America, to relax and regroup. This one-third of each real-world hour is, in external and objective fact, how much time the average American is not plugged in during his or her waking life. Nearly 12 hours of a 16-hour day are spent engaged in some form of mass media, according to the 2004 Ball State study.[11] Even ten years earlier, Leslie Savan estimated that the average city dweller ingests some 16,000 commercial icons, images, ads, jingles, or logos every day.[12] On *24*, the product placement within the show is massive and clearly proportional to the regular advertising budget, both of which are apparently necessary to equal the show's production budget— within the first half of Episode 1 of Season One, we are made conscious by name and logo of Adidas, Coldplay, Greenday, 2Pac, Apple Ibook, Molson Canadian Beer, GMC Yukon XL SUV, Walgreens, AT&T, and Ericsson. The real purpose of the commercial break, as everyone knows by now, is to pick up your cell phone to find out if your friends are watching the same show. You have to get your "Oh my God, I can't believe they killed her!" into your friend's ear before the show resumes.[13]

---

11   The study was done in 2003, the report issued in 2004. See the press release from the Middletown Media Studies Report from the Center for Media Design at Ball State University, online at www.bsu.edu/icommunication/news/stories/february/2_25_03.html.
12   Leslie Savan, *The Sponsored Life* (Philadelphia: Temple University Press, 1994).
13   Some of the dramatic implications of *24*'s "realtime" format are discussed in Paul A. Cantor's chapter.

Today is the Longest Day of My Life

Part of the exhaustion of the show for the viewer is the simultaneity of the events, requiring us to pay attention at all times to all subplots.[14] Jack Bauer is never somewhere, he is always everywhere thanks to being Jacked-in to what Adam Greenfield calls everyware:[15] ubiquitous communication technology that won't allow us the twentieth-century luxury of separating the personal from the professional. What starts out as a split-screen ends up as a four-screen image by the end of the show, and by Episode 2 we are up to five screens. As Jack walks in, he opens this metaphor for the viewer, while conversing on the cell phone with Teri about their marital stress: "I was thinking we should try to remember what it was like when we were kids, you know." She responds, "It's a different world now, Jack." Jack responds, "Yeah, I know." The show is both a celebration and lament of this "different world now" from the parents' point of view. To the younger generation, when not out raving or being killed by the "different world," it is not so shiny. When Jack and Teri have to hack in to their daughter's computer to find out where she is, the first obstacle is her password. Jack says, "We gave her her own password to show that we trusted her, remember?" After hacking in, Jack discovers that his daughter's password is "lifesucks."

This "Everywhere" phenomenon is partly responsible for the peculiar blurring of the lines between fact and fiction; it's as though they no longer inhabit two distinct realms. Indeed, *24* has created some rather unusual conflations of reality and entertainment. Some highlights, which you may recall from the last few years:

---

14 This exhaustion may be evidence of my personal struggle here, and not the common experience: I have never owned a television nor lived in a house with one. Steven Johnson, in *Everything Bad Is Good For You: How Today's Popular Culture Is Actually Making Us Smarter* (New York: Riverhead, 2005) argues that plot complexity and rapidity (in shows like *24*) actually educate us to watching smarter, closer, and with more attention to subtle detail. If this essay is any indication, Johnson is either dead on, or else dropped out of Columbia graduate school just before he got to the good stuff.

15 See Greenfield's book, *Everyware: The Dawning Age of Ubiquitous Computing* (Berkeley: New Riders, 2006).

- Officials at the Council on American-Islamic Relations met with producers back in 2005 when the *24* plot revolved around Muslim fundamentalists, and they were upset again because Season Six seems to portray members of their religion in the same shady light. Council spokesman Rabiah Ahmed says, "The overwhelming impression you get is fear and hatred for Muslims. After watching the premiere, I was afraid to go to the grocery store because I wasn't sure the person next to me would be able to differentiate between fiction and reality."

- *The New Yorker* magazine reported that Brigadier General Patrick Finnegan, Dean of the US Military Academy at West Point and an eminent military lawyer, had flown to California to meet producers of *24*. Finnegan reportedly told the producers that promoting illegal behavior on the show was having a damaging effect on US troops in Iraq. Finnegan told the magazine, "The kids see it and say, 'If torture is wrong, what about *24*?'" In response, Gordon (one of the show's producers) told the *Inquirer*, "The thesis that we are affecting our soldiers in Iraq in their treatment of prisoners is being exaggerated, I think. Hopefully, there are a lot of filters between their watching *24* and their work in the field."

- Dennis Haysbert was furious when he found out that his character on *24*, President David Palmer, was being assassinated and told producers he would refuse to tape the scene. The star argued over the storyline for months because he felt killing the president would send out a dangerous message to viewers. Haysbert appeared on the chat show *The View* where he explained how he left the show saying, "They did it as a stunt to get ratings and it worked. It started at the end of Season Four when I did the last six episodes. Then I thought I was done. I was right in the middle of the fourth episode I was doing when they called me up at lunch time to talk to me and said, 'Dennis, on the first show of next season, we're going to shoot you.' I said, 'Good luck with that. What's it going to be: a CNN (news) report? Because I won't shoot it.' So we went back and forth and back and forth and the season ended and all during the summer the fellows kept calling and then they sent their mercenary, one of my best friends on the show, the show runner Howard Gordon, whom I love, and I have to tell you before I go any further that I love the guys on *24*, both in front of the camera and behind it. We have a legacy of killing our leaders in this country and I said, 'Guys, don't do it.' Howard basically said, 'Dennis, look I understand how you feel. I believe you, I believe in what you're saying, but we need it to start the show, because without it, we don't have a season.'"[16]

That the actors and the audience are increasingly unable to separate reality from fantasy is no small matter. In another context Michael Crichton has said, "The greatest challenge facing mankind is the challenge of distinguishing reality from fantasy, truth from propaganda"[17]—which makes you wonder if he too is a fan of *24*. Is that too paranoid? Well, McLuhan predicted that as well—in his tetrad analysis of the satellite he pointed out that, in retrieving ecology, the satellite simultaneously returns us to primitive man's state, and that "the primitive regards everything as related to everything—a condition we recognize as paranoia."[18] And this paranoia, of course, happens without our conscious awareness: "The effects of technology do not occur at the level of opinions or concepts, but alter sense ratios or patterns of perception without any resistance."[19] If you've never thought of *24* as a documentary of the cell phone's effect on your life until now, well that's why.

Gotta Go

Listen, I can't talk much longer. If you need more, consult the full works of Marshall McLuhan. Meanwhile, maybe turn your cell phone off and try to get some rest—tomorrow's going to be the longest day of your life.

16   All quotes taken from www.imdb.com/title/tt0285331/news.
17   Crichton said this in a speech to the Commonwealth Club, September 15, 2003, available at www.michaelcrichton.com/speeches/speeches_quote05.html.
18   *Laws of Media* (Toronto: University of Toronto Press, 1988), p. 150.
19   *Understanding Media* (New York: McGraw-Hill, 1964), p. 33.

24 and the Ethics of Objectification

Robert Arp and John Carpenter

Doing the Right Thing Without the Necessary Means

Using people as bait, kidnapping innocents, torturing prisoners, hijacking airplanes, holding hostages, threatening to infect someone with a deadly virus, and shooting unarmed individuals—not only are these examples of tactics used by terrorists in 24, but each was also employed by Jack Bauer in his efforts to stop them. Why does he resort to such extreme methods? The answer can be found in the introduction to Season One, when Kiefer Sutherland describes the show as "the story of a man constantly trying to do the right thing, but not having the necessary means to do it."[1] Here *necessary* is not meant literally (after all, how would Jack always be able to get the job done?), but rather in the sense of *preferable*. Again and again, Jack is forced to do things that he would rather not, if there were any other options. Yet, might not the terrorists justify their radical actions with similar sentiments? For the most part, they would prefer *not* to kill millions of civilians but they believe, as Marie Warner says in Season Two, that "people have to die for things to change." The natural question to ask, and the main question that we investigate here, is this: When and to what degree is it permissible to use people as means rather than ends?

Objects—like knives, escalators, and remote controls—are lifeless things that can be used by people as tools to get what they want. In the context of this chapter, the word *objectification* refers to the act

---

1 Season One, DVD number 6, special features.

of treating people as if they were objects—that is, as solely means for some end. For example, in Season One, Alexis Drazen objectifies Elizabeth Nash not only by using her to get privileged information about David Palmer but also, undoubtedly, for sexual gratification. The objectification of Ms. Nash is especially clear when Alexis's brother, Andre, makes him promise to kill her when she is no longer of any use. Ironically, Ms. Nash soon thereafter allows herself to be used by CTU for the purposes of monitoring the Drazens, and is so overcome with rage that she stabs Alexis, thereby treating *him* as an object. Examples like these are found throughout *24* episodes, as characters frequently use each other to gain revenge, information, and power. While treating people as mere means intuitively strikes many of us as wrong, is that belief really warranted?

There are three prominent moral theories in the history of philosophy that can help us understand the ethics of objectification. First, there is the view originated by Immanuel Kant (1724–1804) that persons, by virtue of their conscious rational capacities, are free and autonomous beings having an inalienable worth or dignity. Because of this intrinsic worth, a person should *never* be treated as a mere object. In Season Three, we learn that terrorists are using Kyle Singer not merely as a "mule" to transport drugs, but they have possibly infected him with a virus that would have turned him into a biological weapon. After realizing this, Kyle is so despondent that he tries to commit suicide to prevent the virus from getting out. But even in that case, Kant's philosophy implies that Kyle will have acted wrongly, since if he takes his own life, he will have used *himself* as a mere means.

Second, there is the utilitarian view, found in the philosophy of John Stuart Mill (1806–1873), which asserts that actions are morally good insofar as they maximize the collective happiness of all people. On this view, rampant objectification is immoral because unhappiness typically thrives where everyone is worried that they will be exploited in their social interactions. Consider how trust, safety, and success are often undermined in the CTU when one person decides to withhold vital information from another. For example, in Season One, George Mason justifies keeping the fact that Jack's wife and daughter are missing from him based on the rationale that he needs to stay "focused," so he can do his job. As a result, Jack only finds out that Kim has been recaptured by the Drazens when he is also helplessly in their custody.

Third, there is the classical virtue ethics view, held by Aristotle (384–322 BCE), that sees morally right actions as stemming from virtuous characters. Here, objectification can be considered immoral because it originates from, as well as reinforces, a non-virtuous (vicious) character. Think about how President Logan's vile nature is gradually revealed throughout Seasons Four and Five. At first it just seems as if he is too cowardly to be a reliable leader, and he partially redeems himself by recognizing the fact and bringing Palmer in to help him. However, Logan not only repays Palmer by taking the majority of credit for successfully managing a crisis, but he is later complicit in Palmer's assassination! Such despicable behavior is exactly what a virtue ethicist would expect from someone having a weak or wicked character.

However, there *are* times when each of these theories suggests that someone actually has done the right thing in objectifying another person. First, a Kantian might argue that it's morally acceptable for a person—by virtue of being a rational, autonomous agent—to give permission to be used by others. In Season Two, isn't Kate Warner right to volunteer to go into the mosque and identify Syed Ali, in spite of how risky the situation is? Second, a utilitarian might argue that it's morally acceptable to sacrifice a member of a group in order to save the rest of its members. An emotionally charged example of this is when, later in that season, it becomes clear that it isn't possible to disable the nuclear bomb and someone must fly it to a safe location and crash the plane. At first, Jack takes the role of the pilot and, as his heart-wrenching farewell to Kim shows, he is willing to die to stop the bomb. (It turns out, however, that the terminally ill Mason is hiding on the plane, later convincing Jack to let him take it down.) Finally, virtue ethicists might declare that prudence is the best disposition or character state to exemplify, even if that entails objectifying others. For example, in Season Three, President Palmer wants to get reelected, but Alan Milliken threatens to subvert his campaign. To prevent that from happening, Palmer enlists his ex-wife, Sherry, to dig up dirt on Milliken. Instead, she literally takes matters into her own hands and watches Milliken die while clutching his medicine. While David and Sherry disagree about how much objectification is permissible for the sake of prudence, both agree that *some* objectification is acceptable.

In this chapter, we use examples such as these to illustrate moral "stalemates" or inconsistencies for the Kantian and utilitarian systems.

These stalemates call the legitimacy of the two approaches into question concerning their outlooks on objectification. This leaves virtue ethics as most viable of the three major moral perspectives, if for the primary reason that it does not clearly generate such stalemates. After comparing and contrasting the three different virtue ethics positions advocated by Aristotle, Niccolò Machiavelli (1469–1527) and Friedrich Nietzsche (1844–1900), we ask the reader to decide which of the three provides the best grounds for understanding the ethics of objectification.

Sanctity, Autonomy, and a Kantian Moral Stalemate

Kant grounds morality in the fact that persons are rational beings. Since it is only by reason that we determine and perform our moral obligations, rational will—the expression of our freewill by acting in accordance with rationality instead of irrationality and sensuality—is the only thing that is unconditionally good. By virtue of the fact that all people possess rationality, they are worthy of dignity and respect, and are the only things that are "ends in themselves." Given that people are entirely precious in this way, they always have *intrinsic* value (as ends) and must never be treated as having merely *instrumental* value (as a means to an end) like some instrument. So, it would be immoral for one person to use another exclusively as a means to further some end, goal, or purpose since, by doing so, the used person is reduced to the status of a lowly tool.[2]

A few examples from 24 will make this point clear. First, consider Jack's execution of Ryan Chappelle at the terrorist's behest. Faced with the choice of having a lethal virus unleashed or killing Chappelle, President Palmer, Jack, and even Chappelle all grudgingly agree that the sacrifice is necessary. Second, think about when Tony prevents a terrorist from being captured by CTU in order to save Michelle's life in Season Three. While the terrorist shamelessly uses Michelle as a mere means, Tony won't allow her to be treated as such, even to the

2   See Immanuel Kant, *Foundations of the Metaphysics of Morals*, trans. Lewis White Beck (Upper Saddle River, NJ: Prentice-Hall, 1989). See also Onora O'Neill, *Constructions of Reason: Explorations of Kant's Practical Philosophy* (Cambridge: Cambridge University Press, 1990).

point of endangering his career and national security. Finally, recall that rare instance when, in Season Four, a character in the show both recognizes and objects to being objectified. After CTU agent Curtis Manning promises to protect Behrooz Araz, the son of two key terrorists in that day's attacks, Behrooz complains, "You don't care about me or your word. You're just using me."

Given that persons are conscious, rational beings, capable of making their own free and informed decisions, Kant demands that they also be respected in virtue of being *autonomous* ("self-ruling") beings. Now since a person's innate dignity and worth are tied to rational autonomy, some post-Kantian thinkers have argued that what is most significant in making a moral decision has to do with whether a person's *freedom in rationally informed decision-making* has been respected.[3] The idea here is that if a fully rational person chooses to engage in some action—as long as the action doesn't harm anyone else—then that person is fully justified in doing it, even if it puts him or her in the position of being used like an object. Think of rational adults joining the military knowing that they may die protecting their country. Similarly, as long as the henchmen of the terrorists in *24* know full well the risks that they are assuming by aiding and abetting criminals, there is nothing immoral in the terrorists treating them as if they were dispensable. In other words, as long as these rational agents all freely agree to engage in such behaviors, then there is nothing morally wrong in objectifying them.

But how is one to decide whether we should ever use people as mere instruments, or whether fully rational persons should have the freedom to make their own well-informed decisions? There is one camp of "moral sanctity" Kantians who would argue that it's immoral to objectify a person—no matter what. Thinkers like Dworkin and MacKinnon endorse this position.[4] But there is another group of "moral autonomy" Kantians who would contend that, as long as all parties are fully aware of the risks of the situation, nothing immoral

3 See Thomas Hill, *Autonomy and Self Respect* (New York: Cambridge University Press, 1991); Christine Korsgaard, *The Sources of Normativity* (New York: Cambridge University Press, 1996); and Timothy Madigan, "The Discarded Lemon: Kant, Prostitution and Respect for Persons," *Philosophy Now* 21 (1998): 14–16.
4 Andrea Dworkin, *Pornography: Men Possessing Women* (New York: Perigee Press, 1981); Catherine MacKinnon, *Feminism Unmodified: Discourses on Life and Law* (Cambridge, MA: Harvard University Press, 1988).

occurs in consensual objectification. In fact, they often argue that to deny a person the freedom so to choose would itself be immoral because such a denial violates a person's autonomy as a rational, free decision-maker. In other words, refusing to allow people to make their own choices is to reduce them to objects since, after all, mere objects lack choices. Garry, Madigan, and Schwarzenbach have argued along these lines.[5] Here we have a stalemate, since for a Kantian to say whether Jack was right or wrong in executing Chappelle, he or she would have to assume that autonomy is more valuable than sanctity or vice versa. Based on Kant's philosophy, however, neither can be more important than the other—both are indispensable.

The Absurdity of Maximizing Happiness: A Utilitarian Moral Stalemate

While most utilitarians would admit that both sanctity and autonomy are important,[6] the foundation of morality, as far as they're concerned, is simply happiness—actions are good insofar as, in general, they increase the pleasures or decrease the pains of people. The reason this view is termed *utilitarian* is because the true test of an action's propriety is whether it has useful consequences (utility) with respect to promoting happiness. In opposition to the strict Kantian view that persons should never be used merely as means to some end, the utilitarian position has no problem treating some people as means if, as a result, the sum total of happiness is increased for all people.[7]

24 abounds with examples of actions justified by utilitarian-type reasons. In every season, we find terrorists objectifying people to achieve some goal. In Season Four, for example, Jack explicitly attributes the

---

5   Ann Garry, "Pornography and Respect for Women," in *Morality and Moral Controversies*, ed. John Arthur (Upper Saddle River, NJ: Prentice-Hall, 1993), pp. 395–421; Timothy Madigan, "The Discarded Lemon: Kant, Prostitution and Respect for Persons," *Philosophy Now* 21 (1998): 14–16; Sibyl Schwarzenbach, "On Owning the Body," in *Prostitution: On Whores, Hustlers, and Johns*, ed. James Elias, Vern Bullough, Veronica Elias, and Gwen Brewer (New York: Prometheus Books, 1998), pp. 345–51.

6   See, for example, John Stuart Mill, *On Liberty* (New York: Meridian, 1974).

7   Jeremy Bentham, *An Introduction to the Principles of Morals and Legislation* (Garden City, NY: Doubleday, 1961); John Stuart Mill, *Utilitarianism* (Indianapolis: Hackett, 2002); Peter Singer, *Practical Ethics* (Cambridge: Cambridge University Press, 1993).

following belief to the terrorist Habib Marwan: "the death and destruction of innocent life is the means to an end." Often, even Jack rationalizes aggressive conduct by referring to the outcome. For instance, in Season Three, he justifies putting a gun to Chase Edmunds' head by saying, "Chase, listen to me. You do this job long enough, you're going to have to make choices, and you don't know you've made the right one until the whole scenario plays itself out." Finally, the conflict between Kantianism and utilitarianism is never clearer than when, in Season Two, it appears as if Jack is willing to kill Syed Ali's children and wife in order to get information on the bomb's location. When President Palmer learns about this plan, the following dialogue ensues between him and his Chief of Staff, Mike Novick:

Palmer: Can we let this happen? Condone the murder of innocent people?

Novick: The argument would be that the bomb is an act of war and wars inevitably result in civilian casualties.

Palmer: But I don't want a rationale here Mike. I don't know of a war where a president knowingly targeted children for assassination.

Novick: Compare this to a weapons factory we discover is near a hospital—a situation we have faced. The bombing would still be ordered on the logic that many more people would be saved by the destruction of the factory. Now, the numbers are even more compelling here. A few people may have to die to save millions.

Palmer: How could it have come to this?

In the end, Palmer does *not* sanction the killings, but Jack pretends that the president *has* authorized them and then fakes killing one of Ali's sons. Ali, transforming from killer to Kantian, protects the rest of his family by confessing.

Now, in the last section, we noted that Kant's theory presents us with a moral stalemate because it implies that objectification is *both* right and wrong in some scenarios. Yet another stalemate arises from the utilitarian perspective. A strict utilitarian must admit that an action is good, no matter how horribly some people are treated, so long as more people benefit in the long run.[8] This means that if killing

---

8 That "goods" can result from "evils" has also been argued for by many thinkers to justify the existence of God or the forces of nature in the face of egregious evil. Classical examples are G. W. Leibniz, *Theodicy* (London: Routledge & Kegan Paul, 1996) and Viktor Frankl, *Man's Search for Meaning* (Boston: Beacon Press, 1959). For more contemporary work, see *Dialogues in the Philosophy of Religion*, ed. John Hick (New York: Macmillan, 2001).

certain people will increase the overall happiness of humanity, then murder is not only permissible, but downright advisable. For example, if you are a healthy person, it is likely that more public benefit could come from you donating all of your organs than using them yourself. That is, if they were given up for transplantation, your liver could save one person's life, and your lungs could save another, and so on. Furthermore, if you gave your body to science—say, letting scientists induce a lethal disease in you so that they could study how it develops—the knowledge gained as a result could save *millions*. Thus a utilitarian regards such self-sacrifice as obligatory, and if you decline to give up your life, other people are justified in taking it to get "results" (*à la* Jack killing and decapitating Marshall Goren at the beginning of Season Two).

Maybe a few utilitarians could bite the bullet and claim that this conclusion is acceptable, but most of them would admit that it is too extreme.[9] While mandatory self-sacrifice would create a tremendous amount of happiness for some people, the amount of misery left behind by the widows, families, and friends of the departed would be nonetheless substantial. Such a system would induce paranoia, undermine security, and destroy humanity as we know it, thereby making it worse. Indeed, you can imagine this state of affairs culminating in a single living person, so pleased with his solitude that killing everyone else was warranted. Such an outcome is not merely tragicomic, it is absurd. A utilitarian stalemate, then, results from the fact that by holding the greatest happiness of the greatest number in such high regard, it *unacceptably* advocates decreasing the number of people as a means of increasing the overall happiness of the community.

---

9 See J. J. C. Smart, "An Outline of a System of Utilitarian Ethics," in *Utilitarianism: For and Against*, ed. J. J. C. Smart and Bernard Williams (New York: Cambridge University Press, 1973). Smart's position gave rise to the following infamous entry in *The Philosophical Lexicon*, 8th Edition (1987), ed. Daniel Dennett: "outsmart, v. To embrace the conclusion of one's opponent's *reductio ad absurdum* argument. 'They thought they had me, but I outsmarted them. I agreed that it *was* sometimes just to hang an innocent man.'" This lexicon is available online at www.blackwellpublishing.com/lexicon/.

The Virtue Ethics Perspective

Opposed to these *action-based* moral theories, which first establish what people should do and then assess whether they have actually done so, there are *character-based* theories, centering on how people actually behave and then determining how they should have acted. The idea here—noted by philosophers as far back as Confucius (551–479 BCE) and Plato (427–347 BCE)—is that different people have different characters.[10] Aristotle, in particular, thinks that character development was the key to morality. As he sees things, our characters result from (1) forming certain habits starting in childhood and (2) acquiring practical wisdom in maturity. Ideally, people will cultivate the habits and form the wisdom that will lead them to know how to routinely act in the right way, at the right time, in the right manner, and for the right reasons. He famously believes that the character states grounding such a life form a mean between two extremes. For example, courageous people are neither cowardly nor reckless, but somewhere in between. Unfortunately, many people fail to achieve such a balanced temperament and end up either continent, incontinent, or downright vicious. The first know what is right, act accordingly but occasionally falter; the second are weak-willed and often acting wrongly; and the third simply refuse to do what they know is right.[11]

Aristotle's theory is exemplified by several characters in *24*. Jack's struggle with drug addiction (starting in Season Three) clearly illustrates just how powerful the force of habit can be. Even though he starts doing drugs for the sake of catching the Salazars, he continues to use when the mission ended, even to the point of lying to Kim and the rest of his co-workers. He wants to stop of course; but like all addicts isn't able to simply "will" himself to do so. The only way to overcome such destructive behavior is to strive to change one's character. As Aristotle says, "by abstaining from pleasures we become

---

10 Confucius, *The Analects of Confucius*, trans. Arthur Waley (New York: Vintage Books, 1938); Plato, *The Republic of Plato*, trans. Allan Bloom (New York: Basic Books, 1991).
11 Aristotle, *Nicomachean Ethics*, trans. David Ross, in *The Basic Works of Aristotle*, ed. Richard McKeon (New York: Random House, 1941). See also Alasdair MacIntyre, *After Virtue* (Notre Dame: University of Notre Dame Press, 1981).

temperate, and it is when we have become so that we are most able to abstain from them."[12] Presumably, between Seasons Three and Four, Jack enters a rehabilitation program and is able to recover.

An example of a plainly vicious character was given earlier when we discussed President Logan. However, at the other end of the spectrum, David Palmer provides the quintessential example of Aristotle's virtuous person. Throughout Season One, in particular, Palmer's integrity and resolve betray his disposition. First, we find him confronting vandals in the parking garage, trying to warn Ferragamo that he's in danger, confessing the role that his son played in Lyle Gibson's death, refusing Patty's seduction, and finally leaving Sherry in spite of the likely impact on his campaign. But of course nobody's perfect and even David had his weak moments. In Season Three, after agreeing to pay off his girlfriend Anne's ex-husband not to go public with a rumor, they talk about his decision:

> *Palmer*: Sometimes you have to do the wrong thing for the right reason . . . I have been in this job for nearly four years and I have learned the hard way that there are no absolutes—sometimes you have to make compromises.
> *Anne*: Politically, yes, but when it comes to morality, David, you have to draw the line.
> *Palmer*: I have drawn the line, we're just standing on different sides . . .
> *Anne*: You've never been about what's easy. You've been about what's right. *That's* who you are.

He then yields to this voice of reason and decides not to go through with the pay off.

While some virtue ethicists have held that objectification stems from a lack of virtues such as honesty, courage, generosity, integrity, affability, and respect, other thinkers have argued for the cultivation of different virtues that are consistent with objectifying people. For example, Niccolò Machiavelli sees objectification as the upshot of prudence—and with it, cleverness, manipulation, scheming, and well-placed aggression.[13] Machiavelli was a historian who agreed with Thucydides (460–395 BCE) that "history is philosophy teaching by

12 *Nicomachean Ethics*, Bk. II, Ch. 2.
13 Niccolò Machiavelli, *The Prince*, trans. Daniel Donno (New York: Bantam Classics, 1984).

examples." Machiavelli looks at the history of ancient and contemporary governments and sees a Gibbon-like register of crimes, follies, and misfortunes. While it would be ideal for everyone to respect everyone else and never treat anyone as a mere means, when you look at history, you see that this is simply not the way the world works. Objectification is not only common, but sometimes vital to one's survival, especially for rulers who are constantly in danger of being deposed or worse. Machiavelli's conclusion, then, is that a ruler should preempt people treating her as a means by treating them as such first. Sherry Palmer furnishes a good example of this philosophy in action, for many of her choices stem from the belief that her family's political and personal survival depend on having to use people.

Since Machiavelli has been widely misunderstood, a couple of points are worth noting. First, while "Machiavellian" has come to be synonymous with "ruthlessness" and "cunning," Machiavelli does *not* advocate brutality and deceit for their own sake. He is simply giving honest advice to political leaders whose positions are always precarious. If a ruler needs to lie, steal, or even kill to maintain power, then such behavior is justified as the least of all evils. Secondly, it is important to distinguish Machiavelli's philosophy from Mill's utilitarianism. While both theories insist upon cost-benefit analyses of actions in terms of their consequences, they differ sharply on whom the analyses are meant for and on what counts as good consequences. Recall that Mill's advice is supposed to apply equally to everyone; it amounts to the contention that increased communal happiness is the only benefit and decreased happiness the only cost of actions. In contrast, Machiavelli does *not* preach Machiavellianism as the correct form of morality to all people, but only to a small set of ambitious ears. His insight is that a blanket claim such as Mill's neglects the unique problems presented to unique people in unique positions. The morality of someone trying to be a ruler is necessarily different from that of the common person, since rulers have to cope with dangers that most people never face. Thus, Machiavellianism is *uncharitably* applied to characters like Nina Myers and Mandy, since their cruel behaviors are purely mercenary—that is, they are venal and ignoble people being purchased by the highest bidder. Also in stark contrast to Mill, Machiavelli held neither an egalitarian nor a hedonistic standard of right, but one of *individualistic thriving*. The best actions for a ruler are those that assure maintenance of unfettered power in spite of opposition. It should now be clear that due to the subtle nature of his advice, when Machiavelli is taken out of context, he can be readily misinterpreted.

Friedrich Nietzsche believes the will to power is the ultimate virtue and expressing one's power is not contingent on being a monarch. We all must express power *if we are powerful*.[14] For him, society can be understood in the context of domineering master/slave relationships. Some people have the kind of character that gravitates toward being in control; others are prone to being controlled. For example, to use Nietzschean similes, the chief terrorists in *24* often act as powerful "birds of prey," and their victims succumb like weak "sheep." However, a proclivity for power is not limited to politicians and terrorists. Clearly, Jack is a "take charge" kind of guy who frequently dominates people by virtue of being stronger than they are. Nietzsche's point is that if Jack and others like him deny their powerful nature, they are living lesser lives simply to fall in line with the alleged virtues of conformists. When, in Season Three, Jack breaks Salazar out of prison by starting a riot, he reveals that, in a very real sense, he is superior to those trying to stop him. He objectifies the prison guards, Salazar, and even himself simply because he can.

So, What Kind of Person Do You Want to Be?

Based on these virtue ethics perspectives, can we successfully decide if and when objectification is warranted without encountering the same stalemate traps that befall the Kantian and utilitarian positions? Aristotle escapes the problems facing Kant because even if we suppose that sanctity and autonomy are equally important, a person who encroaches on either simply reveals that they have weak character. A virtuous, well-balanced person tends not to objectify others because

14 Friedrich Nietzsche, *Beyond Good and Evil*, trans. Walter Kaufmann (New York: Random House, 1966) and *The Will To Power*, trans. Walter Kaufmann (New York: Random House, 1967). For contemporary examples of virtue ethics theories employing the concept of power, see Imelda Whelehan, *Modern Feminist Thought: From Second Wave to 'Post-Feminism'* (New York: New York University Press, 1995) and Marti Hohmann, "Prostitution and Sex-Positive Feminism," in *Prostitution: On Whores, Hustlers, and Johns*, pp. 322–332.

objectification is such an extreme action. On rare occasions, however, objectification can be the right course of action. For example, when people courageously (as opposed to rashly) allow themselves to be used by others, they are demonstrating their own virtuous characters. Thus, for Aristotle, the conflict between sanctity and autonomy is illusory: one of the two is always the right target. Since Aristotle would have said that only vicious people achieve happiness at other people's expense, the difficulty that plagues utilitarianism also doesn't apply.

Machiavelli values, not heartlessness, but prudence for the sake of self-preservation. As far as he can see, full autonomy is impossible, since society necessarily restricts the freedom of each individual. Similarly, universal sanctity is a fairy tale because there always has been and always will be people who objectify others. The best we can hope for is to live in a society where, as much as possible, a ruler prevents objectification. Unfortunately, that will sometimes require that the ruler objectify people in the process. But Machiavelli has given the able ruler principles by which that can best be accomplished. Machiavelli evades the utilitarian stalemate on two fronts. First, he values the prosperity of some rather than the happiness of all. Second, since his goal is to reveal the best possible government, its implementation would indirectly promote the greatest happiness of the greatest number without having to advocate significantly decreasing the number.

Finally, Nietzsche advocates living life to your potential. If your greatest attribute is intelligence, don't feign stupidity to appease the masses. Similarly, if you're camera shy, don't try to become a movie star. Rather, just be yourself! Don't let anyone tell you what you should believe, or that sanctity is a virtue. In fact, it is a vice meant to make you live like everyone else. Instead, determine for yourself what to believe, and you will experience joyful wisdom of which most people aren't even capable. Simply put: always express your autonomy, and you will never act "wrong." Nietzsche does not encounter the Kantian stalemate because, for him, autonomy is clearly more important than sanctity. He also sidesteps the utilitarian problem because he is not concerned with egalitarian principles at all. Utilitarians are just those who have been brainwashed into thinking all men are created equal and deserve equality. This is the source of their stalemate.[15]

---

15 For further Nietzschean reflections on *24*, see Stephen Snyder's essay in this volume.

Thus, the three virtue ethics perspectives we've surveyed survive the attacks that plague the moral theories of Kant and Mill. What we have not investigated is whether any of these three perspectives is more reasonable or desirable than the others. We leave the reader to consider this question: Which kind of person do you think it is best to be—Aristotle's *eudaimon* (flourishing man), Machiavelli's *principe* (prince), or Nietzsche's *Übermensch* (higher man)? More to the point, whom do *you* most aspire to be: a David Palmer, a Sherry Palmer, or a Jack Bauer?

Jack in Double Time: 24 in Light of Aesthetic Theory

Paul A. Cantor

As for your twenty-four hours, what a great inconvenience that
a love affair should need to commence at daybreak, and end in
a wedding in the evening.

Tirso de Molina, *Cigaralles de Toledo*

We can only guess what Aristotle (384–322 BCE) might have thought
of American television, but I believe he would have been a fan of *24*.
Coming as he did from Macedonia, he probably would have gotten a
kick out of the anti-Serbian bias of the first season. More importantly, *24* offers confirmation of one of his most famous principles and
indeed one of the best-known rules of aesthetics (the philosophical
treatment of art and beauty). In his *Poetics*, Aristotle contrasts the
literary forms of tragedy and epic in terms of length: "tragedy tends
to fall within a single revolution of the sun or slightly to exceed that,
whereas epic is unlimited in point of time."[1] This is evidently the first
formulation of the rule that a drama should take place within a 24-
hour period, what came to be known as the principle of unity of time.
Few TV viewers are aware that *24* has such a venerable history and is
in fact derived from a formula first articulated by an ancient Greek
philosopher in the fourth century BCE based on his observation of
classical tragedies such as Sophocles' *Oedipus Rex*. *24* is an ideal case

---

1 Aristotle, *The Poetics*, trans. W. Hamilton Fyfe (Cambridge, MA: Harvard University
Press, 1982), p. 21.

for discussing the intersection of philosophy and popular culture. Analyzing the show in light of one of the most famous debates in the history of aesthetics will help us understand and appreciate its distinctive contribution to television.

The Classical Unities and Shakespeare

Aristotle seems to prefer tragedy to epic because of the greater compression and intensity it achieves. Tragedy "attains its end with greater economy of length. What is concentrated is always more effective than what is spread over a long period."[2] Aristotle thus already understood what the producers of *24* rediscovered, that confining a drama to a 24-hour period can generate a level of dramatic excitement easily dissipated when a story is spread out over a longer interval. But the principle of unity of time was not established as a dogma of aesthetic theory until long after Aristotle, namely in the Italian Renaissance. Critics in sixteenth-century Italy such as Lodovico Castelvetro (1505–1571) began to argue that to be good, a play simply has to be written according to strict principles of dramatic construction, what came to be known as the Three Unities or the Classical Unities: (1) unity of action, (2) unity of time, (3) unity of place. The first two unities were derived from Aristotle, with the third being added on grounds of aesthetic probability. If a play is going to be restricted to a 24-hour period, then it also has to be restricted to the limited amount of space that can be covered in such a time span.[3]

The Three Unities provided one of the foundations of what is known as the neoclassical school of criticism, "neo" because it derived its authority from classical sources such as Aristotle and the Roman poet Horace, but also claimed to have refined classical ideas and improved upon them. The neoclassical movement in literature reached its peak in seventeenth-century France, especially in the drama of the royal court. Playwrights such as Racine and Molière observed the Three Unities strictly in both tragedies and comedies, demonstrating

2 Aristotle, *Poetics*, p. 115.
3 The speed and ease of travel made possible by modern technology have made the old arguments for unity of place moot in our day, and a show like *24* need not worry about this issue. For that reason, I have focused on the issue of unity of time in this chapter.

how effective dramas constructed according to these principles can be on the stage. But the Three Unities never caught on in England the way they did in France or other parts of Europe. For a variety of reasons, the English stage was more free-wheeling. Christopher Marlowe's *Doctor Faustus*, for example, deals with 24 years, not 24 hours, in its hero's life, and it ranges in almost cinematic fashion all over the German and Italian states of Renaissance Europe. Thus thinkers in sixteenth-century England who were aware of cutting-edge aesthetic theory in Renaissance Italy could be biting in their criticism of the London theater of their day. In his *Apology for Poetry*, the distinguished courtier Sir Philip Sidney (1554–1586) made fun of the way contemporary dramatists failed to observe the unity of time, and allowed their characters to be conceived and grow to adulthood in the course of a single play:

> Of time they are much more liberal, for ordinary it is that two young princes [a prince and a princess] fall in love. After many traverses, she is got with child, delivered of a fair boy; he is lost, groweth a man, falls in love, and is ready to get another child; and all this in two hours' space; with, how absurd it is in sense, even sense may imagine, and Art hath taught, and all ancient examples justified, and, at this day, the ordinary players in Italy will not err in.[4]

Critics like Sidney could make plausible arguments for observing the unity of time, but they had a big problem in getting the principle established in England, a problem named William Shakespeare. To be sure, Shakespeare showed his respect for the Classical Unities at several points in his career. One of his earliest plays, *The Comedy of Errors*, takes place within a single day and obeys the unities strictly, partly because he was imitating a Roman comedy, Plautus' *The Manaechmi*. In what is perhaps his last play, *The Tempest*, Shakespeare evidently decided to show that he could be a complete master of the unities if he wanted to be. The play virtually unfolds in real time upon the stage—to great dramatic effect. But in most of his plays, Shakespeare is utterly unconcerned about obeying the unities and moves through space and time with reckless abandon.

---

4 "An Apology for Poetry" in *Criticism: The Major Texts*, ed. Walter Jackson Bate (New York: Harcourt, Brace & World, 1952), p. 102.

Paul A. Cantor

For example, *The Winter's Tale* takes us from Sicily to Bohemia, and a 16-year interval occurs between Acts III and IV, time enough for the kind of princes Sidney complained about to reach marriageable age. Aware that he is violating aesthetic law, Shakespeare brings Time himself out on stage as a chorus to apologize:

> Now take upon me, in the name of Time,
> To use my wings. Impute it not a crime
> To me, or my swift passage, that I slide
> O'er sixteen years and leave the growth untried
> Of that wide gap.[5]

In Unity There is Strength

Once Shakespeare became the focus of debates over the unity of time, the principle had little chance of being accepted in English aesthetic theory. In some respects, this development was unfortunate, because, as the example of *24* shows in our day, the restriction of a story to a single 24-hour period can generate genuine dramatic excitement. The fact that Shakespeare could get away with not observing the unities does not prove that all dramatists can do so with impunity, or that the unities could not be useful in writing some kinds of drama. Shakespeare was the greatest dramatist who ever lived and could evidently achieve anything he wanted to on stage. But critics like Sidney may still have been right in laughing at the feeble results when dramatists inferior to Shakespeare flagrantly disregarded the unities and allowed their plots to wander all over time and space.

As Aristotle clearly understood and *24* confirms, observing the unity of time can give focus to a plot and raise the level of dramatic intensity. This is especially true if the author can succeed in generating the effect of the clock ticking away as the action proceeds (something *24* achieves brilliantly by using an actual clock). When the audience has been made aware that an important event must take place within a fixed and brief period of time, their excitement inevitably builds as that moment approaches. Unity of time can thus

---

5 *The Riverside Shakespeare*, ed. G. Blakemore Evans (Boston: Houghton Mifflin, 1974), pp. 1585–1586 (Act IV, scene i, lines 3–7).

supply a potent principle of dramatic pacing. For the plot to be resolved in time, the pace of events must increase as the end approaches. This kind of pacing works very well in comedy, particularly in screwball comedies, where the characters have to work more and more frantically to get themselves out of whatever crazy situation they have landed in—in time to avoid disaster and bring about a happy ending.

Unity of time can also be effective in tragedy with precisely the opposite effect. Confronted with imminent catastrophe, the characters struggle desperately and with increasing urgency to avoid it, with the clock ticking away, only to fail in the end and face disaster. Unity of time is especially effective in a dramatic situation in which essentially everything has happened before the play begins and the plot basically consists of those facts coming to light. *Oedipus Rex* is the classic example of this kind of drama. Sophocles does not do what we might have expected him to do—write a play about how Oedipus came to kill his father and marry his mother. Rather, accepting these facts as the premise of his drama, Sophocles portrays on the stage only how Oedipus comes to *discover* what he has done. And that discovery can easily take place within a 24-hour period and even unfold in more or less real time on stage. It is no accident that Aristotle praises both *Oedipus* and unity of time. Both judgments are based in his principle that action is what is fundamental to drama, and the portrayal of character can be relegated to a secondary function.[6]

Action vs. Character

Thus, as *24* suggests, unity of time works best in the kind of plot that emphasizes action at the expense of character development. In a brilliant essay on unity of time, the Shakespeare scholar Norman Rabkin makes this point about the unities: "The fixed scene and the short time in which the action occurs put the emphasis rather on the playwright's virtuosity in revealing what is already inevitable

6   See Aristotle, *Poetics*, p. 25: "tragedy is not a representation of men but of a piece of action, . . . and the end aimed at is the representation not of qualities of character but of some action."

and ordained at the beginning, or extricating characters from a situation already fully established, than on the growth of character."[7] Rabkin goes on to argue that the deeper aesthetic reason why Shakespeare did not obey the unities of time and place is that he was more interested in character development than in sheer action on the stage.

Development of character takes time, usually more than 24 hours. If you are interested in showing how a young prince grows up to be a king, as Shakespeare is in his *Henry IV* plays, you are not going to be able to focus solely on a single day in his life, but must portray his complex reactions to a whole series of events and encounters over time. The argument for unity of time often stresses the issue of aesthetic probability or credibility. But in many cases to restrict a drama to a 24-hour period may make the action seem less probable to us. For example, to show a man and a woman fall in love, then fall out of love, and then fall back in love again within the space of a single day can strain an audience's belief. Considerations of emotional plausibility in a drama often force a playwright to go beyond the confines of a single day of action, as Shakespeare does in his love tragedy, *Antony and Cleopatra*.

The debate over unity of time thus ultimately points to a kind of aesthetic tradeoff dramatists face. They are basically involved in choosing between compression of action and serious character development. But beginning in the nineteenth century, further studies of Shakespeare's handling of time have explored the possibility that in his genius he tried to combine the best of both worlds, to achieve the dramatic excitement of the unity of time principle while still leaving room for plausible character development. He did this by means of a complex dramatic device that critics have called Double Time. Several of his plays work on what are in effect mutually contradictory time schemes. According to one set of time indicators in the text, events happen very quickly (the so-called Short Time), but according to another set, events are spread out over a longer period of time (the so-called Long Time).

---

7   Norman Rabkin, *Shakespeare and the Common Understanding* (New York: Free Press, 1967), p. 242.

Double Time in *Othello*

The most famous example of this kind of double time scheme can be found in *Othello*, Shakespeare's tragedy about a noble Moor, who is deceived by his seeming friend Iago into believing that his wife Desdemona has been unfaithful to him, leading Othello to murder her. The great Shakespearean critic A. C. Bradley has analyzed the issue of time in the play in elaborate detail in Note I, "The Duration of the Action in *Othello*," in his famous book, *Shakespearean Tragedy*. Following the specific time references in the text carefully, Bradley concludes:

> Thus (1) one set of time-indications clearly shows that Othello murdered his wife within a few days, probably a day and a half, of his arrival in Cyprus and the consummation of his marriage; (2) another set of time-indications implies quite as clearly that some little time must have elapsed, probably a few weeks; and this last is certainly the impression of a reader who has not closely examined the play.[8]

Drawing upon the idea of Double Time as developed by nineteenth-century critics, Bradley explains what Shakespeare was attempting to accomplish in *Othello*:

> Shakespeare, consciously or unconsciously, wanted to produce on the spectator (for he did not aim at readers) two impressions. He wanted the spectator to feel a passionate and vehement haste in the action; but he also wanted him to feel that the action was fairly probable. Consciously or unconsciously he used Short Time . . . for the first purpose, and Long Time . . . for the second. The spectator is affected in the required manner by both, though without distinctly noticing the indications of the two schemes. (341)

Bradley is not entirely happy with this account of the contradictory time schemes in *Othello*, and he raises some telling objections to it, but on the whole he concludes "the notion underlying this theory is

8 A. C. Bradley, *Shakespearean Tragedy* (1904; rpt. New York: Meridian, 1955), pp. 340–341. Subsequent page references to Bradley are to this work. For confirmation of Bradley's analysis of time in *Othello*, see Mable Buland, *The Presentation of Time in the Elizabethan Drama* (New York: Henry Holt, 1912), pp. 4–8. This book is the classic study of Double Time in Shakespeare.

probably true" (341). Playing fast and loose with the time indicators in *Othello*, Shakespeare manages to gain the benefits of unity of time while avoiding the defects. By seeming to confine the action to a day and a half, he achieves dramatic compression and keeps his audience on the edge of their seats as events unfold at a breathless pace. But by supplying a contrary set of indicators that seem to expand the action to several weeks, Shakespeare allows time for the character development his plot demands. If we paused and thought through the implications of having all the events take place within a 36-hour period, we might have a hard time accepting the idea that Othello's feelings about his wife Desdemona could change so radically and so often in such a brief span of time, as he runs the emotional gamut from total romantic devotion to murderous hate and back several times in the course of the play. Thus even as Shakespeare drives events forward relentlessly on the stage, he must simultaneously make us think that enough time is passing for Othello realistically to evolve from the self-possessed commanding figure of Act I to the self-doubting emotionally devastated figure of Act V.

Is It Really Real Time?

The centuries-long debate in aesthetic theory over unity of time, especially in Shakespeare's plays, thus prepares us for thinking about *24*. One wonders how much the creators of the show were aware of this debate, but one thing is clear. They certainly chose to emphasize the issue of unity of time in packaging the show, as evidenced by its title, the decision to call the company that creates it Real Time Productions, and the emphasis in much of the publicity for the show on its restriction to a single day of action. In the feature on the show on the DVD version of the first season, its star, Kiefer Sutherland, explains the consequences of the decision to obey the unity of time: "The freedom of time was gone. But that's what added to the intrigue and tension of the entire story. Now something as small as a long red light at an interchange carried a huge amount of weight, especially when a life was at stake, which it usually was." Aristotle could not have said it better. *24* certainly gets the most out of its decision to restrict its action to a single day, and with its digital clock ticking away throughout each hour, it can build up almost unbearable tension in its audience. But I want to invoke the example of Shakespeare to complicate our view of the series and suggest that *24* actually develops its own version of Shakespearean Double Time to play with its audience and try to compensate for the potential drawbacks of observing unity of time in a season-long television series.

Up to now I have been comparing *24* to conventional dramas and speaking as if there were no difference between a play and a television series. But if one looks at the issue of real time, it is obvious that *24* does not belong in the same category as a drama. When we say that a play unfolds in real time, we mean that *The Tempest*, for example, covers roughly four hours of action and can be performed on stage in almost the same time. *24* bases its claim to being a "realtime production" on the fact that it covers 24 hours' worth of action in 24 episodes, each one hour in length (actually about three quarters of an hour to leave room for commercials and station breaks). But television viewers do not watch all 24 hours of a *24* season in a single 24-hour period. The episodes are spread out over a television season, usually at the rate of one episode per week, with occasional two-hour special broadcasts. The availability of the show on DVDs means that it is theoretically possible for people to watch all 24 hours of action in real time, although it would take physical and psychological endurance of truly Jack Bauer proportions to do so (the most I have been able to watch in a single day on DVD is six episodes in a row, and I needed to be sedated after attempting that).

As a result, almost all viewers do not in fact experience *24* unfold on the screen in real time. In an intriguing variant of Shakespearean Double Time, *24* actually benefits from the tension between the way the action unfolds in time and the way viewers experience it over time. To oversimplify the situation: *24* presents its action in Short Time but viewers experience it in Long Time. The result is that *24* combines the virtues of an action drama with those of a soap opera. It generates intense dramatic excitement while still allowing for character entanglements and complications on the scale of a *Dallas* or a *Dynasty*. It craftily manages to create an entire season out of 24 hours of viscerally exciting action, while at the same time packing a season's worth of soap opera incidents and emotions into that single day.[9]

9   For a "behind the scenes" look at some of the "realtime" oddities connected with filming *24*, see the chapter by Read Mercer Schuchardt.

Days of Our Lives

A television season is at first sight an odd artistic unit. Too long to be absorbed in a single sitting, it presents a fundamental problem of unity to its creators. The simple solution traditionally adopted by television shows is to have a season consist of independent units, so-called "stand-alone" episodes (39 in the earlier days of TV, currently about 22–25 per season). Each episode is a self-contained drama, with the whole season tied together loosely by a continuity of cast, concept, and style. This tried-and-true television formula makes it easy for viewers to miss individual episodes of a program and still watch it on a more or less regular basis. But that pattern can be viewed as a drawback because it means that the average television show is less compelling *as a series* and seldom gets its viewers to feel a compulsion *not to miss a single episode*. As an alternative to the loose form of stand-alone episodes, from the beginning television adopted true serial formats, in which the action is continuous from episode to episode, and the characters keep changing as they face various crises in their lives. This pattern is most clearly evident in the long-running soap operas on daytime TV. In this regard, television was merely following the lead of radio soap operas, as well as movie serials, with their cliffhanger endings designed to hook the audience to keep coming back for more. The serialized novel of the nineteenth century, of which Charles Dickens was the great master, is the grand-daddy of all these serial formats, which have become a mainstay of modern popular culture.[10] As its ancestry in the nineteenth-century novel suggests, the serial television format is particularly suited to portraying character development over time. Serialized television, especially in the form of primetime soap operas, has been hugely successful over the years, bringing back viewers compulsively week after week with variants of the cliffhanging principle, most famously in the "Who Shot JR?" frenzy generated by *Dallas*.

But even the continuity generated by serialized television is relatively loose and unfocused compared to the intensity of a play like

---

10   For an excellent discussion of this subject, see Jennifer Hayward, *Consuming Pleasures: Active Audiences and Serial Fictions from Dickens to Soap Opera* (Lexington: University Press of Kentucky, 1997).

Oedipus Rex. The soap opera is by its nature an open-ended form, offering the artistic equivalent of urban sprawl, headed in many directions at once, with no clear limits to its growth. The virtue of the soap opera is that its plots can go on for years, but therefore they lack concentration and compression. The soap opera trades intensity and focus for range and scope. The genius of the creators of *24* was to come up with a way of redefining a television season. By limiting it to a single day in the life of their hero, they gave it closure and clear limits, allowing them to generate dramatic intensity in ways that were new to a television season. Indeed, with the clock ticking away in every episode, *24* has carried the art of the cliffhanger to new heights. Never have the episodes of a television series been so completely integrated into a single whole, in which each part leads immediately and inexorably to the next.

And yet, like Shakespeare, the creators of *24* wanted to have it all. Even for the sake of the new intensity they were able to generate from their 24-hour format, they were not willing wholly to sacrifice the advantages of a soap opera format. They understand that their audience likes action, but it likes character development as well. Thus, from the beginning, *24* has counterpointed its action plotlines involving terrorists and international politics with soap opera plotlines involving the domestic entanglements of its characters, above all their love lives and their convoluted family histories. The series has repeatedly dwelled on the way Jack and other central figures must choose between political and domestic concerns, for example, between their country and their family. This has given a greater emotional depth and complexity to the show and is no doubt partly responsible for its success. But it has depended on an element of aesthetic sleight-of-hand in the show that is analogous to Double Time in Shakespeare. In a season of *24*, we are watching hours of action but months of emotional development, no matter what the digital clock may tell us. The fact that we are watching the hours of action over months of actual viewing time helps to conceal the nature of the trick that *24* repeatedly brings off. The characters in the series may be able to turn on and shut off their emotions at a moment's notice, but we as viewers need time to absorb emotionally the momentous events that happen in the series every episode—events not just in the public sphere, but in the private lives of the characters we have grown to love and hate. For that reason, having a week between episodes to digest what has happened helps the audience deal with what might otherwise become an emotional overload in watching *24*. We may say we cannot wait for the next episode, but it is actually good to have a week to recover emotionally from the previous one. Viewing all 24 hours of a season of *24* at once could become emotionally numbing.

One Helluva Day

Look at all that happens emotionally in the first season of *24*, for example. The romantic entanglements alone would fill out a whole season of the average soap opera. Jack's daughter has a rebellious teenage romance with the young man who kidnaps her, falling in and out of love with him with each twist of the plot—and all this of course within the regulation 24 hours. Talk of the Stockholm syndrome that affects victims of hostage situations, which makes them bond with their abductors, is meant to make this romance seem plausible to us. But the whole point of the Stockholm syndrome is the *weeks* or *months* the hostage spends with his or her captors—not the *hours*. Meanwhile, presidential candidate David Palmer turns out to have a complete soap opera going on just within his immediate family, including a daughter still reliving the trauma of rape, a son who accidentally killed the rapist and is now being fingered for the crime, and a Lady Macbeth for a wife who wants to cover up all this and more.

If the back stories of the Palmer family are not enough for a single day of complications, the would-be president seems willing to enter into an extramarital affair with a young female aide in his camp—in the middle of a day during which multiple state primaries will determine if he gets his party's nomination—and he has to deal with such minor distractions as multiple assassination attempts on his life and terrorist strikes in LA. The romance is quickly nipped in the bud when it turns out that Palmer has seen through his wife's scheme to use the aide to manipulate him, and he is merely stringing the young woman along. But this is an example of how *24* manipulates its audience. In a soap opera, covering several months of action, we would have time to see a presidential candidate have a torrid affair with an aide. But in the compressed time scheme of *24*, we are merely titillated with the illusion of such a romance developing. We are put through the emotional wringer, and given an additional thrill in the plot, but ultimately over nothing real. That is how the show can seem to give us months of emotional development in what is merely hours of real time action.

The creators of *24* can thus have their cake and eat it too. Or rather they can give their audience all the thrill of a realtime action story with all the emotional twists of a full soap opera season. I am not faulting *24* for this, just trying to explain the trick the producers have cleverly brought off with their new format. As I have shown, this manipulation of their audience actually has the most venerable of cultural precedents in Shakespeare's use of Double Time. Even the ancient Greek philosopher Aristotle had an inkling of what was to make *24* succeed centuries after his death. Sometimes the history of aesthetic theory can illuminate even the most current phenomena of popular culture. Now if only Aristotle were here to explain *Lost* to us . . .

9:00 PM–10:00 PM

Classified:
CTU Personnel

Robert Arp is presently doing a postdoc at the National Center for Biomedical Ontology in Buffalo, NY where he works 24–7. Get it? 24–7 . . . 24–7 has the number 24 in it.

Scott Calef is Professor and Chair of the Department of Philosophy at Ohio Wesleyan University. He has published in ancient philosophy, applied ethics, political philosophy, metaphysics and the philosophy of religion. He has also contributed to *Metallica and Philosophy*. The closest he's ever come to danger was the time he survived an attack of Syntox nerve gas. His proudest moment, after the birth of his children, was the day he took first runner-up in the fourth annual Ohio Wesleyan Edgar Stiles look-alike contest.

Paul A. Cantor is Clifton Waller Barrett Professor of English at the University of Virginia. He is the author of *Gilligan Unbound: Pop Culture in the Age of Globalization*, which was named by the *LA Times* one of the best works of non-fiction in 2001—much to his surprise because he thought he'd written a novel. He has published widely on pop culture, including essays on *The Simpsons*, *South Park*, *Star Trek*, Martin Scorsese, film noir, and pro wrestling. Don't tell the editor, but he wrote his essay for this volume in 24 hours.

John Carpenter is a PhD candidate in Philosophy at Florida State University. His main research interests are metaphilosophy, epistemology, and ethics. John's plans for the near future include completing his book manuscript and rescuing Kim Bauer the next

208

time she gets abducted. He occasionally repeats the longest day of his life by pulling all-nighters; on such occasions, he thrives on the tension engendered by the ticking of an exceptionally loud clock. John has more information, but plans on using it as leverage to stay alive.

Brandon Claycomb's current cover is Associate Professor of Philosophy and Chairperson of the Arts & Humanities Division at Marian College in Fond du Lac, Wisconsin. He discontinued his research for the academic management book *What Would Jack Bauer Do?* after his controversial success formula was leaked to the public: (1) Put employee in holding, (2) Repeatedly shout: "You don't have any more useful information, do you?" (3) If employee answers, interrupt with "Shut up, stupid!" (4) Knock out employee with butt of gun.

Richard Davis is Associate Professor of Philosophy at Tyndale University College (TUC), the Canadian branch of Los Angeles' CTU, where he hones his skills in the critical arts of intellectual trafficking, ontological indoctrination, and philosophical mind control. Much of his time is spent in the field, interrogating suspicious characters in the dark and dangerous world of metaphysics. He has published numerous articles on such crowd pleasers as possible worlds, bare particulars, and the mind of God. His book *The Metaphysics of Theism and Modality* was actually showcased in Season Two, where viewers caught a glimpse of the volume stuffed in Kim Bauer's make-up bag. Don't be alarmed: a free sub-dermal encryption key is included with each copy so that readers can decipher the meaning of the title.

Stephen de Wijze is a lecturer in political theory at the University of Manchester in the UK. He is presently writing a book on the problem of "dirty hands." If pushed, Steve will insist that President David Palmer isn't really dead and that the final season of *24* will have Jack as president. Then we will finally see world peace (within 24 hours) because no one (that's right *no one*) wants to make Jack really angry. Steve particularly likes to watch out of sequence episodes of *24* with his very good friend Jer who, it must be said, utterly fails to understand the exquisite appeal of flying in the face of the *post hoc ergo propter hoc* fallacy.

R. Douglas Geivett is an epistemologist living in Southern California, where he teaches (if you can believe it) epistemology. As you've no doubt noticed, they don't let CTU agents specializing in epistemology appear in any of the episodes of *24*. It's just too risky. So when Doug agreed to write a chapter for this book, the producers of *24* screamed "breach of contract" and the Los Angeles CTU director fretted that it might be a "threat to national security." The producers dropped their allegations when a thorough database investigation revealed that, as far as they can tell, Doug does not work for the network. CTU stopped worrying when the producers of *24* offered to create a whole season based on Doug's chapter. And all parties were scrambling to look up the word "epistemology."

Randall M. Jensen is Associate Professor of Philosophy at Northwestern College in Orange City, Iowa. His philosophical interests include ethics, ancient Greek philosophy, and philosophy of religion. He has also contributed to *South Park and Philosophy* and *The Office and Philosophy*. And the only reason you're still conscious is because he doesn't want to carry you.

Terrence Kelly is a term instructor at the University of Alaska, where he holds the Victor Drazen Endowed Chair of Ethical Research at CTU. A specialist in ethics and political philosophy, he is currently writing *Ordinary Injustice*, a book on the nature of ideology and practical rationality. Tourists to beautiful Alaska are encouraged to take time out to visit him in his office. If you're lucky, you'll catch him during "grading season" and hear his characteristic call: "This is the longest day of my life."

Rob Lawlor is a research fellow in applied ethics at the Inter-Disciplinary Ethics Applied CETL at the University of Leeds. Prior to this, he had been a computer specialist at CTU. During this time, he had a brief relationship with Chloe O'Brian, but the relationship ended when Chloe accused Rob of having an affair with a junior member of staff. Rob denied it, but Chloe didn't believe him, and she asked Jack to get the truth from him—any way possible. Jack insisted he couldn't torture a CTU employee just to find out whether or not he had been unfaithful, but Chloe insisted that Jack owed her and reluctantly Jack agreed to do it. Rob confessed, but later withdrew the confession, saying it was given under duress. He left Chloe, saying she had trust issues, quit his job, and moved back to England. He never forgave Jack, and he wrote his chapter out of spite.

Tom Morris is an independent, freelance, public philosopher—and this doesn't mean he's just an unemployed guy who walks the streets asking deep questions and suggesting people pay him for it. He's actually the second highest paid philosopher in history, outdistanced only by Aristotle, but he'll probably catch up soon, because Aristotle apparently had a very bad agent, possibly as the result of his belief in free agency. Tom holds a PhD from Yale and refuses to let it go. After fifteen years at Notre Dame, he went undercover to save the world and write books like *If Harry Potter Ran General Electric*. Tom wonders why Kiefer Sutherland, one of our finest actors, can't figure out that when you state the time, there is no reason imaginable for putting your emphasis on the letter "M."

Greig Mulberry is currently a Lecturer in Philosophy at Mississippi State University. Still recovering from a thorough search and inter-rogation by Jack Bauer, he now takes more care in choosing what to put into his carryon luggage.

Dónal P. O'Mathúna is Lecturer in Health Care Ethics at Dublin City University, Ireland (or DCU, which is the Irish for CTU). He had agreed with Jack that sometimes you just have to torture students with boring lectures and huge assignments—for their own good, and to save the world. However, having investigated the ethics of torture for this volume, he's not sure if that's the most dignified way to treat students. In addition to thinking about ethics, he also examines issues of evidence in healthcare. It's not as exciting as Jack's search for evidence, but it has led to the book *Alternative Medicine*. There's nothing about truth serums in there, just ways to wade through the evidence in that mine field. Now, back to finding new ways to get papers out of students.

Eric M. Rovie is currently Visiting Analyst at CTU (or Visiting Instructor at Georgia State University, whichever you prefer) where he teaches courses for both the Philosophy and Religious Studies departments. He has graduate degrees in Philosophy from Georgia State University and Washington University in St. Louis and works primarily in ethics and political philosophy. He is the co-editor of *The Morality of War: Classical and Contemporary Readings* and has published papers on abortion, action theory, and the philosophy of Thomas Aquinas. While he has never actually come face to face with a mountain lion or a deranged survivalist in the wild, he's pretty sure he could handle it better than Kim Bauer, and he *knows* he's got better interpersonal skills than Chloe O'Brian.

Read Mercer Schuchardt is the author of *Sinners In The Hands of An Angry Gore (and Other Parables from a Cinematic Cathedral Near You)* and the editor of the collection *Fight Club and Philosophy*. He is founder and publisher of the film interpretation website Metaphilm (www.metaphilm.com), and has taught media courses at New York University, Marymount Manhattan College, and Franklin College Switzerland. He does not own a cell phone.

Stephen Snyder has taught philosophy of art at Washington University and Saint Louis University. Some Eastern European operatives speculate that his current activities involve philosophy at Fatih University on the Marmara Sea. He was last sighted on an Istanbul street corner debating with a *simit* vendor, clutching what appeared to be a Brillo carton. However, reliable sources confirm Snyder has since gone dark.

Georgia Testa is a Lecturer in Medical Ethics and Research Fellow in Applied Ethics at the University of Leeds. Rumor has it that she was once a special advisor at CTU, assigned to educate agents on the ethical treatment of detainees, but resigned in despair when faced with Jack Bauer. She has, unsurprisingly, denied the rumors but does develop an unfortunate facial twitch at the mere mention of Jack.

Jennifer Hart Weed is Assistant Professor of Philosophy at Tyndale University College. She specializes in medieval philosophy and philosophy of religion. She is the author of "Creation as a Foundation of Analogy in Aquinas," forthcoming in *Divine Transcendence and Immanence in the Thought of St. Thomas Aquinas*. Like Chloe, Jennifer is not a field agent. But after what happened to George Mason, Chappelle, Edgar, Lynn, and Milo, she has transferred out of CTU headquarters.

Ronald Weed is Assistant Professor of Philosophy at Tyndale University College. He specializes in ancient philosophy, ethics, and political philosophy. He is the author of *Aristotle on Stasis: A Moral*

Psychology of Political Conflict. He has also published articles on Aristotle, Rousseau, Kant, and contemporary philosophy. After spending a brief tour of duty at CTU, he has requested a transfer to a group with a greater level of Congressional supervision, such as Colonel Samuel's Coral Snake Unit. His most memorable moment at CTU was when he was forced to attend a division-sponsored sensitivity training seminar alongside Jack and Chloe.

10:00 PM–11:00 PM

Classified:
Assets and Sources

Adorno, Theodor and Horkheimer, Max. *Dialectic of Enlightenment*. New York: Continuum Publishing, 1997.

Aquinas, St. Thomas. *Summa theologiae*. Translated by the Fathers of the English Dominican Province. Notre Dame, IN: Ave Maria Press, 1948.

Aristotle. *The Poetics*. Translated by W. Hamilton Fyfe. Cambridge, MA: Harvard University Press, 1982.

Aristotle. *Nicomachean Ethics*. Translated and edited by C. Rowe and S. Broadie. Oxford: Oxford University Press, 2002.

Augustine of Hippo, St. *Political Writings*. Edited by E M. Atkins and R. J. Dodaro. Cambridge: Cambridge University Press, 2001.

Bentham, Jeremy. *An Introduction to the Principles of Morals and Legislation*. Garden City, NY: Doubleday, 1961.

Bufacchi, Vittorio and Arrigo, Jean Maria. "Torture, Terrorism and the State: A Refutation of the Ticking-Bomb Argument." *Journal of Applied Philosophy* 23 (2006): 360.

Carney, Brian. "Jack Bauer's Dilemmas—and Ours: Watching '24' as a Primer on Moral Philosophy." *Wall Street Journal*, January 26, 2007.

Foot, Phillipa. *Virtues and Vices*. New York: Oxford University Press, 2002.

Habermas, Jürgen. *The Theory of Communicative Action: Volume One*. Translated by Thomas McCarthy. Boston: Beacon Press, 1984.

Hampshire, Stuart. *Innocence and Experience*. Cambridge, MA: Harvard University Press, 1989.

Hegel, G. W. F. *The Philosophy of Right*. Translated by H. B. Nisbet. New York: Cambridge University Press, 1991.

Hill, Thomas. *Autonomy and Self Respect*. New York: Cambridge University Press, 1991.

Hobbes, Thomas. *Leviathan*. Edited by Richard Tuck. New York: Cambridge University Press, 1991.

Hume, David. *An Enquiry Concerning Human Understanding.* Edited by Tom Beauchamp. Oxford: Oxford University Press, 1999.

Hurka, Thomas. "Proportionality and the Morality of War." *Philosophy and Public Affairs* 33 (2005): 34–66.

Ignatieff, Michael. *The Lesser Evil: Political Ethics in an Age of Terror.* Edinburgh: Edinburgh University Press, 2005.

Kamm, Frances. "Nonconsequentialism, the Person as End-in-Itself, and the Significance of Status." *Philosophy and Public Affairs* 21 (1992): 354–389.

Kant, Immanuel. *Foundations of the Metaphysics of Morals.* Translated by Lewis White Beck. Upper Saddle River, NJ: Prentice-Hall, 1993.

Korsgaard, Christine. *The Sources of Normativity.* New York: Cambridge University Press, 1996.

Machiavelli, Niccolò. *The Prince.* Translated by Harvey C. Mansfield. Chicago: Chicago University Press, 1998.

MacIntyre, Alasdair. *After Virtue.* Notre Dame, IN: University of Notre Dame Press, 1981.

Mayer, Jane. "Whatever It Takes: The Politics of the Man Behind '24'." *The New Yorker*, February 19, 2007.

Mill, John Stuart. *On Liberty.* New York: Meridian, 1974.

Mill, John Stuart. *Utilitarianism.* Indianapolis: Hackett, 2002.

Moore, G. E. *Principia Ethica.* Cambridge: Cambridge University Press, 1948.

Nagel, Thomas. "War and Massacre." Reprinted in his *Mortal Questions.* Cambridge: Cambridge University Press, 1979.

Nietzsche, Friedrich. *Beyond Good and Evil.* Translated by Walter Kaufmann. New York: Random House, 1966.

Nozick, Robert. *Anarchy, State, and Utopia.* New York: Basic Books, 1974.

Nussbaum, Martha C. *The Fragility of Goodness: Luck and Ethics in Greek Tragedy and Philosophy.* Cambridge: Cambridge University Press, 1986.

O'Neill, Onora. *Constructions of Reason: Explorations of Kant's Practical Philosophy.* Cambridge: Cambridge University Press, 1990.

Rawls, John. *A Theory of Justice.* Oxford: Oxford University Press, 1972.

Shue, Henry. "Torture." *Philosophy and Public Affairs* 7 (1978): 124–143.

Walzer, Michael. *Just and Unjust Wars.* New York: Basic Books, 1977.

Weber, Max. "Politics as a Vocation." In *From Max Weber: Essays in Sociology.* Translated and edited by H. H. Gerth and C. Wright Mills. New York: Oxford University Press, 1958.

Williams, Bernard. *Moral Luck.* Cambridge: Cambridge University Press, 1981.

Žižek, Slavoj. "The Depraved Heroes of *24* are the Himmlers of Hollywood." *Guardian Unlimited*, January 10, 2006.

Classified: The Codes

abduction 139n
Abu Ghraib 20, 100, 103
Acheson, Dean 25
act utilitarianism 10, 14
Adorno, Theodor 143–4, 152, 153
Ahmed, Rabiah 179
Al-Assad, Hamri 50, 93, 145, 153
Ali, Syed 37, 98, 101–2, 132, 138, 183, 187
Allhoff, Fritz 98
Almeida, Tony 6, 8, 14, 37, 71, 109, 131, 135, 146
altruism 53, 159, 184–5
  paternalistic 73
Apollonian-Dionysian duality 44–5, 46, 47–8, 49, 51–2
Araz, Behrooz 185
Arendt, Hannah 69, 70
Aristotle 107n, 183, 184, 189–90, 192, 193, 194, 195, 196, 198, 199, 202, 207
Arp, Robert 181–94, 208
Aurelius, Marcus 41n
authoritarian societies 144
auto-immunities 142, 143, 146, 147, 149, 151, 152, 154
autonomy 185, 186, 193

banality of evil 69
Basin, Dr. 22, 23
Bauer, Graem 21, 100
Bauer, Jack
  anti-authoritarianism 68, 75
  anti-liberalism 68, 69, 70
  bureaucratic agent 144–5
  loyalty 109, 145
  moral deformation 24, 146
  self-sacrifice 32, 50, 54, 72–3, 83, 84
  tragic hero xii, 18, 20, 30, 53
Bauer, Kim 12–13, 21, 35, 37, 73, 74, 106, 109, 182, 206
Bauer, Phillip 126
Bauer, Teri 33, 73, 74, 171, 178
Bentham, Jeremy 7n
Biko, Steve 101
Bin Laden, Osama 150
Bouphonia ritual 50
Bradley, A. C. 201–2
Brecht, Bertold 21n
Buchanan, Bill 6, 14, 38, 46, 92, 97
bureaucratic systems 143, 144–5
Burke, Agent 99

Calef, Scott   39n, 129–47, 208
Camus, Albert   21n
Cantor, Paul A.   195–207, 208
Carpenter, John   181–94, 208–9
Carter, Jimmy   26
Castelvestro, Ludovico   196
cell phone primacy in contemporary
    life   169, 170, 171, 172, 176,
    178, 180
Chappelle, Ryan   6, 8, 32, 34–5,
    61, 109, 114, 137, 138, 184
character development   189–90
Cheng Zi   35, 41, 49, 119, 126
Cicero   93
classical unities   196–8
    see also unity of time
Claycomb, Brandon   67–75, 209
Clifford, William   132, 133, 135,
    137, 140
Clinton, Bill   xv
Coca–Cola "You Can Win, But
    You Can't Hide!" campaign
    173n
Coetzee, J. M.   21n
communcative rationality   153,
    154
Confucius   189
consent, and moral permissibility
    81–4
consequentialism   77–80, 87, 140
    means-end justification   79–80
    non-consequentialism   79, 80,
    193
    strict impartiality   77–9
    see also means-end dilemmas
Correspondence Theory of Truth
    134n
cost-benefit analyses   191
creative exit strategies   7
Crichton, Michael   180
Cruise, Tom   42
Cummings, Walt   25

Dallas (television show)   203, 204
Davis, Richard   31–42, 209
de Wijze, Stephen   17–30, 209
decisions
    forced   136, 137
    momentous   146
deduction   139n
deontology   9–10, 11, 12, 13, 18,
    91
Derrida, Jacques   142, 149, 150,
    151
Descartes, René   129, 137
Dessler, Michelle   xvi, 6, 70, 71,
    109, 131, 135, 163, 184–5
Dickens, Charles   204
"dirty hands" phenomenon   8, 18,
    20, 22–3, 23, 24, 30
Doctrine of Double Effect (DDE)
    80–1, 83, 85–6
Doyle, Mike   125, 126
Drazen, Alexis   182
Drazen, Andre   182
Driscoll, Erin   157, 158, 159
Dworkin, Andrea   185

Edmunds, Chase   106, 113, 114,
    116, 136, 187
Eichmann, Adolf   69, 70
Eisenhower, Dwight D.   35n
"end of history"   150
enlightenment rationality   144, 153
epic   195
epistemology   4, 156–7
    sensory perception   160
    testimonial evidence   157,
    160–4, 165
ethic of responsibility   18, 19
ethics   3, 8, 91
    see also consequentialism;
    deontology; utilitarianism
euthanasia   86n
    voluntary   82, 84n

evidentialism   131–2
expertise   156, 157, 158, 160, 165

Fayed, Abu   92, 103, 149
Finnegan, Brigadier General Patrick   19–20, 179
Fukuyama, Francis   150

Gagarin, Yuri   157n
Garry, Ann   186
Gavin, Sarah   146
Geivett, R. Douglas   155–65, 210
Get Smart (television series)   155
Gibson, Lyle   190
God, belief in   137n, 157n
Gordon, Howard   179, 180
Goren, Marshall   17, 21, 49–50, 188
Greenfield, Adam   178

Habermas, Jürgen   151, 153
Habib, General   100, 103, 152
Hades   47, 49
Hampshire, Stuart   23n, 28, 29
Hayes, Karen   46, 97, 102
Haysbert, Dennis   179–80
Hegel, G. W. F.   150
Heller, James   xvi, 54, 71, 73, 130, 146
Henderson, Christopher   5, 25, 72, 94, 99, 100, 130n
Heraclitus   171
Hewitt, Alex   138–9
Heyd, David   40
Hobbes, Thomas   108n, 109–12, 114–15, 116, 117
Homeland Security Act 2002   35
Homeric moral code   74
Horace   196
Horkheimer, Max   143–4, 152–3
Hume, David   107n, 131

Hurka, Thomas   59, 60, 61, 64, 65
hypothesis formation   139n, 140

Ignatieff, Michael   63, 65
impartiality   77–9
indeterminacy   142
induction   139n
instrumental rationality   143, 154
instrumental value   184
instrumentality   147
intrinsic value   184

James, William   132n, 133, 134, 135, 138, 140
Japan, bombing of (1945)   118–19
Jensen, Randall M.   3–16, 210
Johnson, Steven   178n
just war theory   xvii, 57–66
   authority condition   59, 60–1
   classical and medieval roots   59
   just cause condition   59, 62–3
   just intention condition   59, 63–4
   proportionality condition   59, 60, 64–6

Kant, Immanuel   9n, 146, 182, 183, 185–6
Keeler, President   57
Kelly, Terrence   142–54, 210
Khrushchev, Nikita   157n
knowledge   156
   goal-directed   158
   hunches   159–60
   see also epistemology
Kresge, Lynne   140

Labelle, Ronnie   157, 158
Lawlor, Rob   42n, 118–26, 210–11
laws of nature   111–12
Lee Jong   23, 58, 63, 64, 65

Lennox, Tom 97
"lesser evil" approach to politics 61
liberalism 74, 83n
  anti-liberalism 68, 69, 70
  core features 74
  defined 68
  naïve optimism 74
libertarianism 83n
Limbaugh, Rush xv
Logan, Charles 2, 25, 57–8, 61, 64, 130, 136, 183, 190
love and friendship 13, 141
loyalty 105–17
  blind 106, 107
  defining 113
  and impartiality 107
  nature of 105–6
  and trust 107–9, 112
  see also promise-keeping

McCain, John xv
McCarthy, Darren 149
McGill, Lynn 32, 39, 40, 136, 137
Machiavelli, Niccolò 21, 22, 23, 27, 28, 184, 190, 191–2, 193, 194
MacKinnon, Catherine 185
McLuhan, Marshall 169, 170, 171, 172, 175, 180
Madigan, Timothy 186
Manning, Curtis 15, 93, 145, 185
Marlowe, Christopher 197
Marsyas 51
Marwan, Habib 57, 58, 60, 63, 187
Marxist revolutionary theory 151
Mason, George 17, 21, 37–8, 49, 71, 135, 162–3, 182, 183
master/slave relationships 192
means-end dilemmas 5, 6, 23, 79–80, 83–4, 91

Kantian view 185–6
  utilitarian view 186
media ecology perspective 170–80
Meiwes, Armen 82
Melville, Herman 21n
metaphysical dualism 52
Mill, John Stuart 7n, 182, 191
Milliken, Alan 183
modernity 142, 143, 150, 152
  auto-immunities 142, 143, 146, 147, 149, 151, 154
  characteristics 143
  iron cage thesis 143, 152
Molière 196
Moore, G. E. 36
moral actions 33
moral blind alley 15
moral dilemmas 3, 4–5, 5, 6, 11, 14, 18–19, 23
  compromise strategies 11
  means-end dilemmas 5, 6, 7, 8, 23, 79–80, 83–4, 91, 185–6
  personal dilemmas 6, 7
moral judgment 50
moral luck 118–26
moral obligations 33
moral permissibility, consent and 81–4
moral personality 9, 146, 153
moral pollution 24
moral prohibitions 33
moral reasons 5
moral stalemates 183–4, 187–8, 193
moral taboos 8
moral theories 4, 7, 9, 76
  action-based 189
  character-based 189
  impersonal theories 12
  see also ethics
morally neutral actions 33

Morris, Tom   xi–xiii, 211
Mulberry, Greig   67–75, 211
Murdoch, Rupert   170n
Myers, Nina   4, 33, 49, 50, 76, 77,
    79, 80, 81, 82, 83, 85, 87, 108,
    136, 145, 146, 162, 163–4,
    171, 172

Nagel, Thomas   15–16
Nash, Elizabeth   182
National Emergency Entertainment
    State   173–4
Nazism   100
Nietzsche, Friedrich   43, 44, 46,
    51, 52, 53–4, 184, 192, 194
Novick, Mike   38, 93, 138, 187
nuclear weapons, and just war
    theory   63
Nussbaum, Martha   19

objectification   181–94
    consensual   185–6
    Kantian view   182, 183, 185–6
    moral stalemates   183–4,
        187–8
    utilitarian view   182, 183,
        186–8
    virtue ethics view   183, 184,
        189–92
O'Brien, Chloe   71, 106, 109, 131,
    136
O'Brien, Morris   9, 95
O'Donnell, Rosie   xv
Odysseus myth   144, 145–6
Oedipus Rex (Sophocles)   195,
    199, 205
O'Mathúna, Dónal P.   91–104,
    211

Palmer, David   vii, viii, 6, 11, 22,
    38, 44, 49, 50, 57, 58, 60, 61,
    62, 64, 65, 66, 70, 76, 77–8,
    79, 81, 82, 83, 85, 86, 87, 91,
    100, 109, 131, 136, 138, 139,
    140, 141, 147, 153, 162, 172,
    179, 183, 187, 190, 192, 206
Palmer, Sherry   183, 190, 191
Palmer, Wayne   33, 42, 50, 70,
    102, 108
Papazian, Miles   97
parent-child relationship   78, 79
Park, Jason   47
passions   135, 140, 141
Peirce, Charles Sanders   139n
Plato   31, 189
Plautus   197
plurality   142
political morality   18, 19, 20, 24,
    27
    anti-morality view   25, 26, 29
    morality as seamless approach
        26
political naïvety   26, 27
Postman, Neil   170n
postmodernism   142, 143, 148
pragmatism   133–4
prediction, nature of   107n
Prescott, Jim   138, 140–1
Pressman, Milo   32
probabilities   77n
promise-keeping   112, 113,
    114–16
    fear of reprisal   115, 117
    fear of social consequences   115
    non self-contradiction   112, 115,
        116, 117
proportionality condition   59, 60,
    64–6, 81

Rabkin, Norman   199–200
Racine   196
Raines, Audrey   10, 14, 21, 33,
    41–2, 54, 71, 73, 74, 97, 101,
    119

Raines, Paul   22, 23, 91, 101
rationality
  abduction   139n
  communicative   153, 154
  deduction   139n
  enlightenment   144, 153
  induction   139n, 143
  instrumental   143, 154
  Kantian   184
  modern   153
Realist School of International
  Relations   25n, 124
reapolitik   22, 27, 28, 29, 30
resurrection   51
right to life   79, 80
risk management   154
Rovie, Eric M.   105–17, 211–12
Rovner, Victor   171
Royal Navy marines, Iranian
  capture of (2007)   31
rule utilitarianism   10–11, 14
Rumsfeld, Donald   xvi

St. Augustine   93
St. Francis   53
St. Thomas Aquinas   59
Salazar, Ramon   11, 136,
  192
Sartre, Jean-Paul   21, 22
Saunders, Jane   67–8
Saunders, Stephen   32, 34, 35, 52,
  114, 116, 137
Savan, Leslie   177
Scalia, Antonin   xv
Scarry, Elaine   91n, 102
Schmitt, Carl   68, 69, 72, 74
Schopenhauer, Arthur   53
Schuchardt, Read Mercer   169–80,
  212
Schwarzenbach, Sibyl   186
Scientology   42
The Searchers (film)   73–4

self-sacrifice   32, 35, 39, 50, 54,
  72–3, 83
  Always Better Principle   38
  argument for   36
  immorality of   38
  moral permissibility   83
  One for Many Principle   39, 40,
  42
  utilitarian view   188
sensory perception   160
September 11, 2001 terrorist attacks
  57, 151, 170
  post-9/11 world   43, 46, 74
Shakespeare, William   197–8,
  200–2
  Antony and Cleopatra   200
  The Comedy of Errors   197
  Henry IV plays   200
  Othello   201–2
  The Tempest   197, 203
  The Winter's Tale   198
Shue, Henry   97n, 98, 102
Sidney, Sir Philip   197, 198
The Siege (film)   170n
Singer, Kyle   182
Singer, Peter   7n
Smart, J. J. C.   188n
Snyder, Stephen   43–54, 212
soap operas   185, 204, 205
social contract theory   110–11
social determinism   152
Socrates   xvi
Stanton, Roger   37, 91, 94, 98,
  100
Stiles, Edgar   70
Stockholm syndrome   206
Stoicism   41
Streisand, Barbra   xv
Styron, William   21n
superogatory acts   34
superstition   8
surveillance society   171

suspicion   130, 137, 140
Sussman, David   95
Sutherland, Kiefer   xiii, 181, 202
Suvarov, President   41
Swinton, Harry   40

television shows
   serial formats   204
   stand-alone episodes   204
terror   52–3
terrorism
   communicative and deliberative
      responses to   152, 154
   contemporary   150, 152
   postmodernism and   142, 148
   specter of   147–9, 150
Testa, Georgia   76–87, 212
testimonial evidence   157, 160–4,
   165
Thucydides   190–1
ticking time bomb scenario   6–7,
   98, 99, 101, 102
torture   xiv, xv, xvi, 19–20, 23,
   48–9, 52, 53, 91–104, 146,
   151, 179
   arguments against   98–102
   arguments for   96–8
   cultural context   92–4
   defining   94–6
   dehumanizing effects of   100,
      102
   deontological prohibition   11, 91
   efficacy   100–1, 161–2
   institutionalization   103
   interrogational torture   94, 96,
      99
   military tradition and   93
   post-9/11 world   93–4
   prohibitions against   92–3
   reasons for   96
   survivors, psychological damage
      in   95–6

ticking time bomb scenario   6–7,
   98, 99, 101, 102
training the torturer   100
   utilitarian argument for   11, 92
tragedy   195, 196–7, 199
   see also classical unities
Trump, Donald   106n
trust   130, 137, 141, 182
   and loyalty   107–9, 112
   predictive element   107–8,
      112–13, 114
   see also promise-keeping
truth
   correspondence theory of   134n
   defining   133, 135n
   and illusion   44, 45, 51, 52, 54
   truth-value of a proposition   157
   utility   135n
24
   action plotlines   205
   criticisms of   xv–xvi, 19
   fan base   xv
   political even-handedness   xvi
   reality/entertainment conflation
      178–80
   realtime format   xvi, 97, 176–7,
      202–3
   soap opera plotlines   205, 206
   stereotypes   xv
   temporal compression   74,
      206–7

United Nations, *Convention Against
   Torture and Other Cruel,
   Inhuman or Degrading
   Treatment or Punishment*
   92–3
unity of time   196–207
   classical drama   196–202
   double time scheme   200, 201,
      203, 205
   long time scheme   200, 203

short time scheme 200, 203
24 202–3, 205–7
Urmson, J. O. 33–4, 36
US Army *Code of Conduct* 35n
USA PATRIOT Act 2001 170
utilitarianism 7–9, 10, 12–13, 48,
  92, 97, 147, 186, 193
  act utilitarianism 10, 14
  and consequentialism 182, 183,
  186–8
  cost-benefit analyses 191
  and objectification 182, 183,
  186–8
  rule utilitarianism 10–11, 14
  and self-sacrifice 188
  and torture 11, 92

virtue ethics 92
  and consequentialism 183, 184,
  189–92
  and objectification 183

Wag The Dog (film) 170n
Wald, Joseph 21, 35, 162
Walsh, Richard 44, 172
Walzer, Michael 22, 63
war on terror 57, 65, 93, 97, 98,
  101
Warner, Kate 10, 74, 183
Warner, Marie 37, 92, 94, 132,
  181
Wayne, John 73
Weber, Max 17, 18, 21, 29, 143,
  152
Weed, Jennifer Hart 57–66,
  212
Weed, Ronald xiv–xvii, 212–13
Williams, Bernard 13, 24, 118

Yasir, Nadia 32
Yolkien 75

Žižek, Slavoj xv, 20